STAR WARS®

KNIGHTS OF THE OLD REPUBLIC

VOLUME EIGHT
DESTROYER

The Old Republic
(25,000–1,000 YEARS BEFORE THE BATTLE OF YAVIN)

The Old Republic was the legendary government that united a galaxy under the rule of the Senate. In this era, the Jedi are numerous, and serve as guardians of peace and justice. The **Tales of the Jedi** *comics series takes place in this era, chronicling the immense wars fought by the Jedi of old, and the ancient Sith.*

The events in this story take place approximately 3,963 years before the Battle of Yavin.

STAR WARS®

KNIGHTS OF THE OLD REPUBLIC

VOLUME EIGHT
DESTROYER

SCRIPT **JOHN JACKSON MILLER**

ART **RON CHAN, BRIAN CHING** & **BONG DAZO**

COLORS **MICHAEL ATIYEH**

LETTERING **MICHAEL HEISLER**

FRONT & BACK COVER ART **BENJAMIN CARRÉ**

Dark Horse Books®

PUBLISHER MIKE RICHARDSON

COLLECTION DESIGNER STEPHEN REICHERT

ASSISTANT EDITOR FREDDYE LINS

EDITOR DAVE MARSHALL

*Special thanks to Elaine Mederer, Jann Moorhead, David Anderman, Leland Chee,
Sue Rostoni, and Carol Roeder at Lucas Licensing.*

STAR WARS: KNIGHTS OF THE OLD REPUBLIC VOLUME EIGHT—DESTROYER

This volume collects issues #42–#46 of the Dark Horse
comic-book series *Star Wars: Knights of the Old Republic*.

Published by
Dark Horse Books
A division of Dark Horse Comics, Inc.
10956 SE Main Street
Milwaukie, OR 97222

darkhorse.com | starwars.com

To find a comics shop in your area, call the Comic Shop Locator Service toll-free at 1-888-266-4226

publisher **Mike Richardson** • executive vice president **Neil Hankerson** • chief financial officer **Tom Weddle** • vice president of publishing
Randy Stradley • vice president of business development **Michael Martens** • vice president of marketing, sales, and licensing **Anita Nelson** • vice
president of product development **David Scroggy** • vice president of information technology **Dale LaFountain** • director of purchasing **Darlene
Vogel** • general counsel **Ken Lizzi** • editorial director **Davey Estrada** • senior managing editor **Scott Allie** • senior books editor **Chris Warner** •
executive editor **Diana Schutz** • director of design and production **Cary Grazzini** • art director **Lia Ribacchi** • director of scheduling **Cara Niece**

First edition: February 2010
ISBN 978-1-59582-419-6

1 3 5 7 9 10 8 6 4 2
Printed in China

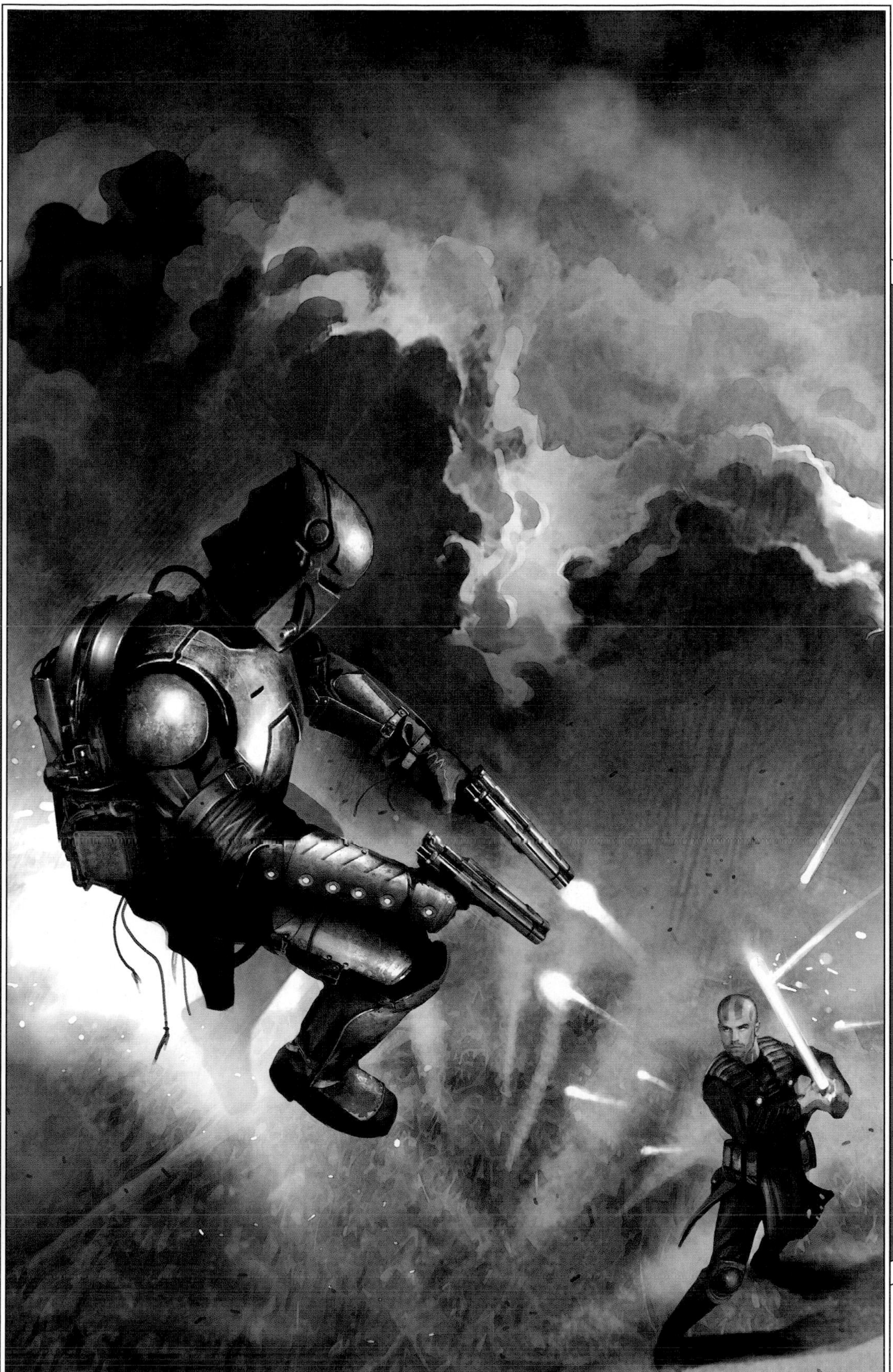

ILLUSTRATION BY BENJAMIN CARRÉ

MASKS

art by Ron Chan

Zayne Carrick believes he has left the Mandalorians and their war far behind. The setback for the armored nomads at Jebble has briefly made the Core Worlds a peaceful place for a former Padawan to find fortune as a freelance adventurer.

But the Jedi Knight now known as Malak never abandons his drive to get the Jedi to enter the war—an effort expressly forbidden by the High Council. Nor does he give up his quest to convince Zayne's fierce and beautiful ally, Jarael, to join the crusade at his side.

But much has changed since their last meeting. Rohlan, the Mandalorian deserter, has discovered Jarael's latent Force powers. And Zayne has learned something Jarael never wanted anyone to know: her past association with the slaver gang known as the Crucible. Not as a slave—but as a *slaver* . . .

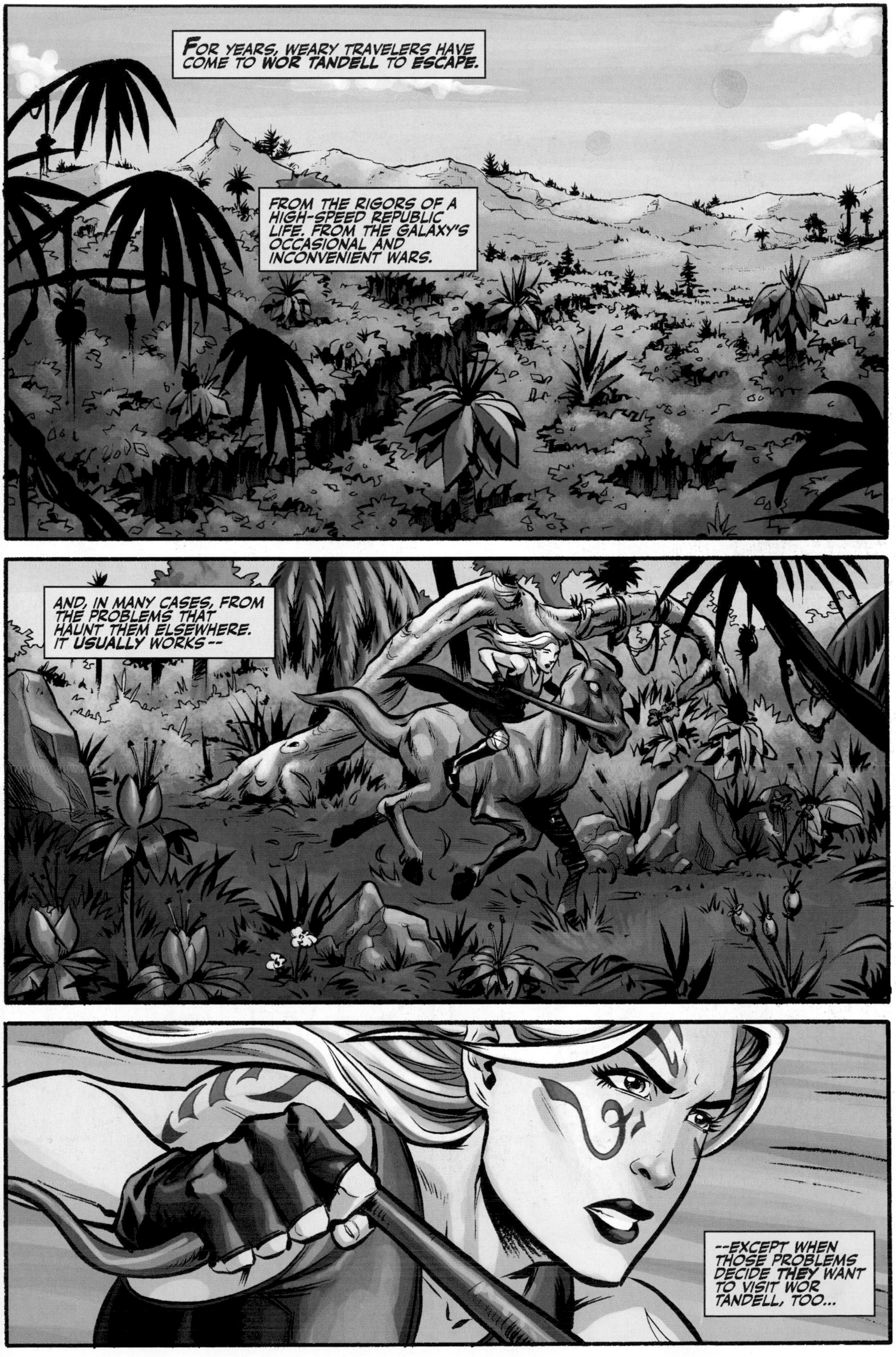
FOR YEARS, WEARY TRAVELERS HAVE COME TO WOR TANDELL TO ESCAPE.
FROM THE RIGORS OF A HIGH-SPEED REPUBLIC LIFE. FROM THE GALAXY'S OCCASIONAL AND INCONVENIENT WARS.
AND, IN MANY CASES, FROM THE PROBLEMS THAT HAUNT THEM ELSEWHERE. IT USUALLY WORKS--
--EXCEPT WHEN THOSE PROBLEMS DECIDE THEY WANT TO VISIT WOR TANDELL, TOO...

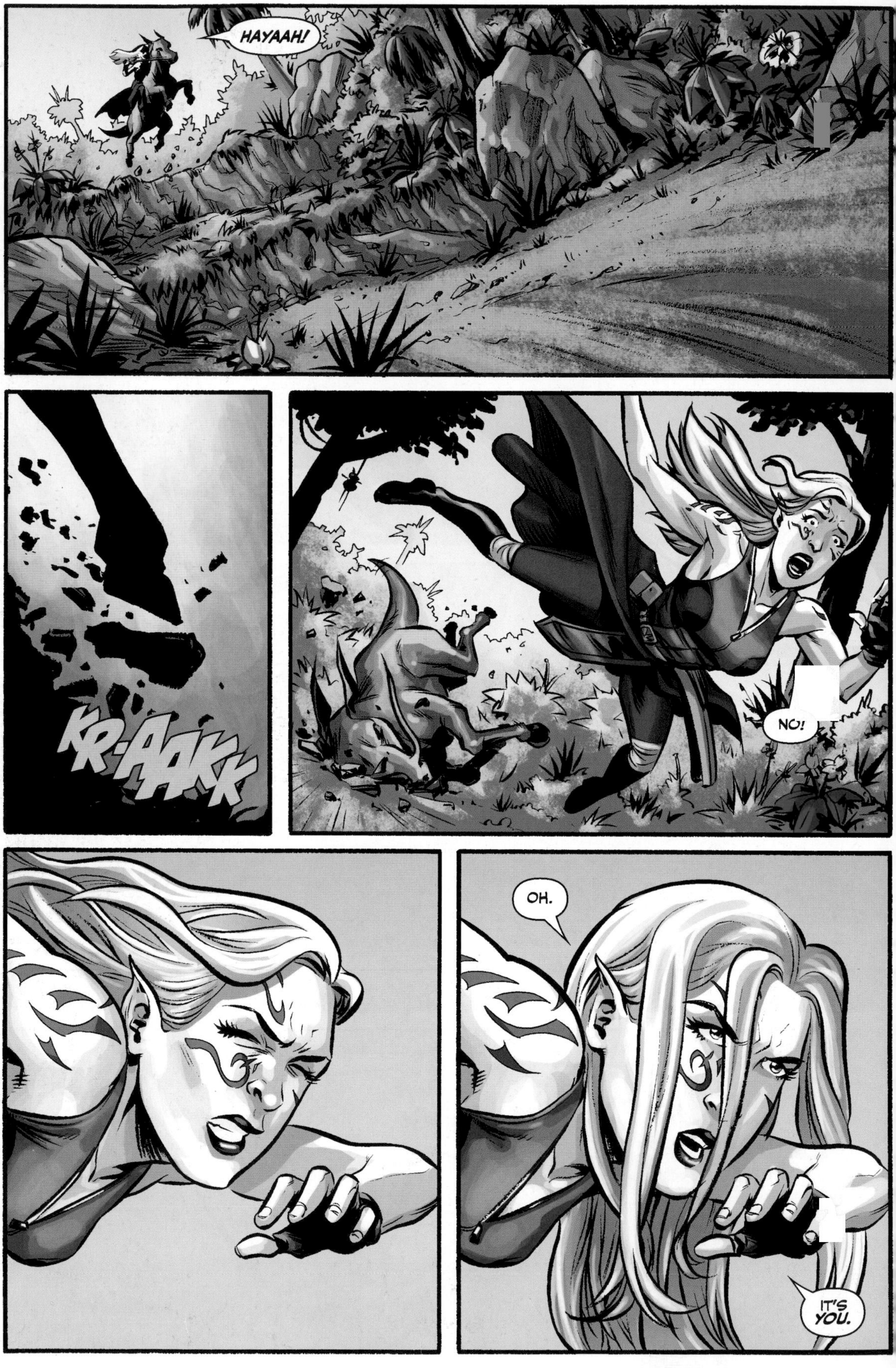
HAYAAH!
KR-AAKK
NO!
OH.
IT'S YOU.

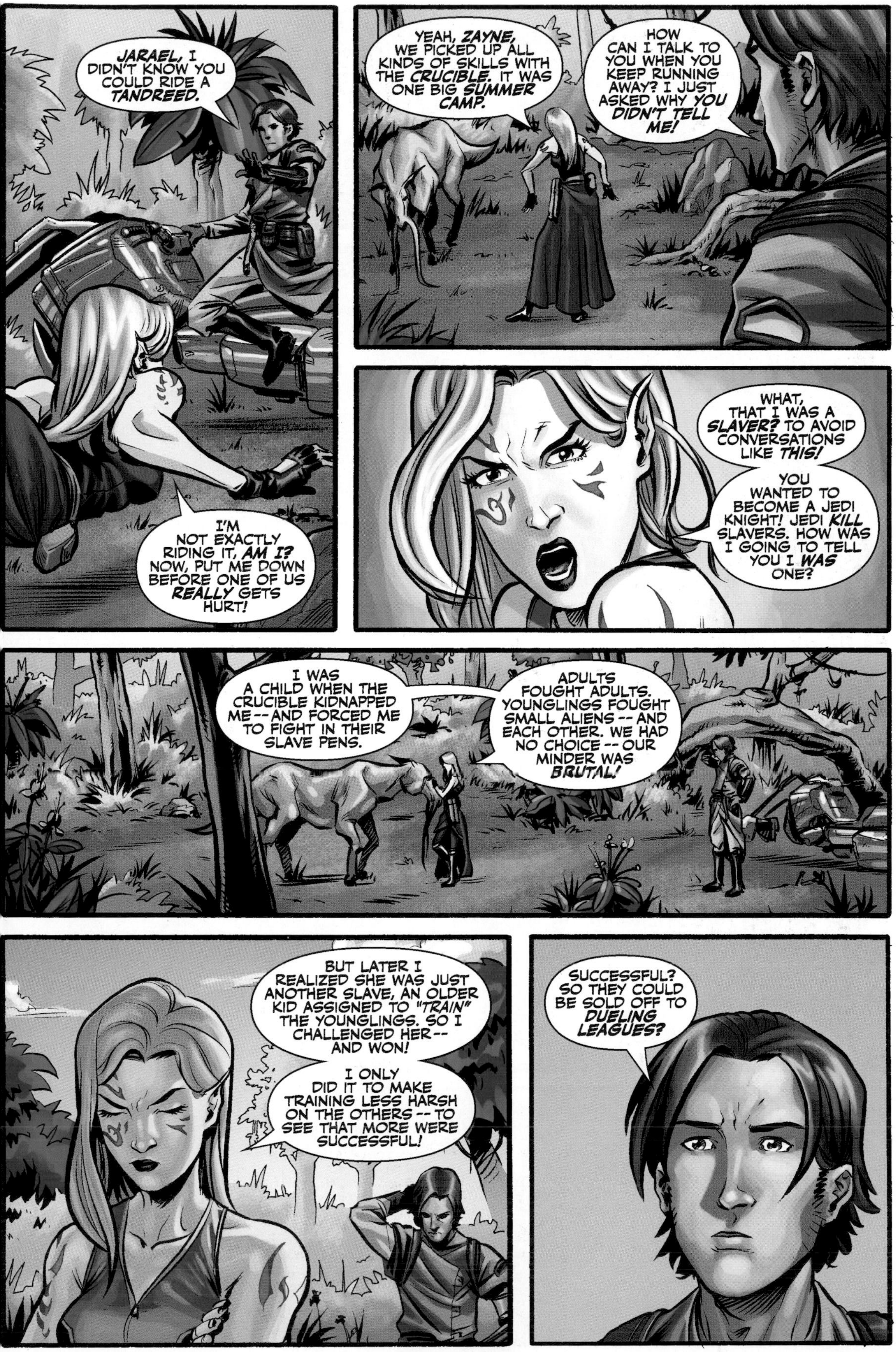
JARAEL, I DIDN'T KNOW YOU COULD RIDE A TANDREED.
I'M NOT EXACTLY RIDING IT, AM I? NOW, PUT ME DOWN BEFORE ONE OF US REALLY GETS HURT!
YEAH, ZAYNE, WE PICKED UP ALL KINDS OF SKILLS WITH THE CRUCIBLE. IT WAS ONE BIG SUMMER CAMP.
HOW CAN I TALK TO YOU WHEN YOU KEEP RUNNING AWAY? I JUST ASKED WHY YOU DIDN'T TELL ME!
WHAT, THAT I WAS A SLAVER? TO AVOID CONVERSATIONS LIKE THIS!
YOU WANTED TO BECOME A JEDI KNIGHT! JEDI KILL SLAVERS. HOW WAS I GOING TO TELL YOU I WAS ONE?
I WAS A CHILD WHEN THE CRUCIBLE KIDNAPPED ME -- AND FORCED ME TO FIGHT IN THEIR SLAVE PENS.
ADULTS FOUGHT ADULTS. YOUNGLINGS FOUGHT SMALL ALIENS -- AND EACH OTHER. WE HAD NO CHOICE -- OUR MINDER WAS BRUTAL!
BUT LATER I REALIZED SHE WAS JUST ANOTHER SLAVE, AN OLDER KID ASSIGNED TO "TRAIN" THE YOUNGLINGS. SO I CHALLENGED HER -- AND WON!
I ONLY DID IT TO MAKE TRAINING LESS HARSH ON THE OTHERS -- TO SEE THAT MORE WERE SUCCESSFUL!
SUCCESSFUL? SO THEY COULD BE SOLD OFF TO DUELING LEAGUES?

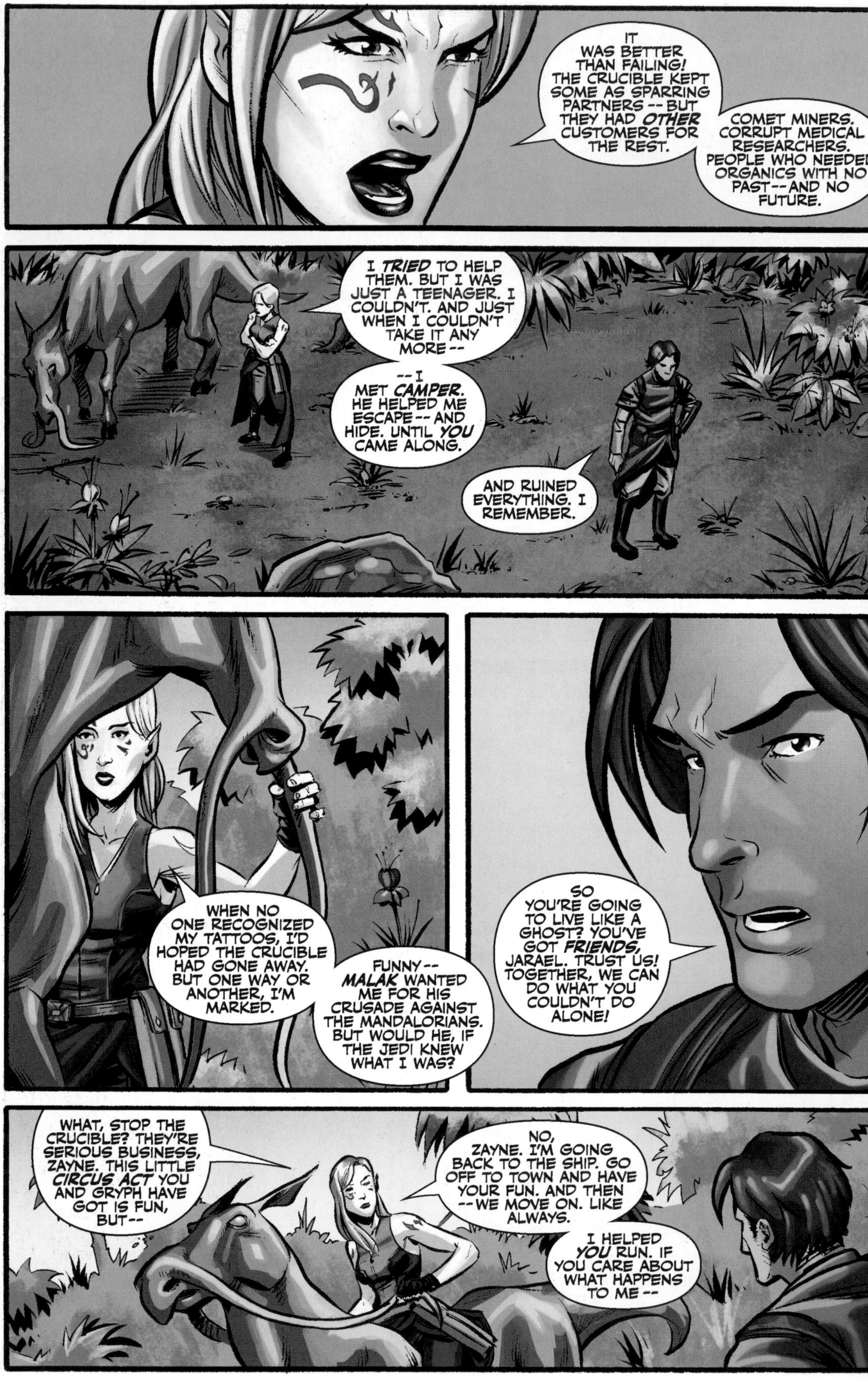
IT WAS BETTER THAN FAILING! THE CRUCIBLE KEPT SOME AS SPARRING PARTNERS -- BUT THEY HAD OTHER CUSTOMERS FOR THE REST.
COMET MINERS. CORRUPT MEDICAL RESEARCHERS. PEOPLE WHO NEEDED ORGANICS WITH NO PAST--AND NO FUTURE.
I TRIED TO HELP THEM. BUT I WAS JUST A TEENAGER. I COULDN'T. AND JUST WHEN I COULDN'T TAKE IT ANY MORE--
--I MET CAMPER. HE HELPED ME ESCAPE--AND HIDE. UNTIL YOU CAME ALONG.
AND RUINED EVERYTHING. I REMEMBER.
WHEN NO ONE RECOGNIZED MY TATTOOS, I'D HOPED THE CRUCIBLE HAD GONE AWAY. BUT ONE WAY OR ANOTHER, I'M MARKED.
FUNNY-- MALAK WANTED ME FOR HIS CRUSADE AGAINST THE MANDALORIANS. BUT WOULD HE, IF THE JEDI KNEW WHAT I WAS?
SO YOU'RE GOING TO LIVE LIKE A GHOST? YOU'VE GOT FRIENDS, JARAEL. TRUST US! TOGETHER, WE CAN DO WHAT YOU COULDN'T DO ALONE!
WHAT, STOP THE CRUCIBLE? THEY'RE SERIOUS BUSINESS, ZAYNE. THIS LITTLE CIRCUS ACT YOU AND GRYPH HAVE GOT IS FUN, BUT--
NO, ZAYNE. I'M GOING BACK TO THE SHIP. GO OFF TO TOWN AND HAVE YOUR FUN. AND THEN --WE MOVE ON. LIKE ALWAYS.
I HELPED YOU RUN. IF YOU CARE ABOUT WHAT HAPPENS TO ME--

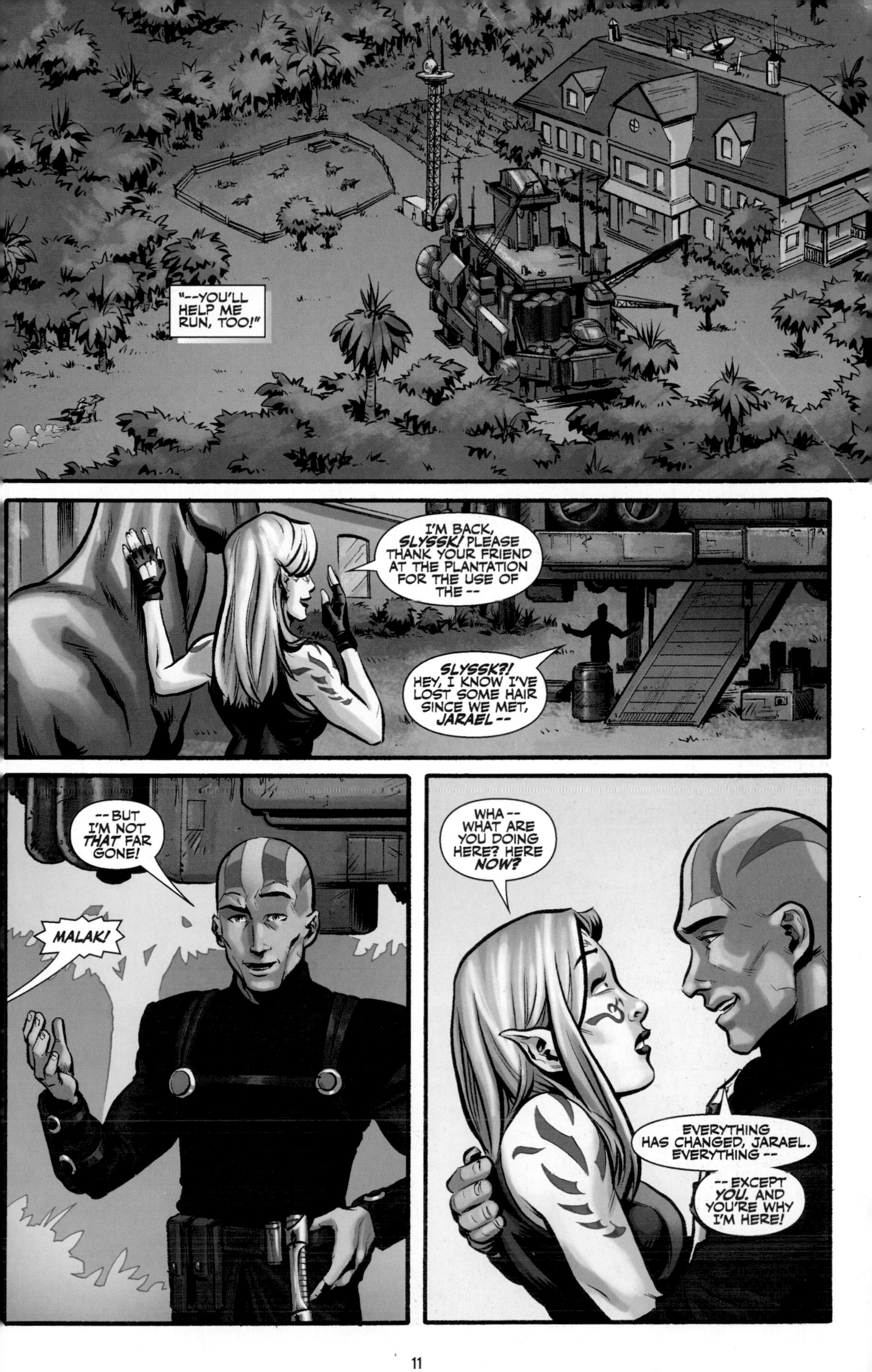
"--YOU'LL HELP ME RUN, TOO!"
I'M BACK, SLYSSK! PLEASE THANK YOUR FRIEND AT THE PLANTATION FOR THE USE OF THE --
SLYSSK?! HEY, I KNOW I'VE LOST SOME HAIR SINCE WE MET, JARAEL --
-- BUT I'M NOT THAT FAR GONE!
MALAK!
WHA -- WHAT ARE YOU DOING HERE? HERE NOW?
EVERYTHING HAS CHANGED, JARAEL. EVERYTHING --
-- EXCEPT YOU. AND YOU'RE WHY I'M HERE!

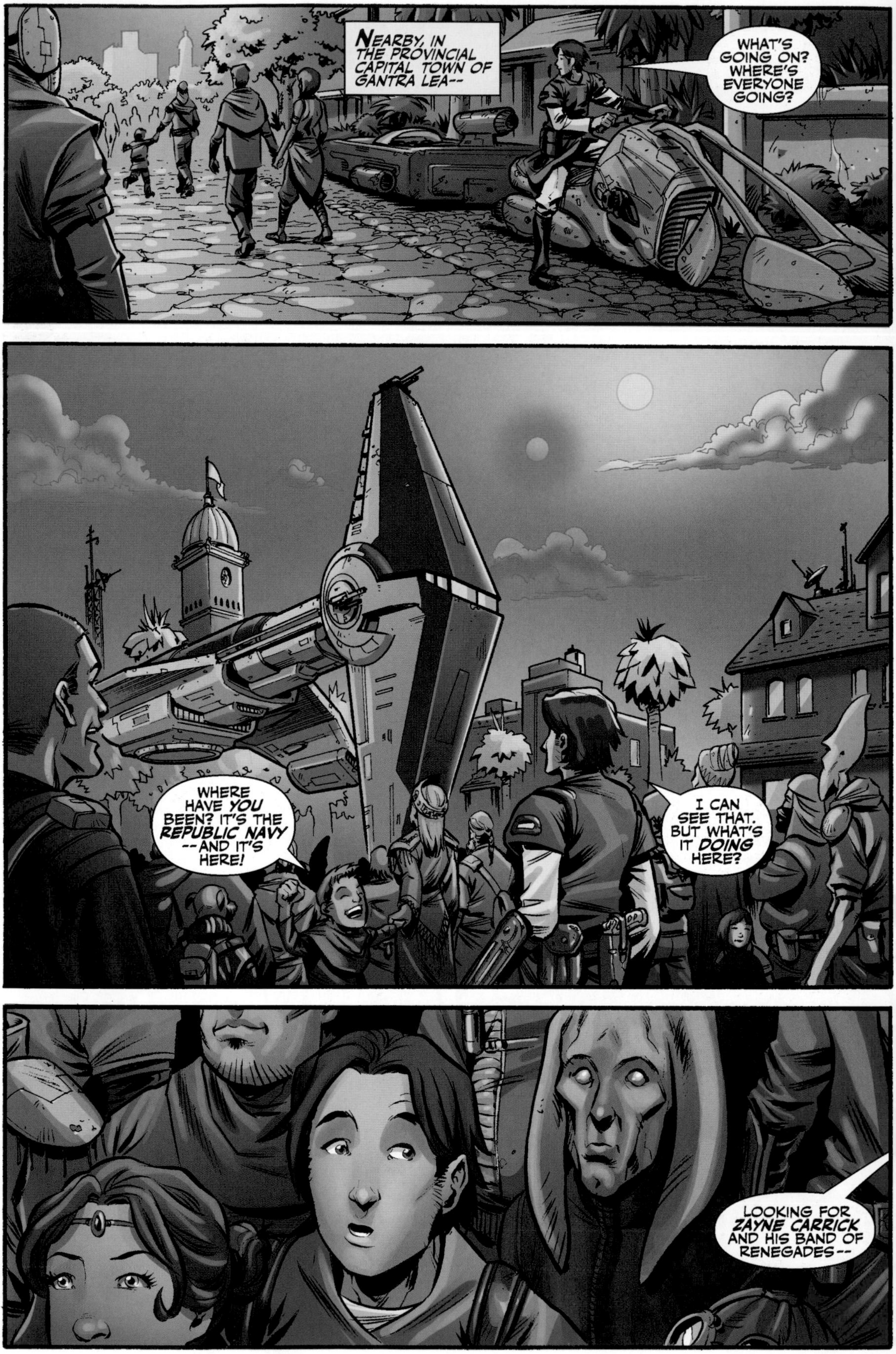
NEARBY, IN THE PROVINCIAL CAPITAL TOWN OF GANTRA LEA--
WHAT'S GOING ON? WHERE'S EVERYONE GOING?
WHERE HAVE YOU BEEN? IT'S THE REPUBLIC NAVY --AND IT'S HERE!
I CAN SEE THAT. BUT WHAT'S IT DOING HERE?
LOOKING FOR ZAYNE CARRICK AND HIS BAND OF RENEGADES--

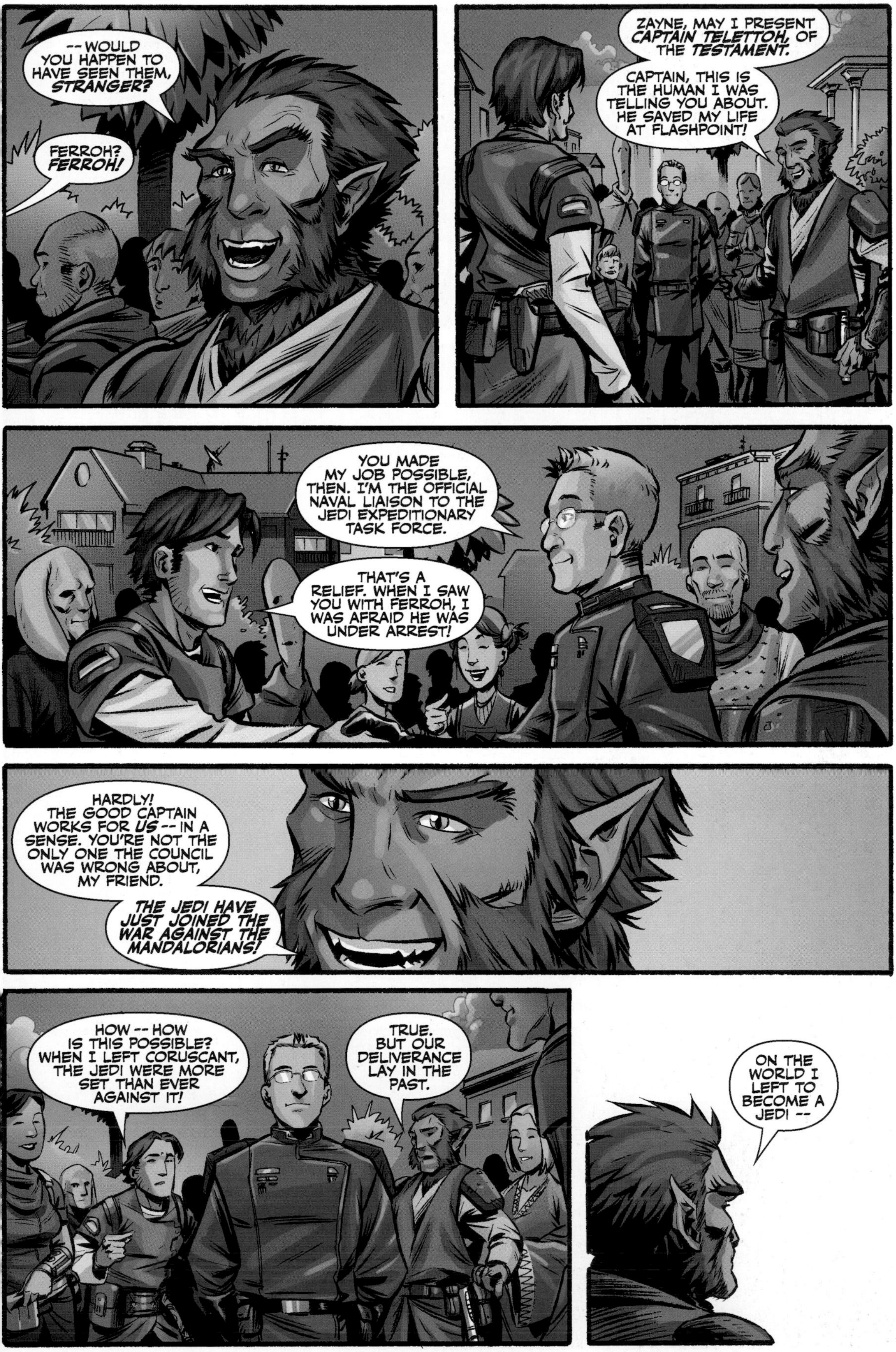
--WOULD YOU HAPPEN TO HAVE SEEN THEM, *STRANGER?*
FERROH? *FERROH!*
ZAYNE, MAY I PRESENT *CAPTAIN TELETTOH,* OF THE *TESTAMENT.*
CAPTAIN, THIS IS THE HUMAN I WAS TELLING YOU ABOUT. HE SAVED MY LIFE AT FLASHPOINT!
YOU MADE MY JOB POSSIBLE, THEN. I'M THE OFFICIAL NAVAL LIAISON TO THE JEDI EXPEDITIONARY TASK FORCE.
THAT'S A RELIEF. WHEN I SAW YOU WITH FERROH, I WAS AFRAID HE WAS UNDER ARREST!
HARDLY! THE GOOD CAPTAIN WORKS FOR *US* -- IN A SENSE. YOU'RE NOT THE ONLY ONE THE COUNCIL WAS WRONG ABOUT, MY FRIEND.
THE JEDI HAVE JUST JOINED THE WAR AGAINST THE MANDALORIANS!
HOW -- HOW IS THIS POSSIBLE? WHEN I LEFT CORUSCANT, THE JEDI WERE MORE SET THAN EVER AGAINST IT!
TRUE. BUT OUR DELIVERANCE LAY IN THE PAST.
ON THE WORLD I LEFT TO BECOME A JEDI --

"--CATHAR. WHEN I RETURNED, A DOZEN YEARS AGO, MY PEOPLE HAD SIMPLY VANISHED. ALL OF THEM. ONLY THE BUILDINGS REMAINED. THE REPUBLIC ASSUMED A MASS MIGRATION DUE TO DISEASE--

"-- BUT OFFWORLD, OTHER CATHAR REFUGEES TOLD ME FRAGMENTED TALES OF HARASSMENT BY THE MANDALORIANS, WHO'D HATED US SINCE THE SITH WAR. I WAS CERTAIN THE MANDALORIANS WERE RESPONSIBLE --

"--AS WAS MY MASTER, WHO KNEW THE JEDI WOULD NEVER JOIN US UNLESS THEY CAME FACE TO FACE WITH MANDALORIAN ATROCITIES.

"WE COULDN'T SHOW THEM WORLDS BEHIND THE LINES, LIKE SERROCO AND JEBBLE. BUT CATHAR KNEW -- IF ONLY IT WOULD TELL US!

"BUT TIME RAN OUT. SOON AFTER MALAK RETURNED, THE JEDI MASTERS CAME. THEY SAID THERE WAS NOTHING SPECIAL ABOUT THE MANDALORIANS--

"--NOTHING WARRANTING JEDI AID IN ANOTHER WAR. WE WERE TO ABANDON OUR EFFORTS AND DISPERSE, FOREVER.

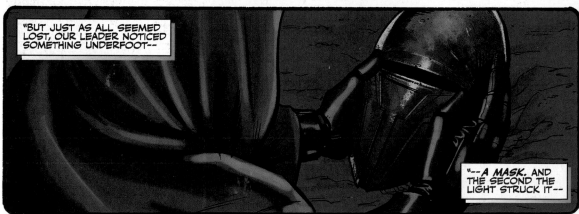

"BUT JUST AS ALL SEEMED LOST, OUR LEADER NOTICED SOMETHING UNDERFOOT--

"-- A MASK. AND THE SECOND THE LIGHT STRUCK IT--

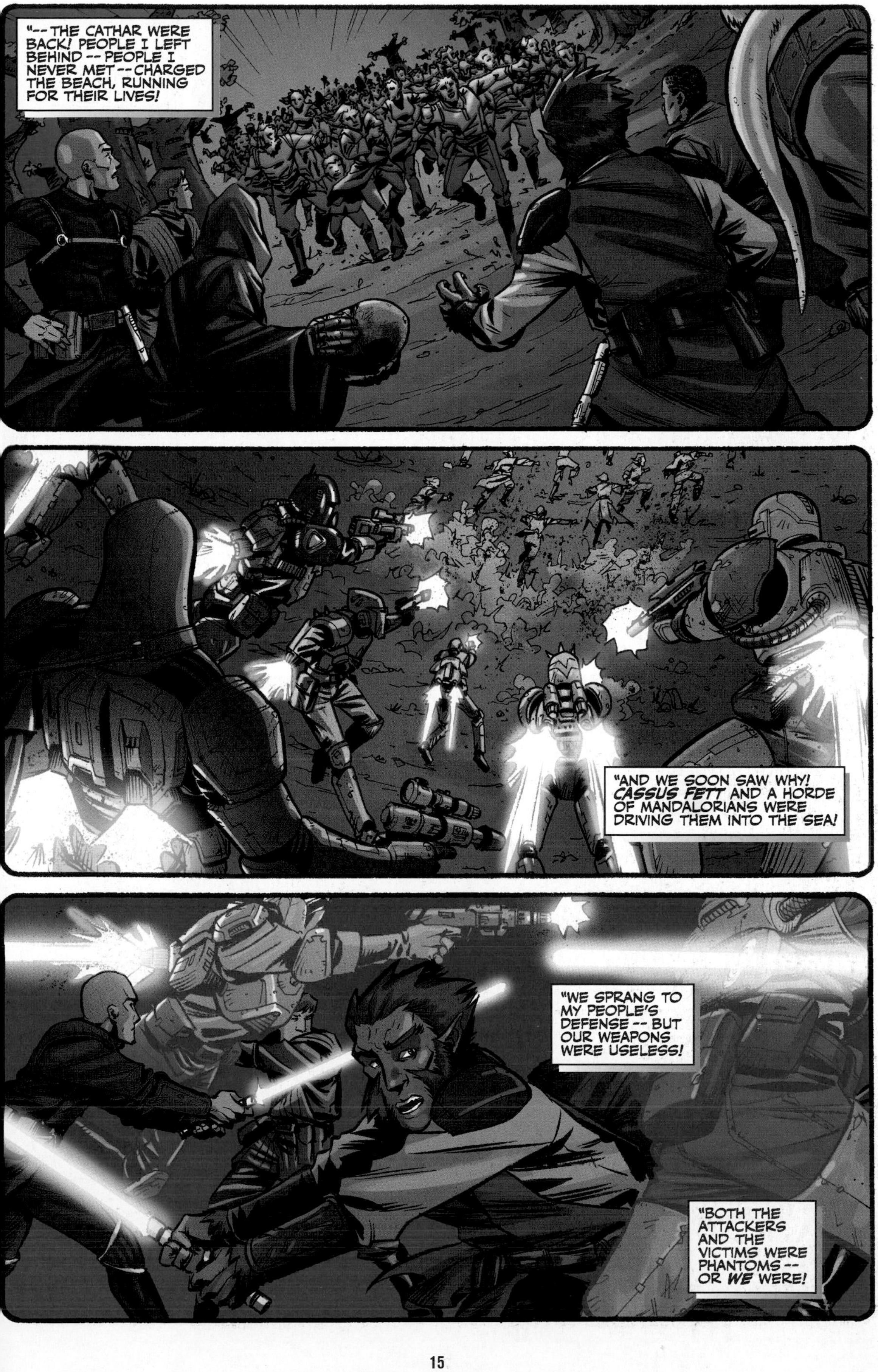
"--THE CATHAR WERE BACK! PEOPLE I LEFT BEHIND--PEOPLE I NEVER MET--CHARGED THE BEACH, RUNNING FOR THEIR LIVES!
"AND WE SOON SAW WHY! *CASSUS FETT* AND A HORDE OF MANDALORIANS WERE DRIVING THEM INTO THE SEA!
"WE SPRANG TO MY PEOPLE'S DEFENSE--BUT OUR WEAPONS WERE USELESS!
"BOTH THE ATTACKERS AND THE VICTIMS WERE PHANTOMS--OR *WE* WERE!

"IT WAS A *JEDI* *VISION* OF EVENTS FROM YEARS BEFORE -- A VISION WE WERE ALL NOW SHARING!"

"WE YELLED AS THE MANDALORIANS WITHDREW, LEAVING THE CATHAR IN THE WATER. BUT NO ONE HEARD! WE WERE NEVER HERE--

"-- BUT PERHAPS THEY WOULD LISTEN TO SOMEONE WHO WAS THERE. ONE OF THEIR OWN, WHO DARED TO SPEAK!"

CASSUS -- *WAIT!* THEY'RE *DEFEATED!* WE DON'T HAVE TO DO THIS!

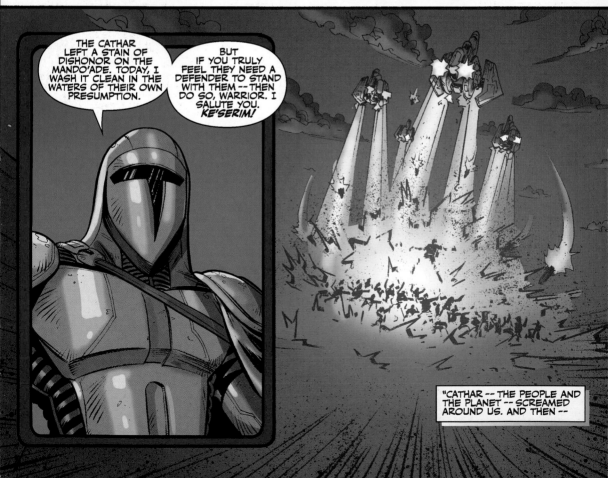

THE CATHAR LEFT A STAIN OF DISHONOR ON THE MANDO'ADE. TODAY, I WASH IT CLEAN IN THE WATERS OF THEIR OWN PRESUMPTION.

BUT IF YOU TRULY FEEL THEY NEED A DEFENDER TO STAND WITH THEM -- THEN DO SO, WARRIOR. I SALUTE YOU. *KE'SERIM!*

"CATHAR -- THE PEOPLE AND THE PLANET -- SCREAMED AROUND US. AND THEN --

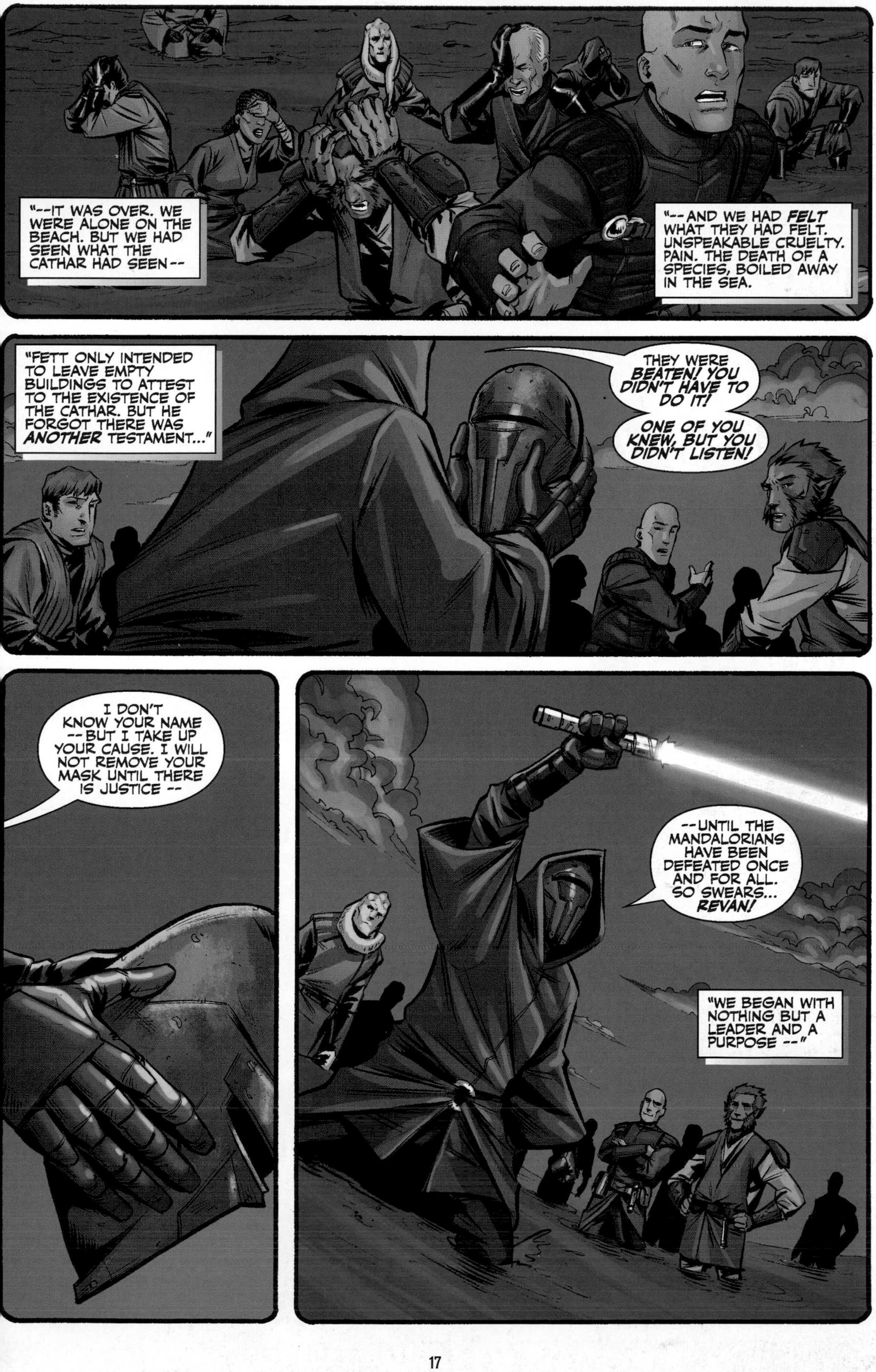
"--IT WAS OVER. WE WERE ALONE ON THE BEACH. BUT WE HAD SEEN WHAT THE CATHAR HAD SEEN--
"--AND WE HAD *FELT* WHAT THEY HAD FELT. UNSPEAKABLE CRUELTY. PAIN. THE DEATH OF A SPECIES, BOILED AWAY IN THE SEA.
"FETT ONLY INTENDED TO LEAVE EMPTY BUILDINGS TO ATTEST TO THE EXISTENCE OF THE CATHAR. BUT HE FORGOT THERE WAS *ANOTHER* TESTAMENT..."
THEY WERE *BEATEN! YOU DIDN'T HAVE TO DO IT!*
ONE OF YOU KNEW, BUT YOU DIDN'T LISTEN!
I DON'T KNOW YOUR NAME --BUT I TAKE UP YOUR CAUSE. I WILL NOT REMOVE YOUR MASK UNTIL THERE IS JUSTICE --
--UNTIL THE MANDALORIANS HAVE BEEN DEFEATED ONCE AND FOR ALL. SO SWEARS... *REVAN!*
"WE BEGAN WITH NOTHING BUT A LEADER AND A PURPOSE --"

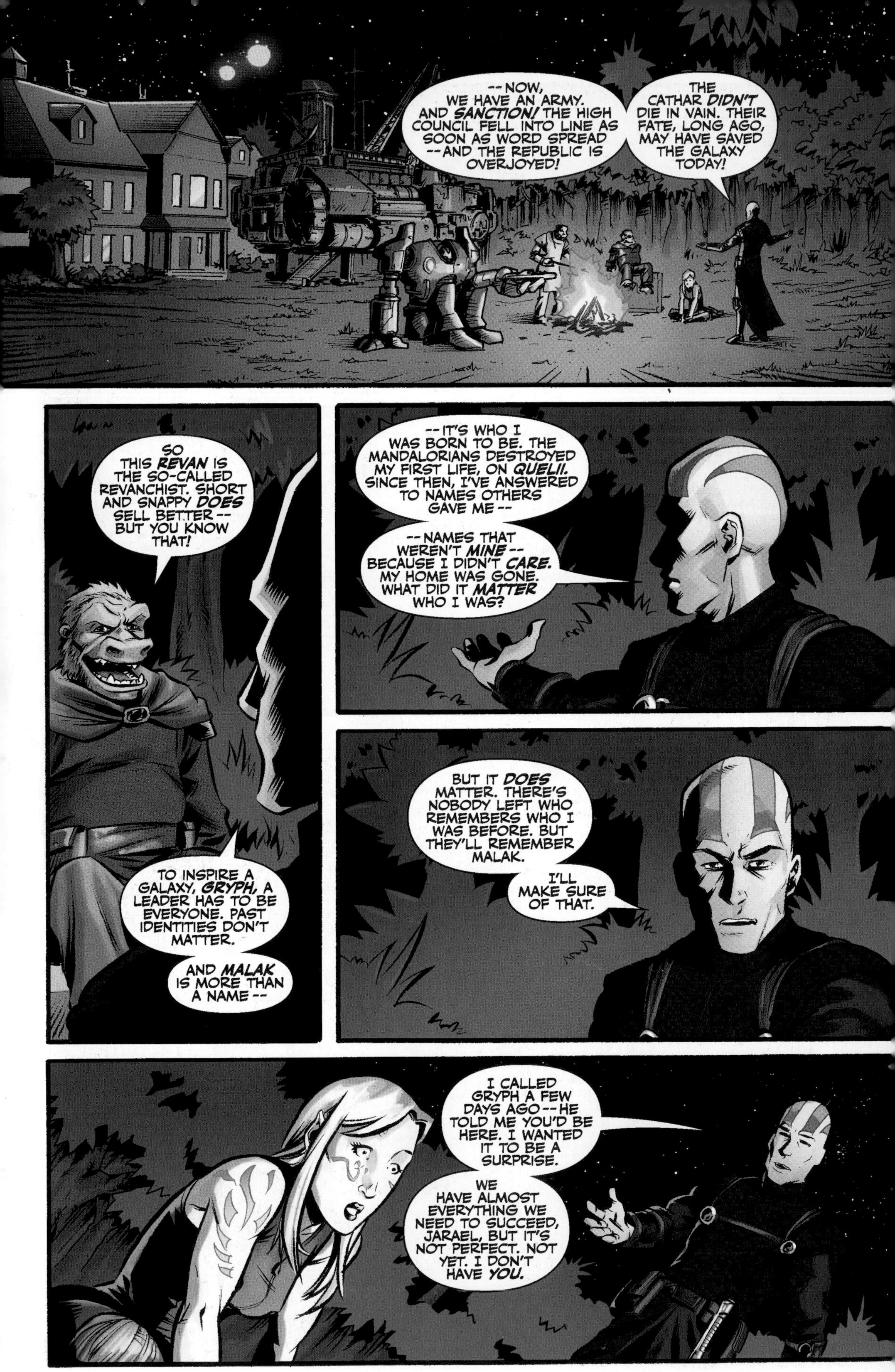
--NOW, WE HAVE AN ARMY. AND SANCTION! THE HIGH COUNCIL FELL INTO LINE AS SOON AS WORD SPREAD --AND THE REPUBLIC IS OVERJOYED!
THE CATHAR DIDN'T DIE IN VAIN. THEIR FATE, LONG AGO, MAY HAVE SAVED THE GALAXY TODAY!
SO THIS REVAN IS THE SO-CALLED REVANCHIST. SHORT AND SNAPPY DOES SELL BETTER-- BUT YOU KNOW THAT!
TO INSPIRE A GALAXY, GRYPH, A LEADER HAS TO BE EVERYONE. PAST IDENTITIES DON'T MATTER.
AND MALAK IS MORE THAN A NAME--
--IT'S WHO I WAS BORN TO BE. THE MANDALORIANS DESTROYED MY FIRST LIFE, ON QUELII. SINCE THEN, I'VE ANSWERED TO NAMES OTHERS GAVE ME--
--NAMES THAT WEREN'T MINE-- BECAUSE I DIDN'T CARE. MY HOME WAS GONE. WHAT DID IT MATTER WHO I WAS?
BUT IT DOES MATTER. THERE'S NOBODY LEFT WHO REMEMBERS WHO I WAS BEFORE. BUT THEY'LL REMEMBER MALAK.
I'LL MAKE SURE OF THAT.
I CALLED GRYPH A FEW DAYS AGO--HE TOLD ME YOU'D BE HERE. I WANTED IT TO BE A SURPRISE.
WE HAVE ALMOST EVERYTHING WE NEED TO SUCCEED, JARAEL, BUT IT'S NOT PERFECT. NOT YET. I DON'T HAVE YOU.

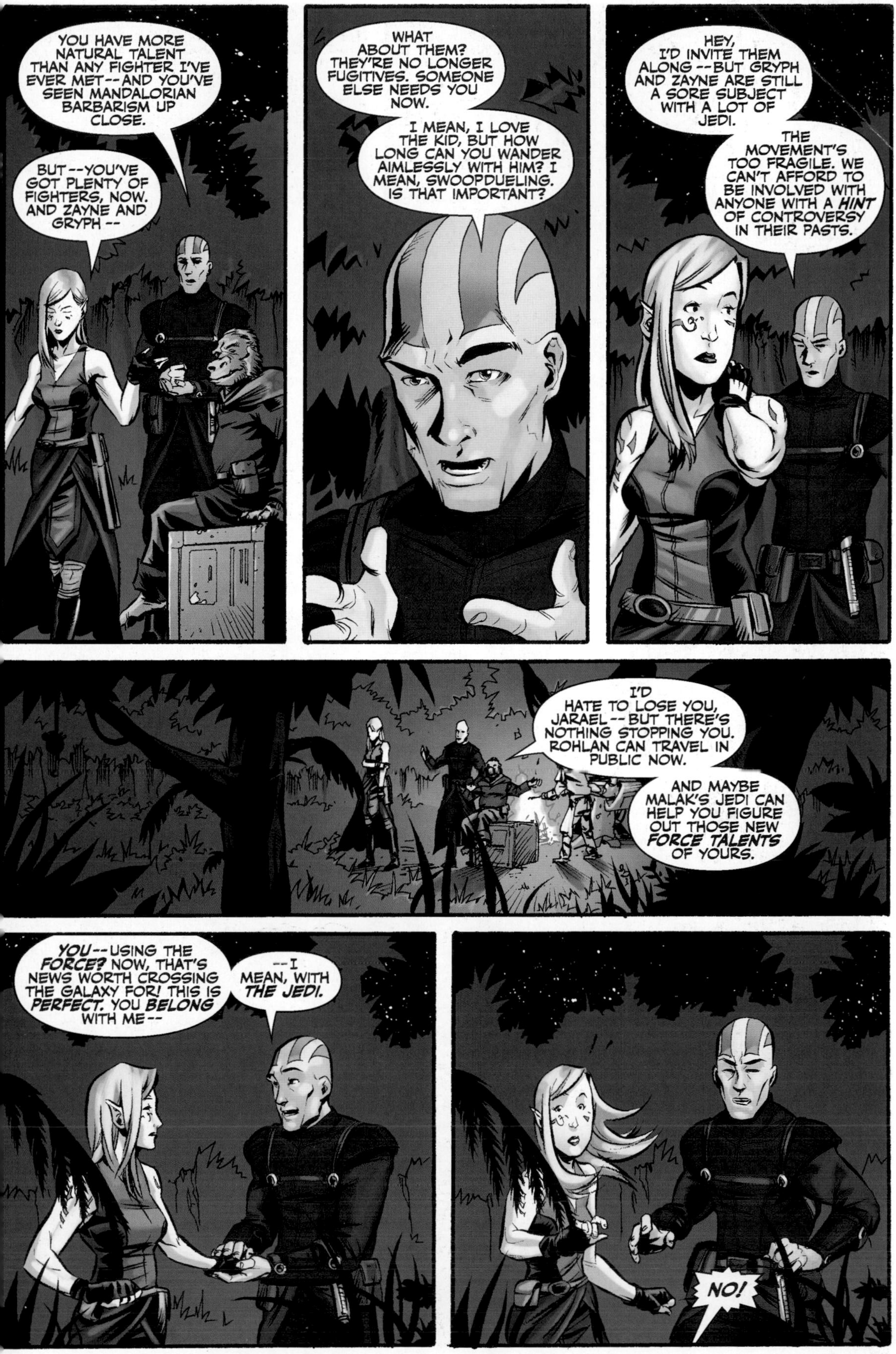
YOU HAVE MORE NATURAL TALENT THAN ANY FIGHTER I'VE EVER MET--AND YOU'VE SEEN MANDALORIAN BARBARISM UP CLOSE.
BUT--YOU'VE GOT PLENTY OF FIGHTERS, NOW. AND ZAYNE AND GRYPH --
WHAT ABOUT THEM? THEY'RE NO LONGER FUGITIVES. SOMEONE ELSE NEEDS YOU NOW.
I MEAN, I LOVE THE KID, BUT HOW LONG CAN YOU WANDER AIMLESSLY WITH HIM? I MEAN, SWOOPDUELING. IS THAT IMPORTANT?
HEY, I'D INVITE THEM ALONG--BUT GRYPH AND ZAYNE ARE STILL A SORE SUBJECT WITH A LOT OF JEDI.
THE MOVEMENT'S TOO FRAGILE. WE CAN'T AFFORD TO BE INVOLVED WITH ANYONE WITH A HINT OF CONTROVERSY IN THEIR PASTS.
I'D HATE TO LOSE YOU, JARAEL--BUT THERE'S NOTHING STOPPING YOU. ROHLAN CAN TRAVEL IN PUBLIC NOW.
AND MAYBE MALAK'S JEDI CAN HELP YOU FIGURE OUT THOSE NEW FORCE TALENTS OF YOURS.
YOU--USING THE FORCE? NOW, THAT'S NEWS WORTH CROSSING THE GALAXY FOR! THIS IS PERFECT. YOU BELONG WITH ME--
--I MEAN, WITH THE JEDI.
NO!

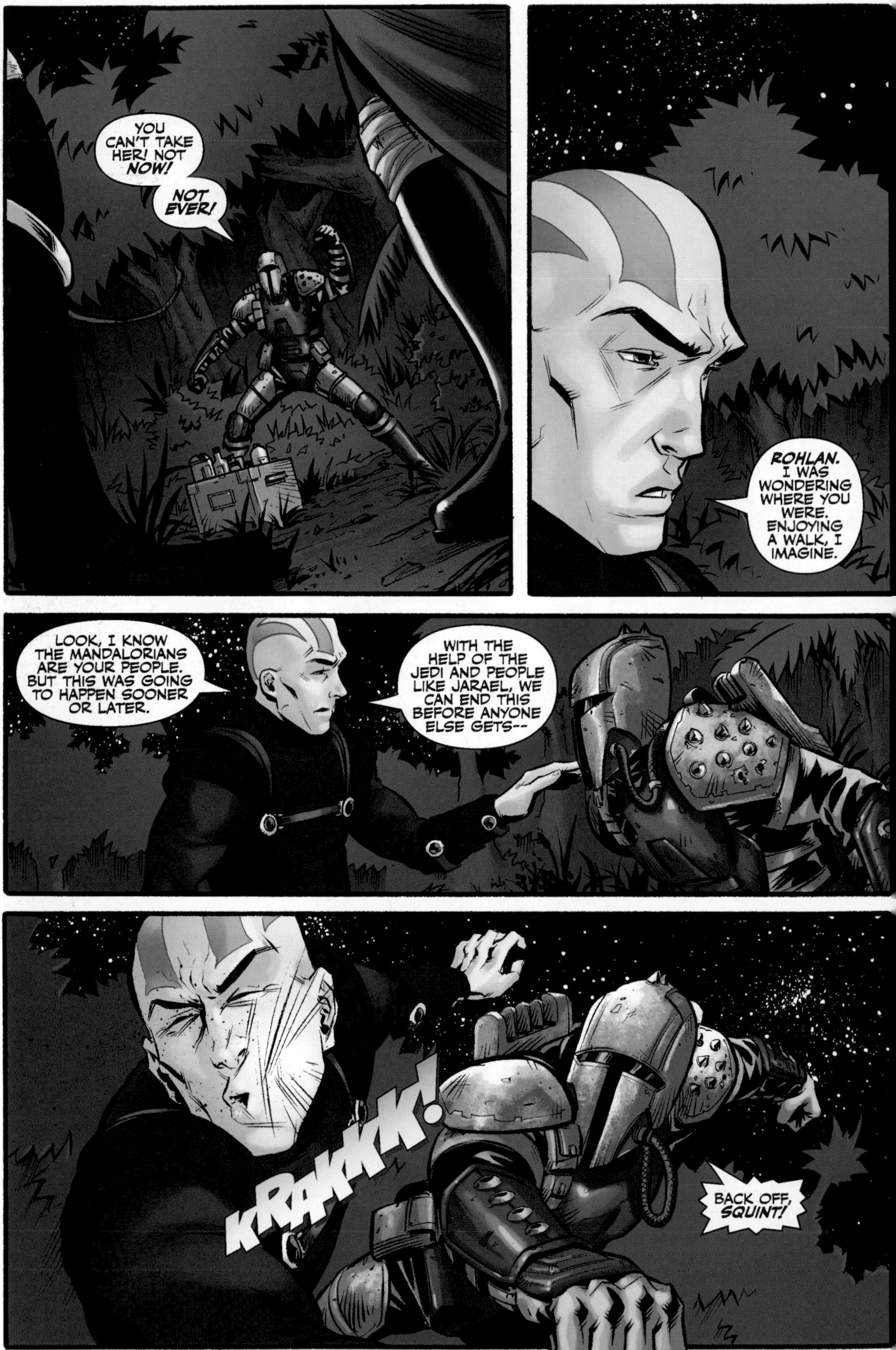
YOU CAN'T TAKE HER! NOT NOW!
NOT EVER!
ROHLAN. I WAS WONDERING WHERE YOU WERE. ENJOYING A WALK, I IMAGINE.
LOOK, I KNOW THE MANDALORIANS ARE YOUR PEOPLE. BUT THIS WAS GOING TO HAPPEN SOONER OR LATER.
WITH THE HELP OF THE JEDI AND PEOPLE LIKE JARAEL, WE CAN END THIS BEFORE ANYONE ELSE GETS--
KRAKKK!
BACK OFF, SQUINT!

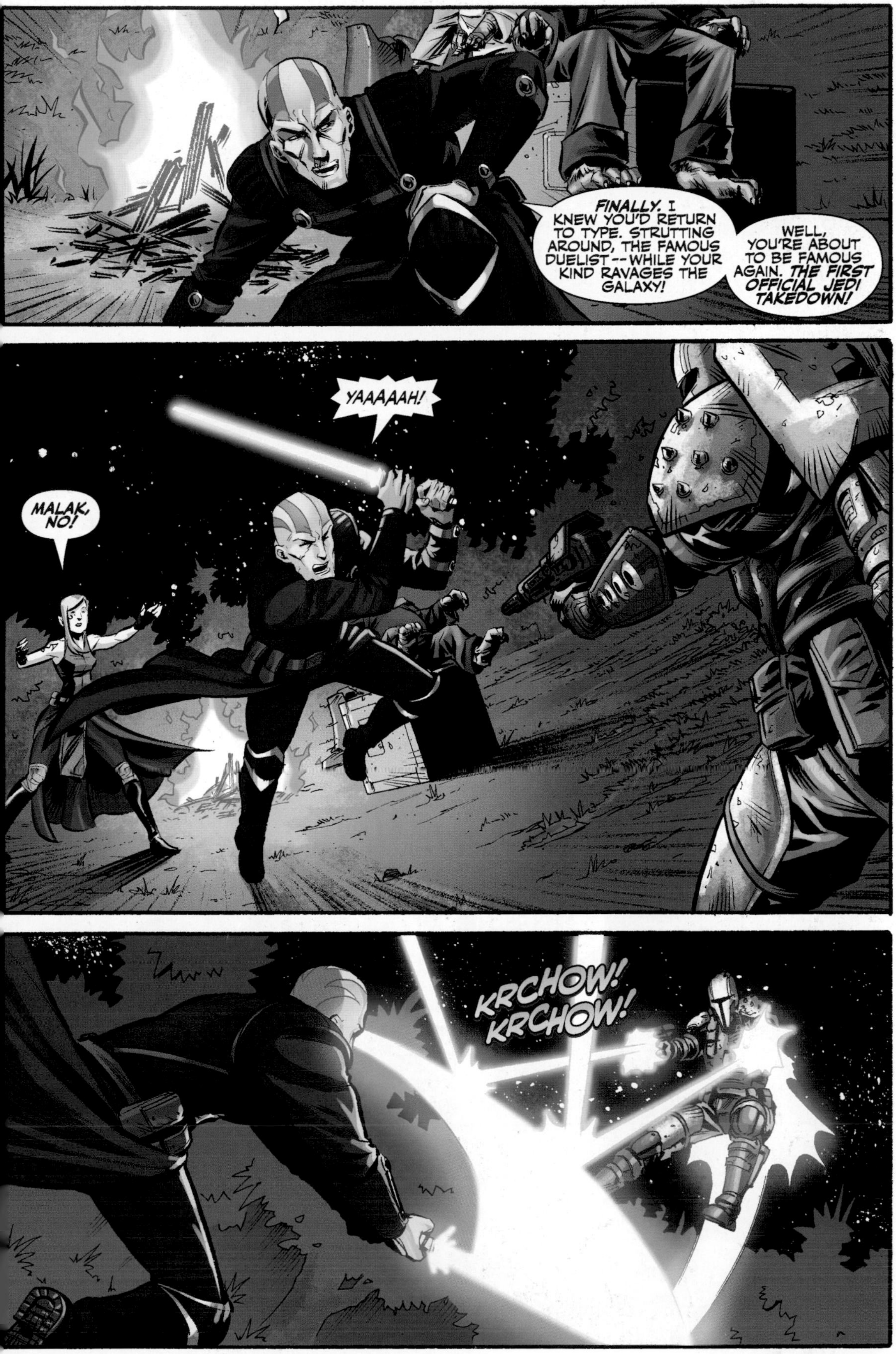
FINALLY. I KNEW YOU'D RETURN TO TYPE. STRUTTING AROUND, THE FAMOUS DUELIST--WHILE YOUR KIND RAVAGES THE GALAXY!
WELL, YOU'RE ABOUT TO BE FAMOUS AGAIN. THE FIRST OFFICIAL JEDI TAKEDOWN!
YAAAAAH!
MALAK, NO!
KRCHOW! KRCHOW!

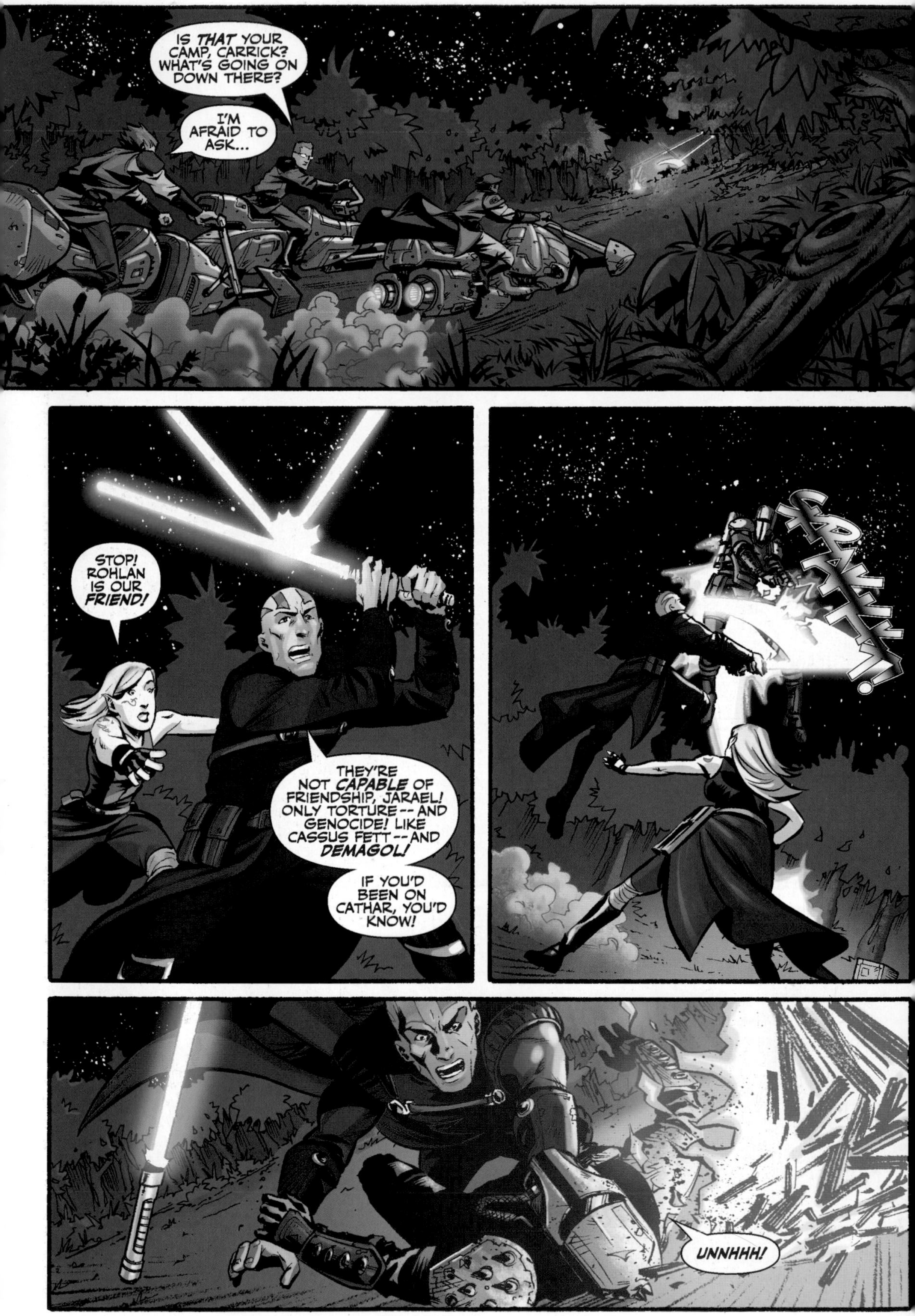
IS THAT YOUR CAMP, CARRICK? WHAT'S GOING ON DOWN THERE?
I'M AFRAID TO ASK...
STOP! ROHLAN IS OUR FRIEND!
THEY'RE NOT CAPABLE OF FRIENDSHIP, JARAEL! ONLY TORTURE -- AND GENOCIDE! LIKE CASSUS FETT -- AND DEMAGOL!
IF YOU'D BEEN ON CATHAR, YOU'D KNOW!
UNNHHH!

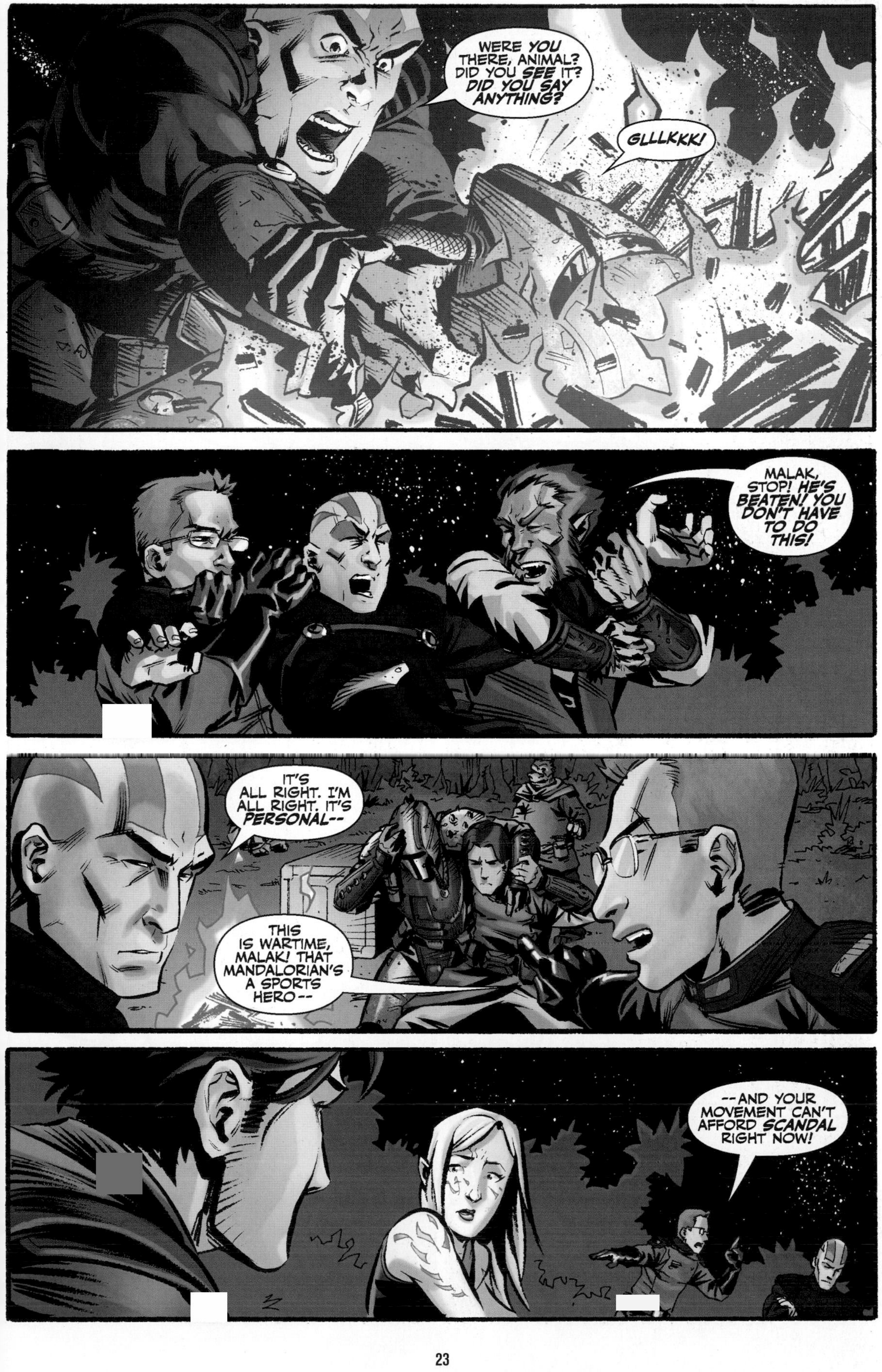
WERE YOU THERE, ANIMAL? DID YOU SEE IT? DID YOU SAY ANYTHING?
GLLLKKK!
MALAK, STOP! HE'S BEATEN! YOU DON'T HAVE TO DO THIS!
IT'S ALL RIGHT. I'M ALL RIGHT. IT'S PERSONAL--
THIS IS WARTIME, MALAK! THAT MANDALORIAN'S A SPORTS HERO--
--AND YOUR MOVEMENT CAN'T AFFORD SCANDAL RIGHT NOW!

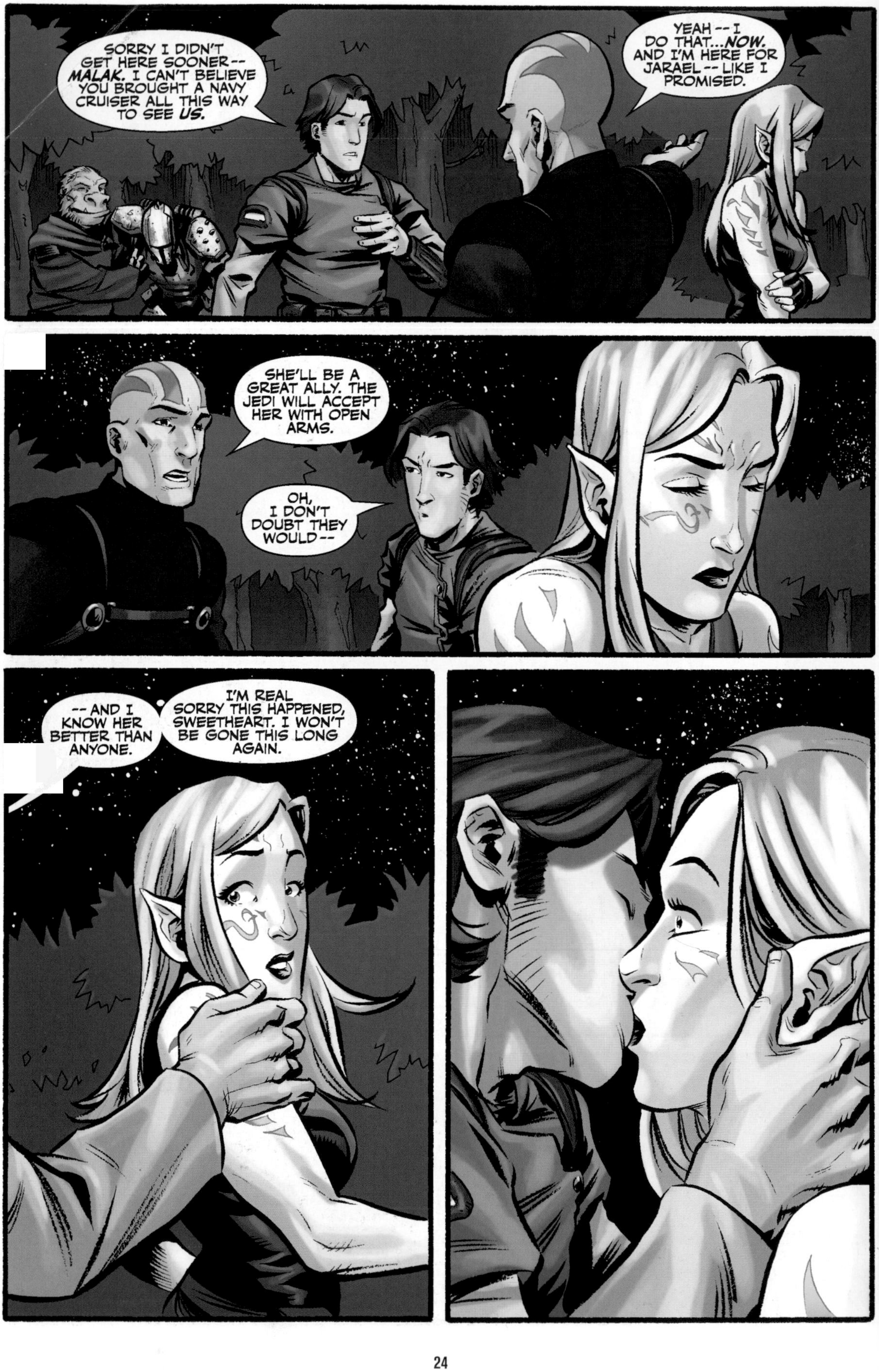

SORRY I DIDN'T GET HERE SOONER-- MALAK. I CAN'T BELIEVE YOU BROUGHT A NAVY CRUISER ALL THIS WAY TO SEE US.
YEAH -- I DO THAT...NOW. AND I'M HERE FOR JARAEL -- LIKE I PROMISED.
SHE'LL BE A GREAT ALLY. THE JEDI WILL ACCEPT HER WITH OPEN ARMS.
OH, I DON'T DOUBT THEY WOULD--
-- AND I KNOW HER BETTER THAN ANYONE.
I'M REAL SORRY THIS HAPPENED, SWEETHEART. I WON'T BE GONE THIS LONG AGAIN.

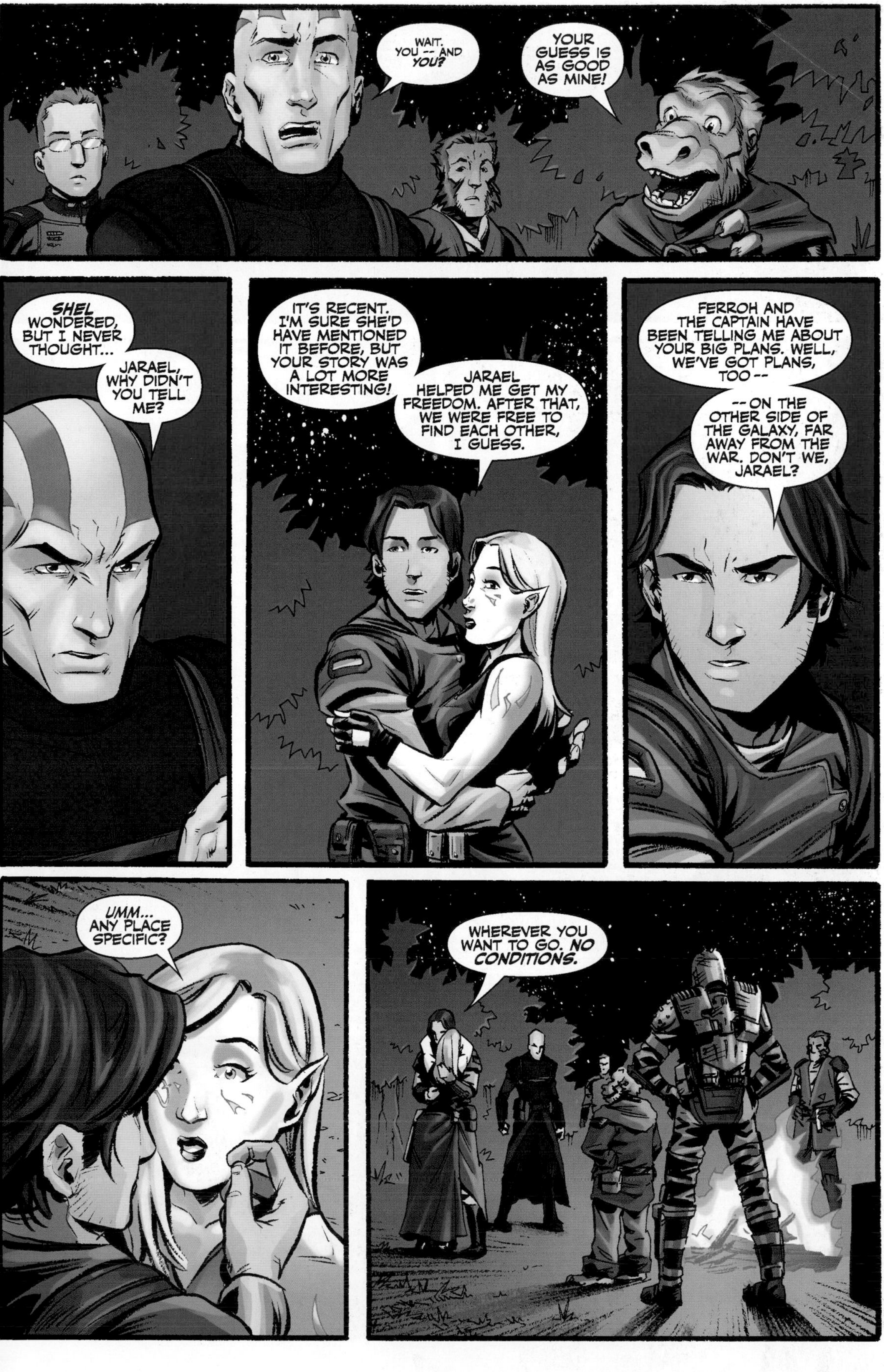
WAIT. YOU -- AND *YOU?*
YOUR GUESS IS AS GOOD AS MINE!
SHEL WONDERED, BUT I NEVER THOUGHT...
JARAEL, WHY DIDN'T YOU TELL ME?
IT'S RECENT. I'M SURE SHE'D HAVE MENTIONED IT BEFORE, BUT YOUR STORY WAS A LOT MORE INTERESTING!
JARAEL HELPED ME GET MY FREEDOM. AFTER THAT, WE WERE FREE TO FIND EACH OTHER, I GUESS.
FERROH AND THE CAPTAIN HAVE BEEN TELLING ME ABOUT YOUR BIG PLANS. WELL, WE'VE GOT PLANS, TOO --
-- ON THE OTHER SIDE OF THE GALAXY, FAR AWAY FROM THE WAR. DON'T WE, JARAEL?
UMM... ANY PLACE SPECIFIC?
WHEREVER YOU WANT TO GO. ***NO CONDITIONS.***

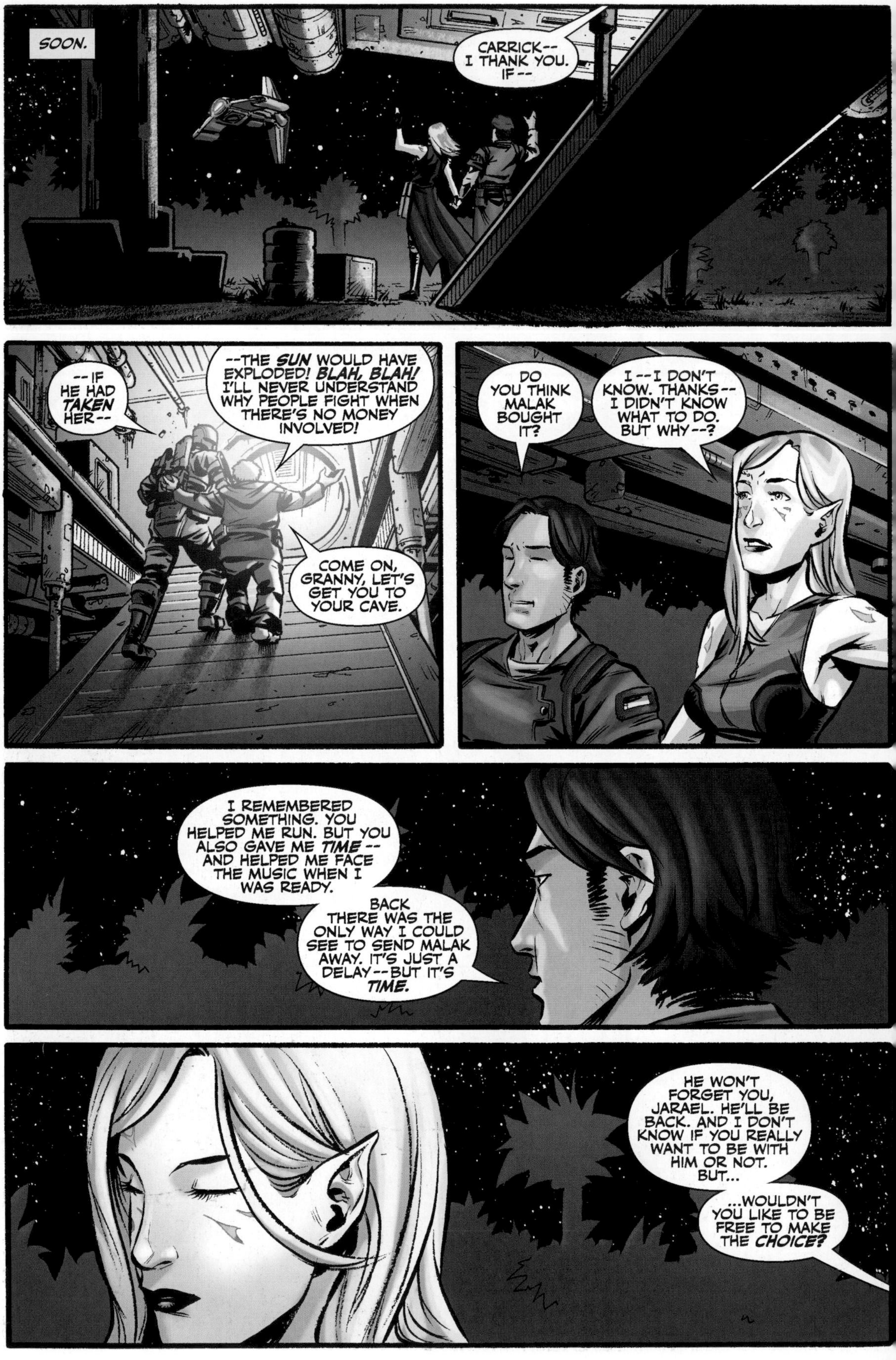
SOON.
CARRICK-- I THANK YOU. IF--
--IF HE HAD TAKEN HER--
--THE SUN WOULD HAVE EXPLODED! BLAH, BLAH! I'LL NEVER UNDERSTAND WHY PEOPLE FIGHT WHEN THERE'S NO MONEY INVOLVED!
COME ON, GRANNY, LET'S GET YOU TO YOUR CAVE.
DO YOU THINK MALAK BOUGHT IT?
I--I DON'T KNOW. THANKS-- I DIDN'T KNOW WHAT TO DO. BUT WHY--?
I REMEMBERED SOMETHING. YOU HELPED ME RUN. BUT YOU ALSO GAVE ME TIME-- AND HELPED ME FACE THE MUSIC WHEN I WAS READY.
BACK THERE WAS THE ONLY WAY I COULD SEE TO SEND MALAK AWAY. IT'S JUST A DELAY--BUT IT'S TIME.
HE WON'T FORGET YOU, JARAEL. HE'LL BE BACK. AND I DON'T KNOW IF YOU REALLY WANT TO BE WITH HIM OR NOT. BUT...
...WOULDN'T YOU LIKE TO BE FREE TO MAKE THE CHOICE?

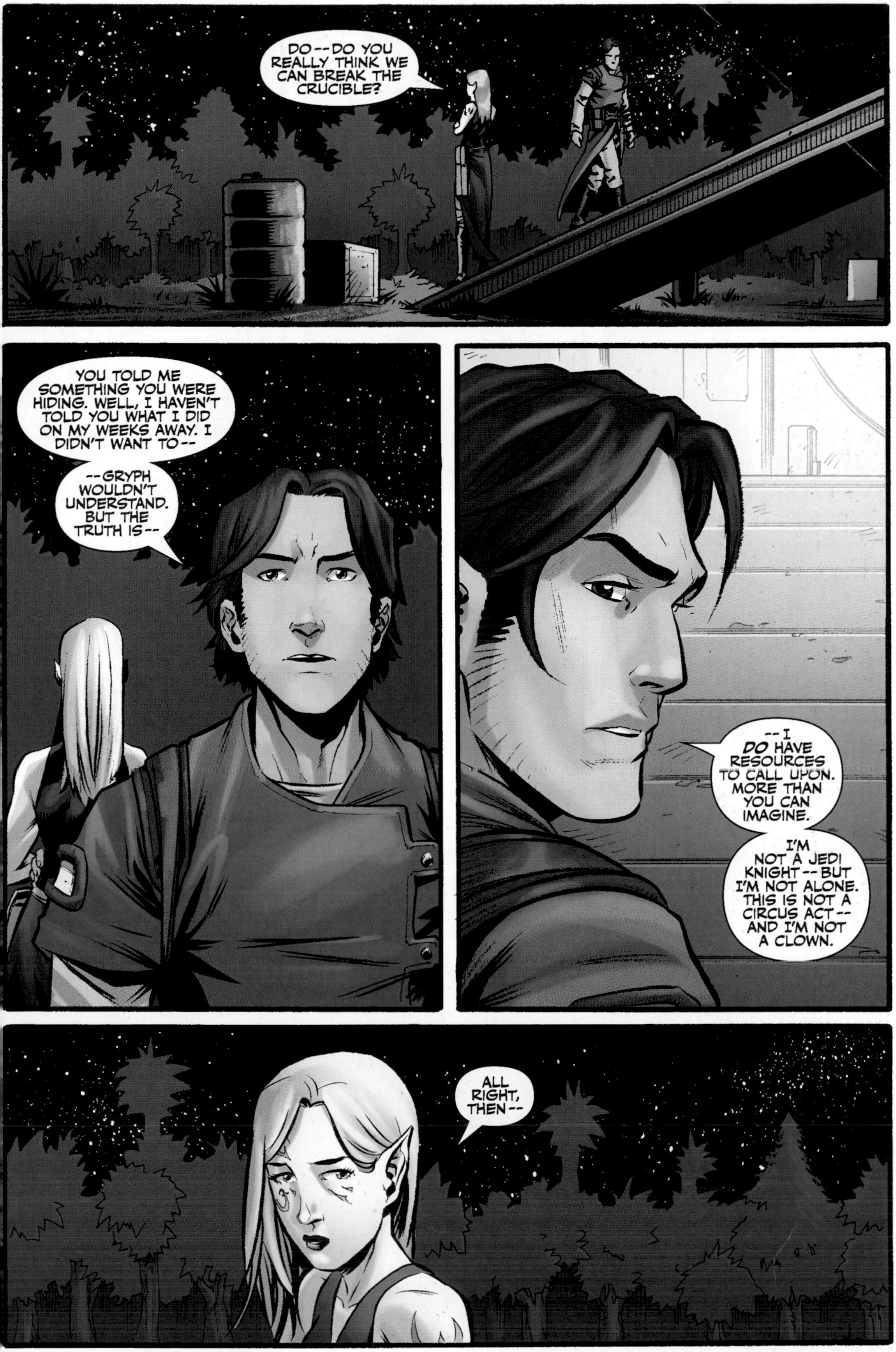
DO--DO YOU REALLY THINK WE CAN BREAK THE CRUCIBLE?
YOU TOLD ME SOMETHING YOU WERE HIDING. WELL, I HAVEN'T TOLD YOU WHAT I DID ON MY WEEKS AWAY. I DIDN'T WANT TO--
--GRYPH WOULDN'T UNDERSTAND. BUT THE TRUTH IS--
--I *DO* HAVE RESOURCES TO CALL UPON. MORE THAN YOU CAN IMAGINE.
I'M NOT A JEDI KNIGHT--BUT I'M NOT ALONE. THIS IS NOT A CIRCUS ACT--AND I'M NOT A CLOWN.
ALL RIGHT, THEN--

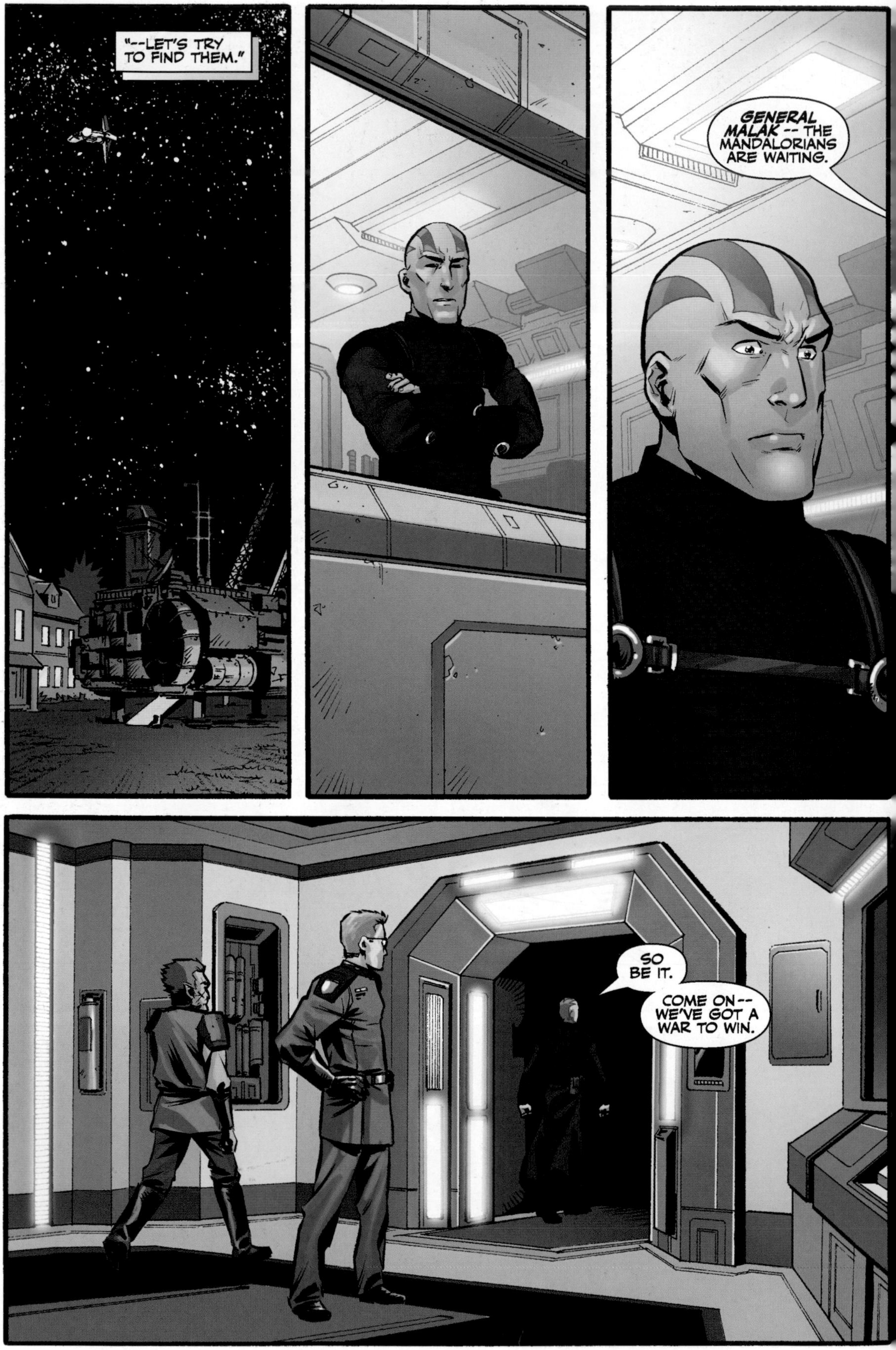
"--LET'S TRY TO FIND THEM."
GENERAL MALAK -- THE MANDALORIANS ARE WAITING.
SO BE IT.
COME ON-- WE'VE GOT A WAR TO WIN.

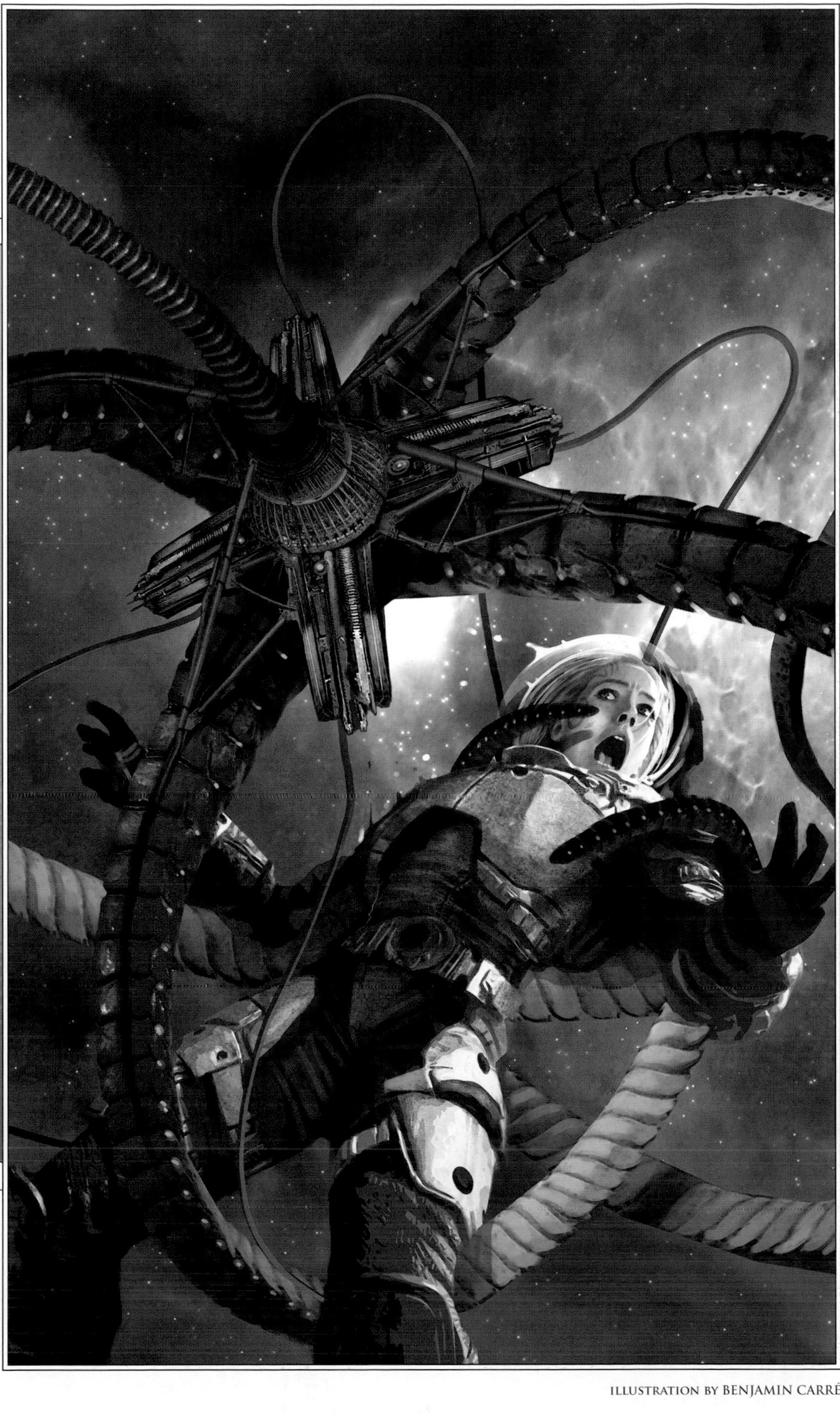

ILLUSTRATION BY BENJAMIN CARRÉ

THE REAPING

art by Bong Dazo

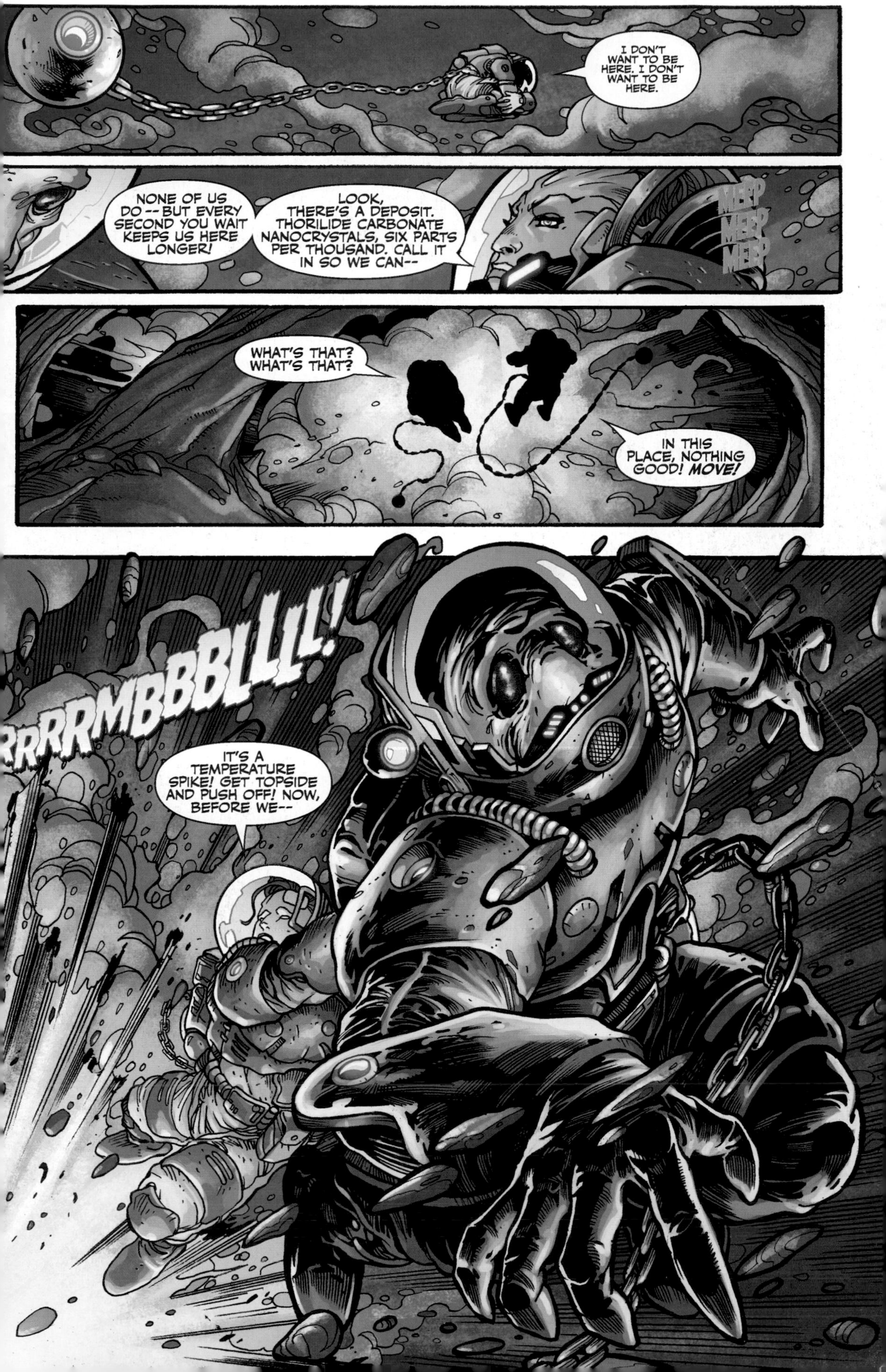
I DON'T WANT TO BE HERE. I DON'T WANT TO BE HERE.
NONE OF US DO--BUT EVERY SECOND YOU WAIT KEEPS US HERE LONGER!
LOOK, THERE'S A DEPOSIT. THORILIDE CARBONATE NANOCRYSTALS, SIX PARTS PER THOUSAND. CALL IT IN SO WE CAN--
MEEP MEEP MEEP
WHAT'S THAT? WHAT'S THAT?
IN THIS PLACE, NOTHING GOOD! MOVE!
RRRRMBBBLLLL!
IT'S A TEMPERATURE SPIKE! GET TOPSIDE AND PUSH OFF! NOW, BEFORE WE--

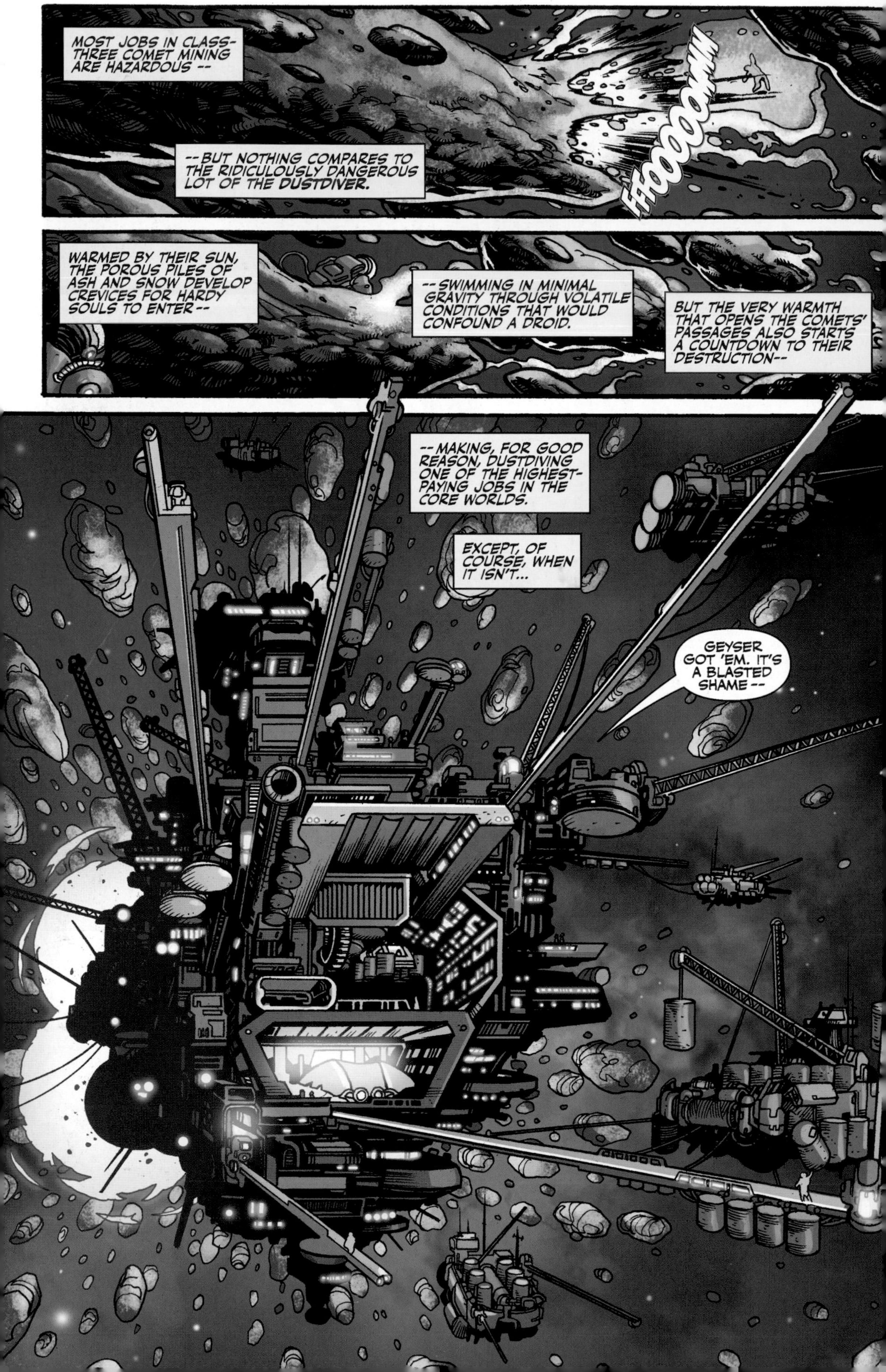
MOST JOBS IN CLASS-THREE COMET MINING ARE HAZARDOUS --
--BUT NOTHING COMPARES TO THE RIDICULOUSLY DANGEROUS LOT OF THE DUSTDIVER.
FFOOOOOOMM
WARMED BY THEIR SUN, THE POROUS PILES OF ASH AND SNOW DEVELOP CREVICES FOR HARDY SOULS TO ENTER--
--SWIMMING IN MINIMAL GRAVITY THROUGH VOLATILE CONDITIONS THAT WOULD CONFOUND A DROID.
BUT THE VERY WARMTH THAT OPENS THE COMETS' PASSAGES ALSO STARTS A COUNTDOWN TO THEIR DESTRUCTION--
--MAKING, FOR GOOD REASON, DUSTDIVING ONE OF THE HIGHEST-PAYING JOBS IN THE CORE WORLDS.
EXCEPT, OF COURSE, WHEN IT ISN'T...
GEYSER GOT 'EM. IT'S A BLASTED SHAME --

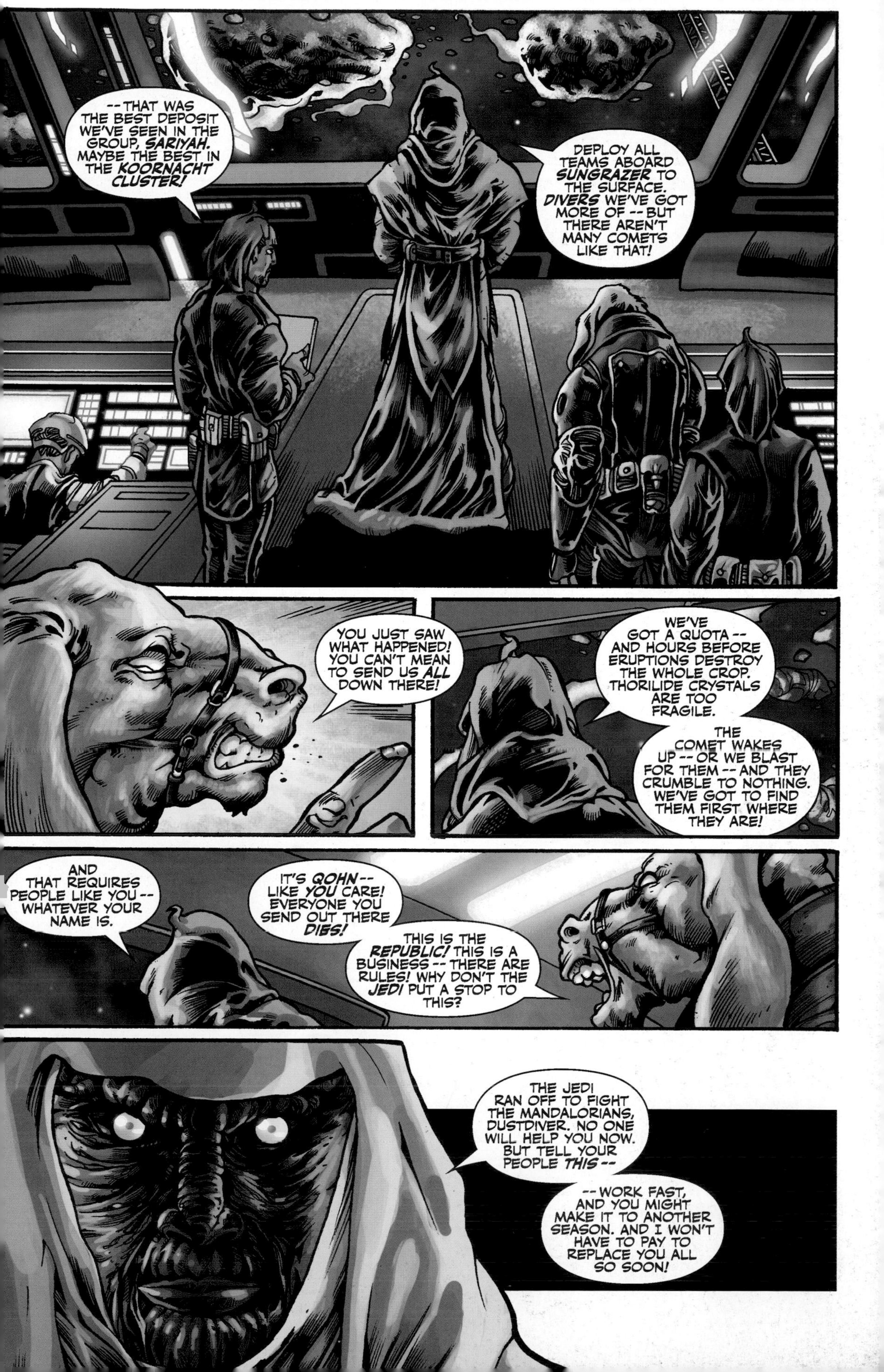
--THAT WAS THE BEST DEPOSIT WE'VE SEEN IN THE GROUP, SARIYAH. MAYBE THE BEST IN THE KOORNACHT CLUSTER!
DEPLOY ALL TEAMS ABOARD SUNGRAZER TO THE SURFACE. DIVERS WE'VE GOT MORE OF -- BUT THERE AREN'T MANY COMETS LIKE THAT!
YOU JUST SAW WHAT HAPPENED! YOU CAN'T MEAN TO SEND US ALL DOWN THERE!
WE'VE GOT A QUOTA -- AND HOURS BEFORE ERUPTIONS DESTROY THE WHOLE CROP. THORILIDE CRYSTALS ARE TOO FRAGILE.
THE COMET WAKES UP -- OR WE BLAST FOR THEM -- AND THEY CRUMBLE TO NOTHING. WE'VE GOT TO FIND THEM FIRST WHERE THEY ARE!
AND THAT REQUIRES PEOPLE LIKE YOU -- WHATEVER YOUR NAME IS.
IT'S QOHN -- LIKE YOU CARE! EVERYONE YOU SEND OUT THERE DIES!
THIS IS THE REPUBLIC! THIS IS A BUSINESS -- THERE ARE RULES! WHY DON'T THE JEDI PUT A STOP TO THIS?
THE JEDI RAN OFF TO FIGHT THE MANDALORIANS, DUSTDIVER. NO ONE WILL HELP YOU NOW. BUT TELL YOUR PEOPLE THIS --
-- WORK FAST, AND YOU MIGHT MAKE IT TO ANOTHER SEASON. AND I WON'T HAVE TO PAY TO REPLACE YOU ALL SO SOON!

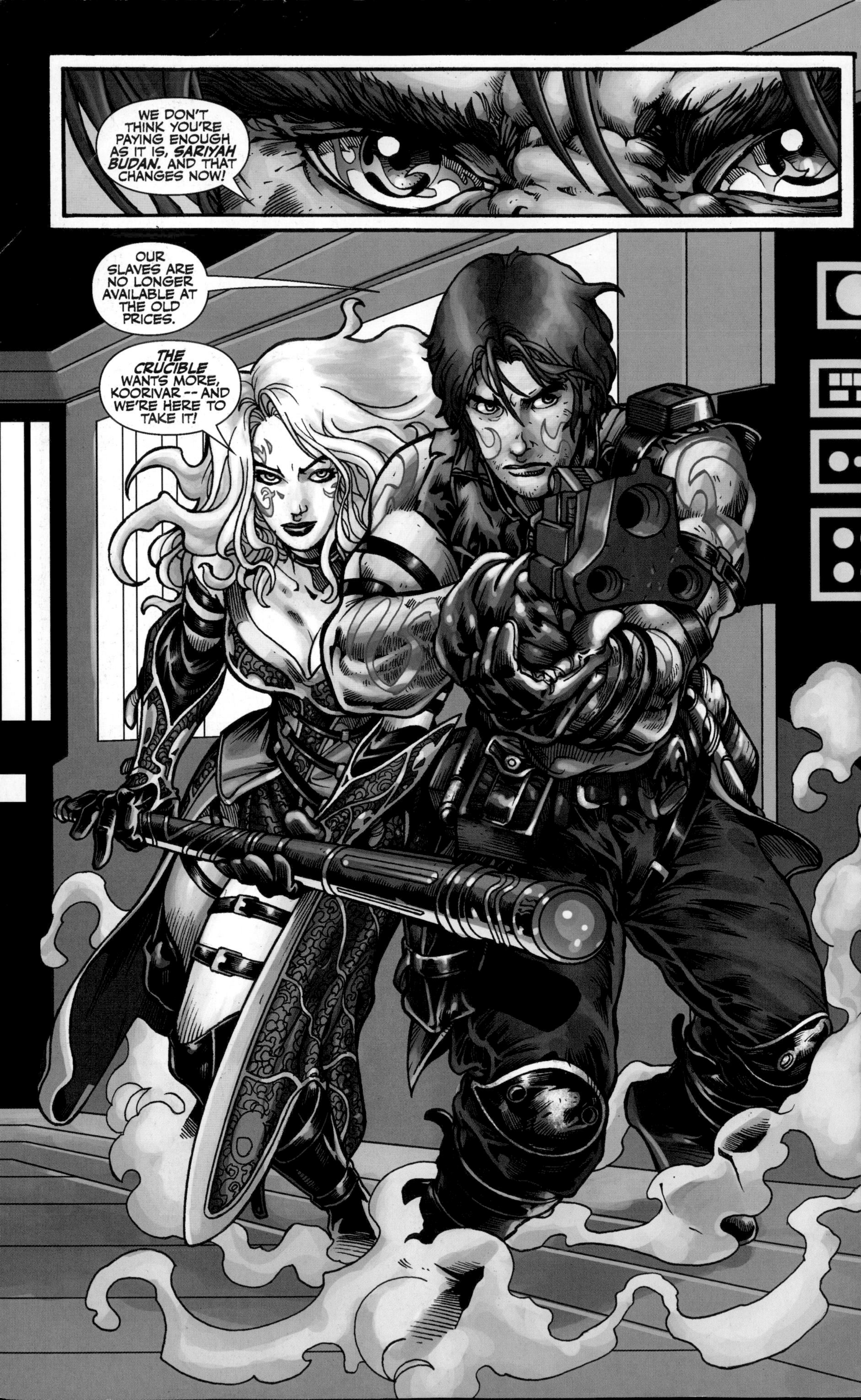
WE DON'T THINK YOU'RE PAYING ENOUGH AS IT IS, *SARIYAH BUDAN.* AND THAT CHANGES NOW!
OUR SLAVES ARE NO LONGER AVAILABLE AT THE OLD PRICES.
THE CRUCIBLE WANTS MORE, KOORIVAR -- AND WE'RE HERE TO TAKE IT!

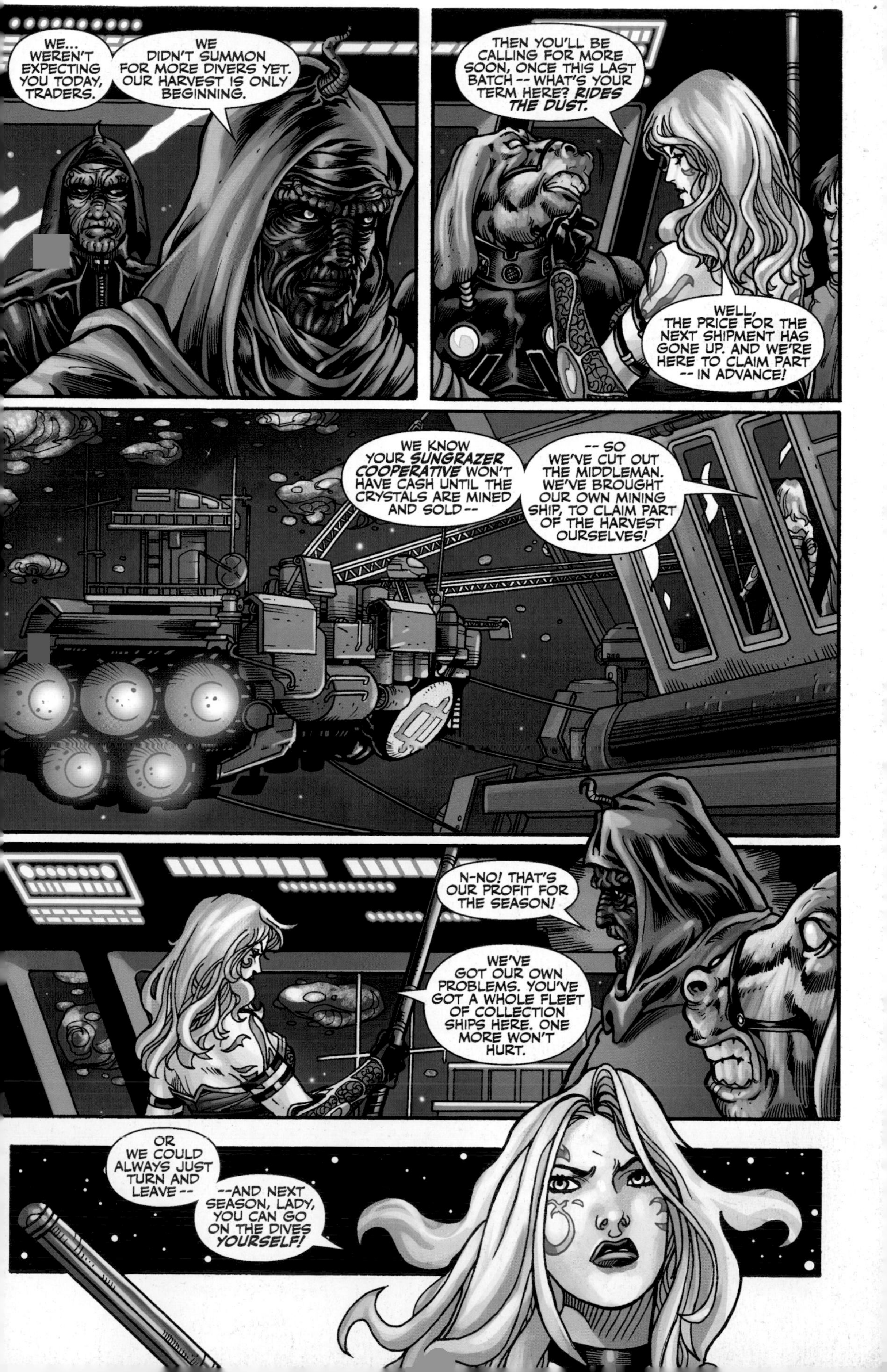
WE... WEREN'T EXPECTING YOU TODAY, TRADERS.
WE DIDN'T SUMMON FOR MORE DIVERS YET. OUR HARVEST IS ONLY BEGINNING.
THEN YOU'LL BE CALLING FOR MORE SOON, ONCE THIS LAST BATCH -- WHAT'S YOUR TERM HERE? RIDES THE DUST.
WELL, THE PRICE FOR THE NEXT SHIPMENT HAS GONE UP. AND WE'RE HERE TO CLAIM PART -- IN ADVANCE!
WE KNOW YOUR SUNGRAZER COOPERATIVE WON'T HAVE CASH UNTIL THE CRYSTALS ARE MINED AND SOLD --
-- SO WE'VE CUT OUT THE MIDDLEMAN. WE'VE BROUGHT OUR OWN MINING SHIP, TO CLAIM PART OF THE HARVEST OURSELVES!
N-NO! THAT'S OUR PROFIT FOR THE SEASON!
WE'VE GOT OUR OWN PROBLEMS. YOU'VE GOT A WHOLE FLEET OF COLLECTION SHIPS HERE. ONE MORE WON'T HURT.
OR WE COULD ALWAYS JUST TURN AND LEAVE --
--AND NEXT SEASON, LADY, YOU CAN GO ON THE DIVES YOURSELF!

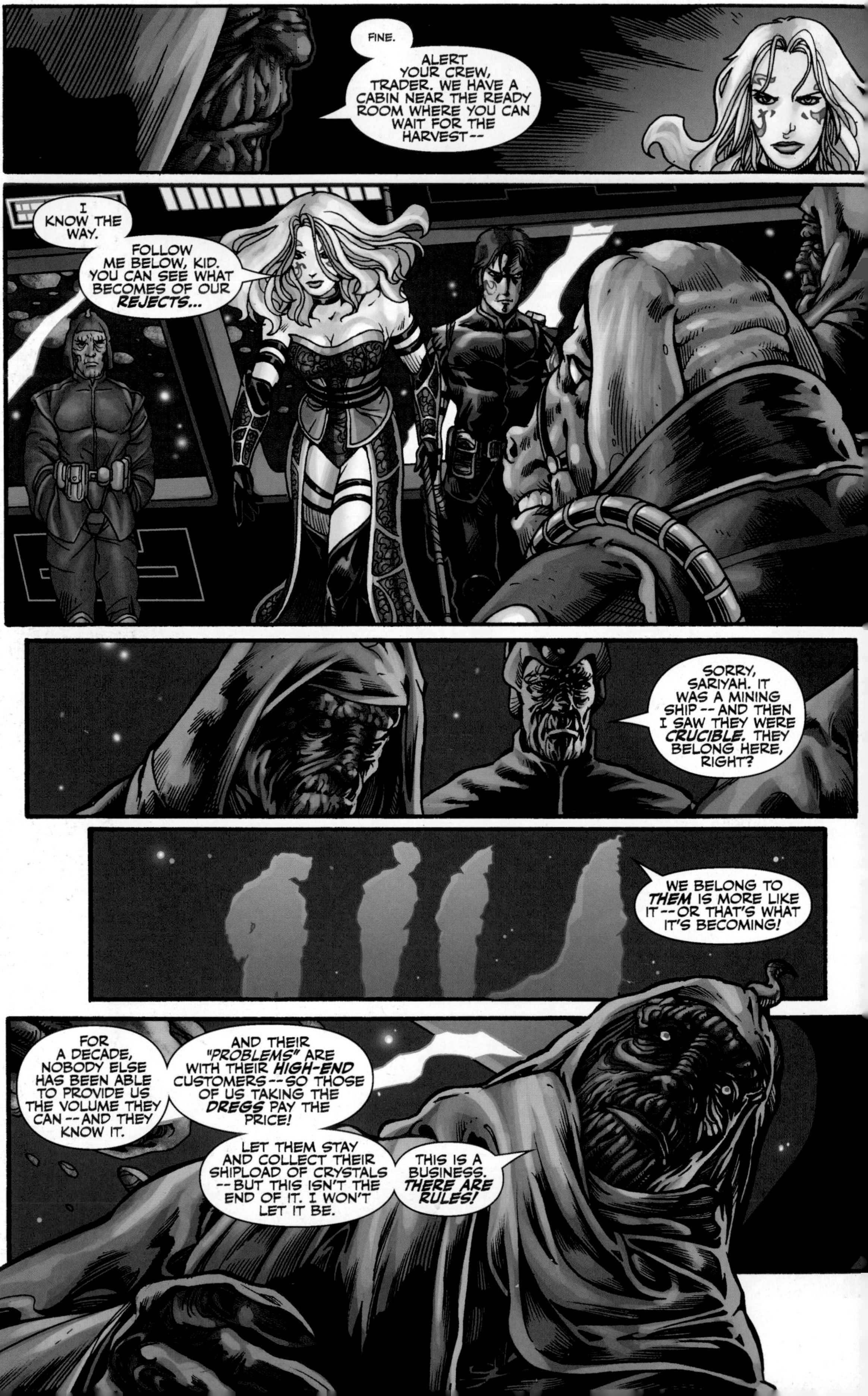
FINE.
ALERT YOUR CREW, TRADER. WE HAVE A CABIN NEAR THE READY ROOM WHERE YOU CAN WAIT FOR THE HARVEST--
I KNOW THE WAY.
FOLLOW ME BELOW, KID. YOU CAN SEE WHAT BECOMES OF OUR REJECTS...
SORRY, SARIYAH. IT WAS A MINING SHIP--AND THEN I SAW THEY WERE CRUCIBLE. THEY BELONG HERE, RIGHT?
WE BELONG TO THEM IS MORE LIKE IT--OR THAT'S WHAT IT'S BECOMING!
FOR A DECADE, NOBODY ELSE HAS BEEN ABLE TO PROVIDE US THE VOLUME THEY CAN--AND THEY KNOW IT.
AND THEIR "PROBLEMS" ARE WITH THEIR HIGH-END CUSTOMERS--SO THOSE OF US TAKING THE DREGS PAY THE PRICE!
LET THEM STAY AND COLLECT THEIR SHIPLOAD OF CRYSTALS--BUT THIS ISN'T THE END OF IT. I WON'T LET IT BE.
THIS IS A BUSINESS. THERE ARE RULES!

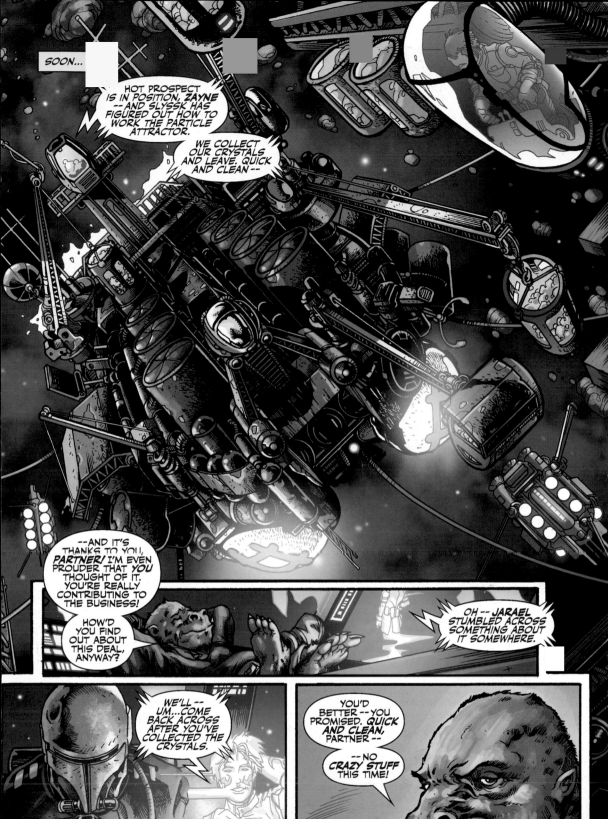

SOON...

HOT PROSPECT IS IN POSITION, *ZAYNE* --AND *SLYSSK* HAS FIGURED OUT HOW TO WORK THE PARTICLE ATTRACTOR.

WE COLLECT OUR CRYSTALS AND LEAVE. QUICK AND CLEAN--

--AND IT'S THANKS TO *YOU*, *PARTNER!* I'M EVEN PROUDER THAT *YOU* THOUGHT OF IT. YOU'RE REALLY CONTRIBUTING TO THE BUSINESS!

HOW'D YOU FIND OUT ABOUT THIS DEAL, ANYWAY?

OH -- JARAEL STUMBLED ACROSS SOMETHING ABOUT IT SOMEWHERE.

WE'LL -- UM...COME BACK ACROSS AFTER YOU'VE COLLECTED THE CRYSTALS.

YOU'D BETTER -- YOU PROMISED. QUICK AND CLEAN, PARTNER --

-- NO *CRAZY STUFF* THIS TIME!

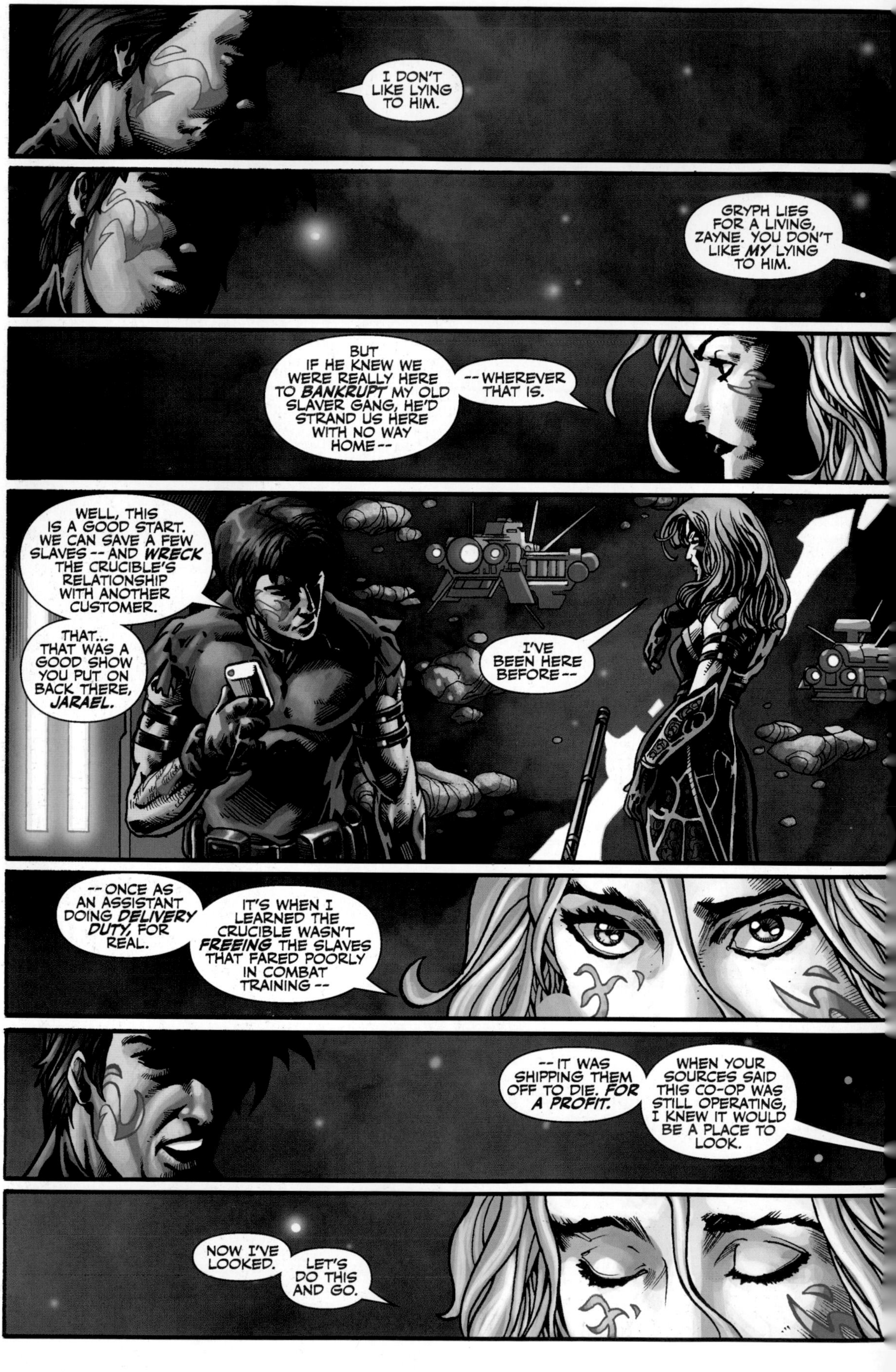
I DON'T LIKE LYING TO HIM.
GRYPH LIES FOR A LIVING, ZAYNE. YOU DON'T LIKE *MY* LYING TO HIM.
BUT IF HE KNEW WE WERE REALLY HERE TO *BANKRUPT* MY OLD SLAVER GANG, HE'D STRAND US HERE WITH NO WAY HOME--
--WHEREVER THAT IS.
WELL, THIS IS A GOOD START. WE CAN SAVE A FEW SLAVES--AND *WRECK* THE CRUCIBLE'S RELATIONSHIP WITH ANOTHER CUSTOMER.
THAT... THAT WAS A GOOD SHOW YOU PUT ON BACK THERE, *JARAEL.*
I'VE BEEN HERE BEFORE--
--ONCE AS AN ASSISTANT DOING *DELIVERY DUTY,* FOR REAL.
IT'S WHEN I LEARNED THE CRUCIBLE WASN'T *FREEING* THE SLAVES THAT FARED POORLY IN COMBAT TRAINING--
--IT WAS SHIPPING THEM OFF TO DIE. *FOR A PROFIT.*
WHEN YOUR SOURCES SAID THIS CO-OP WAS STILL OPERATING, I KNEW IT WOULD BE A PLACE TO LOOK.
NOW I'VE LOOKED.
LET'S DO THIS AND GO.

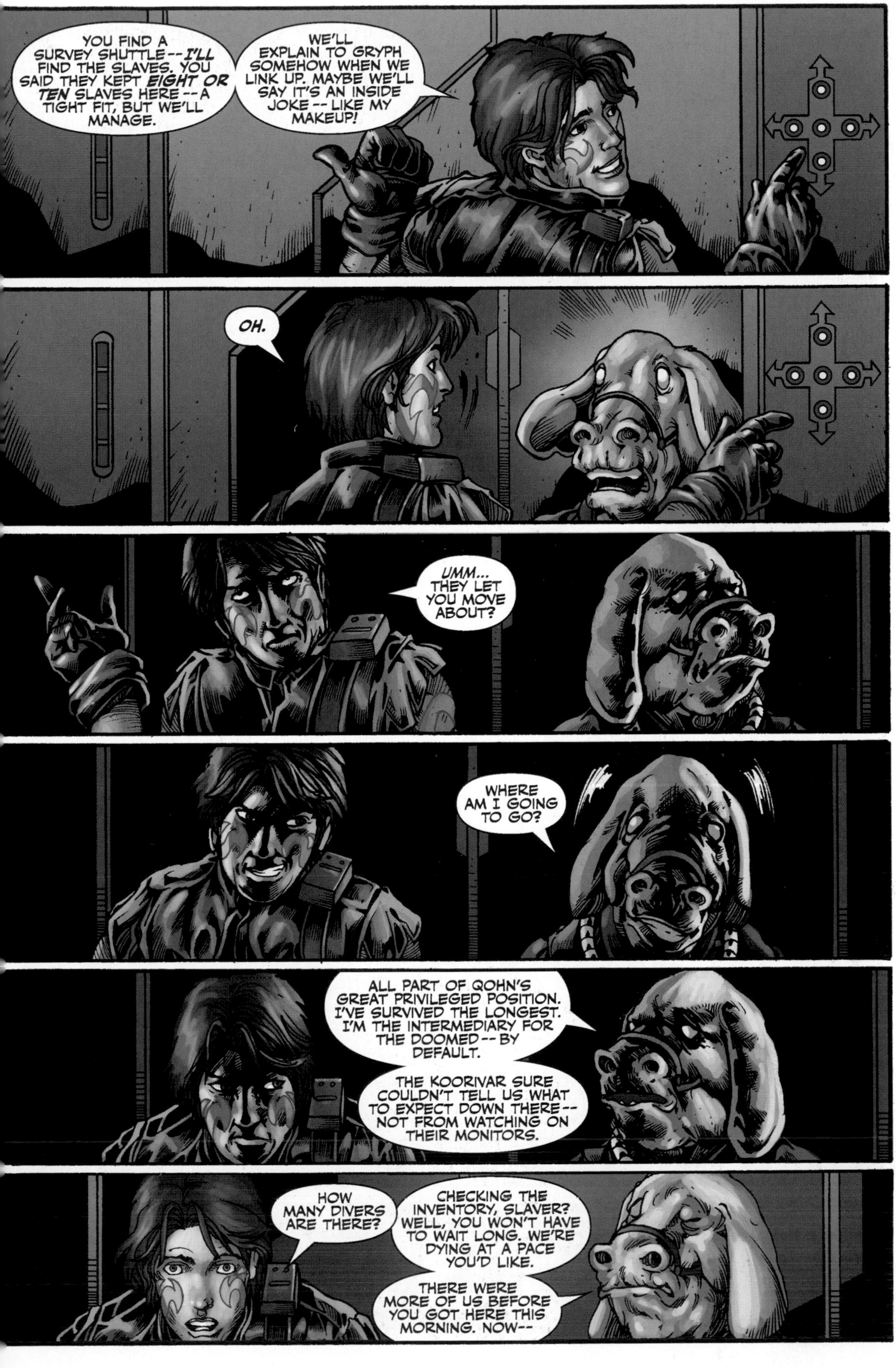
YOU FIND A SURVEY SHUTTLE--I'LL FIND THE SLAVES. YOU SAID THEY KEPT EIGHT OR TEN SLAVES HERE--A TIGHT FIT, BUT WE'LL MANAGE.
WE'LL EXPLAIN TO GRYPH SOMEHOW WHEN WE LINK UP. MAYBE WE'LL SAY IT'S AN INSIDE JOKE--LIKE MY MAKEUP!
OH.
UMM... THEY LET YOU MOVE ABOUT?
WHERE AM I GOING TO GO?
ALL PART OF QOHN'S GREAT PRIVILEGED POSITION. I'VE SURVIVED THE LONGEST. I'M THE INTERMEDIARY FOR THE DOOMED--BY DEFAULT.
THE KOORIVAR SURE COULDN'T TELL US WHAT TO EXPECT DOWN THERE--NOT FROM WATCHING ON THEIR MONITORS.
HOW MANY DIVERS ARE THERE?
CHECKING THE INVENTORY, SLAVER? WELL, YOU WON'T HAVE TO WAIT LONG. WE'RE DYING AT A PACE YOU'D LIKE.
THERE WERE MORE OF US BEFORE YOU GOT HERE THIS MORNING. NOW--

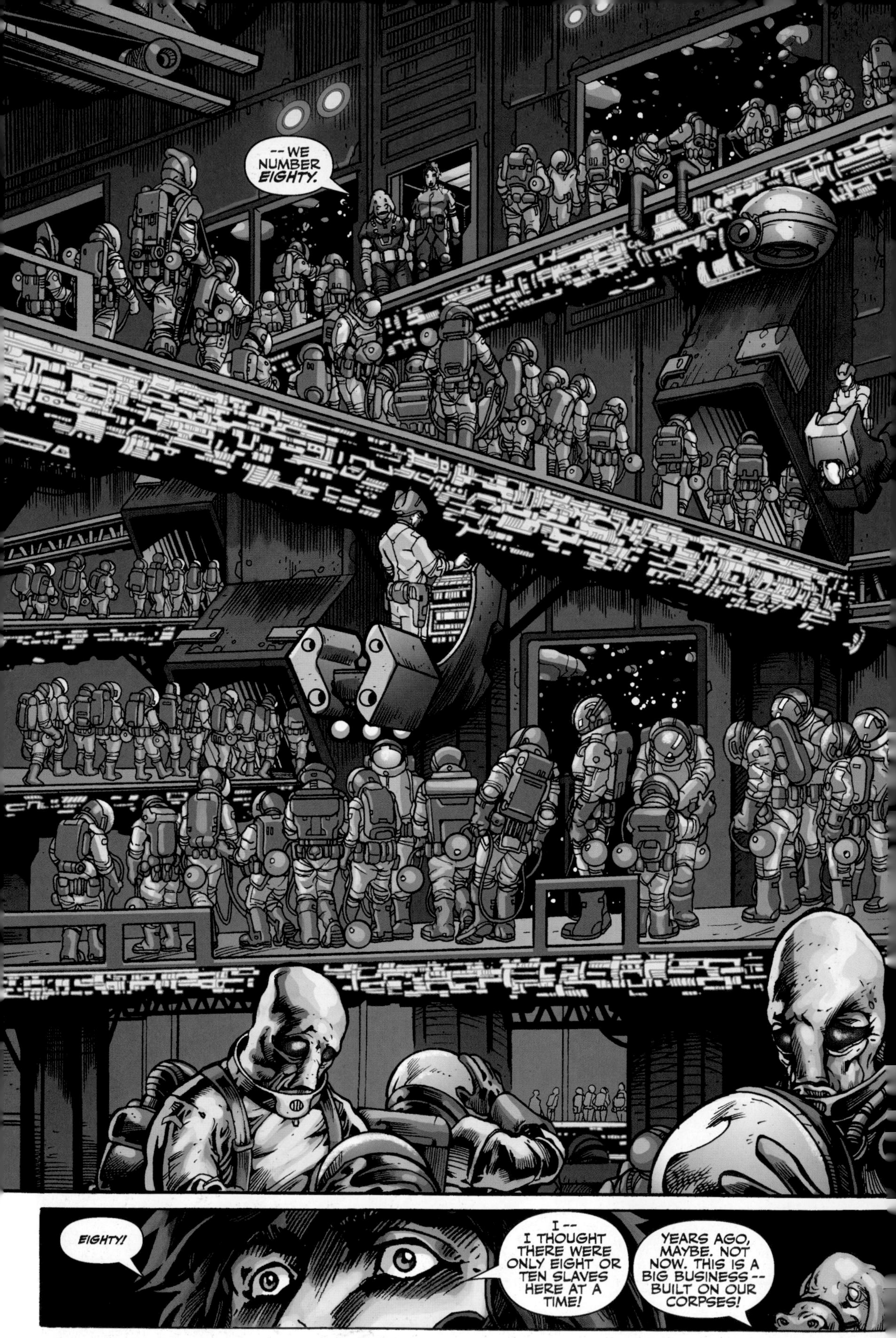
-- WE NUMBER EIGHTY.
EIGHTY!
I -- I THOUGHT THERE WERE ONLY EIGHT OR TEN SLAVES HERE AT A TIME!
YEARS AGO, MAYBE. NOT NOW. THIS IS A BIG BUSINESS -- BUILT ON OUR CORPSES!

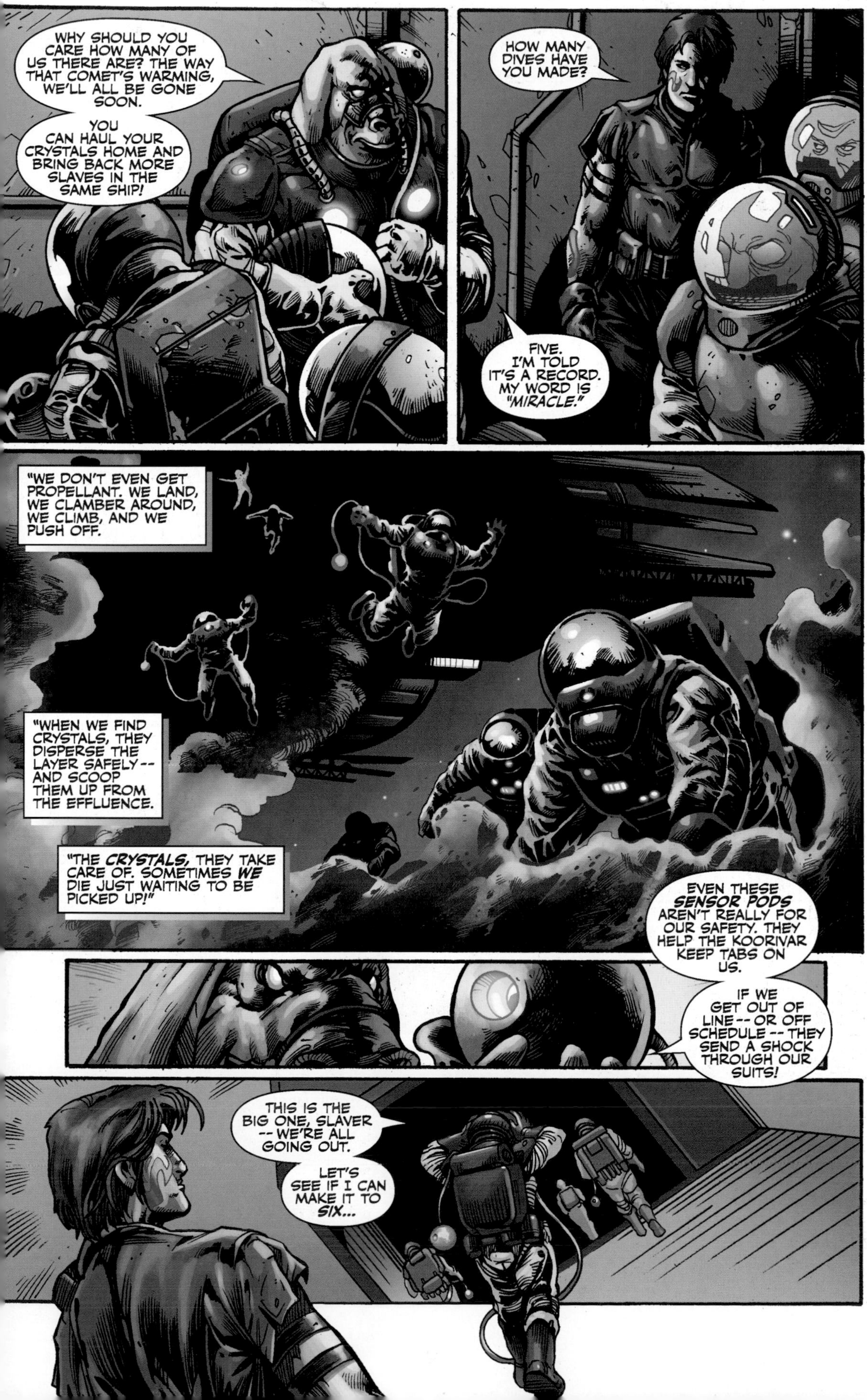

WHY SHOULD YOU CARE HOW MANY OF US THERE ARE? THE WAY THAT COMET'S WARMING, WE'LL ALL BE GONE SOON.
YOU CAN HAUL YOUR CRYSTALS HOME AND BRING BACK MORE SLAVES IN THE SAME SHIP!
HOW MANY DIVES HAVE YOU MADE?
FIVE. I'M TOLD IT'S A RECORD. MY WORD IS "MIRACLE."
"WE DON'T EVEN GET PROPELLANT. WE LAND, WE CLAMBER AROUND, WE CLIMB, AND WE PUSH OFF.
"WHEN WE FIND CRYSTALS, THEY DISPERSE THE LAYER SAFELY-- AND SCOOP THEM UP FROM THE EFFLUENCE.
"THE CRYSTALS, THEY TAKE CARE OF. SOMETIMES WE DIE JUST WAITING TO BE PICKED UP!"
EVEN THESE SENSOR PODS AREN'T REALLY FOR OUR SAFETY. THEY HELP THE KOORIVAR KEEP TABS ON US.
IF WE GET OUT OF LINE-- OR OFF SCHEDULE -- THEY SEND A SHOCK THROUGH OUR SUITS!
THIS IS THE BIG ONE, SLAVER -- WE'RE ALL GOING OUT.
LET'S SEE IF I CAN MAKE IT TO SIX...

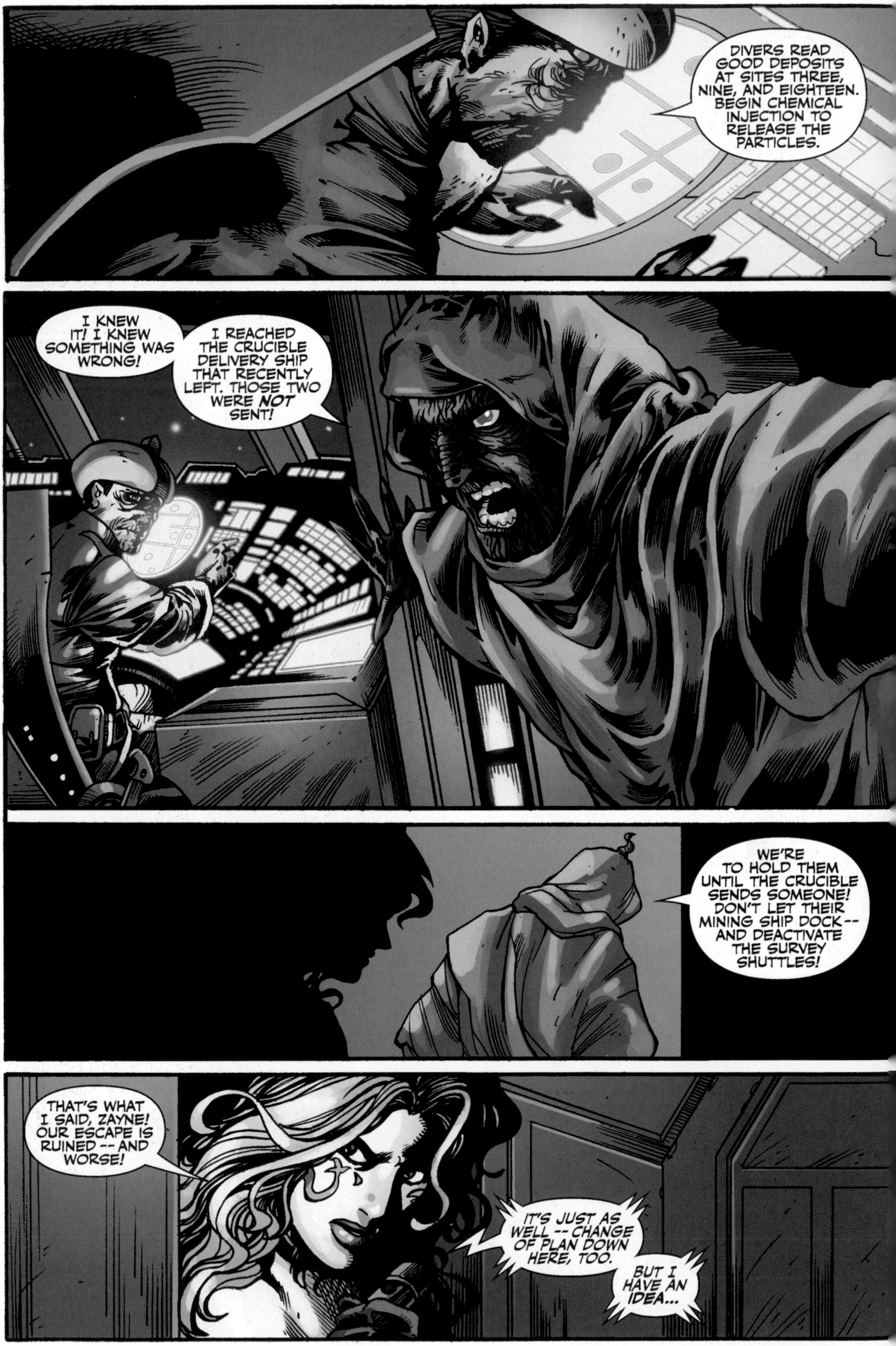
DIVERS READ GOOD DEPOSITS AT SITES THREE, NINE, AND EIGHTEEN. BEGIN CHEMICAL INJECTION TO RELEASE THE PARTICLES.
I KNEW IT! I KNEW SOMETHING WAS WRONG!
I REACHED THE CRUCIBLE DELIVERY SHIP THAT RECENTLY LEFT. THOSE TWO WERE *NOT* SENT!
WE'RE TO HOLD THEM UNTIL THE CRUCIBLE SENDS SOMEONE! DON'T LET THEIR MINING SHIP DOCK -- AND DEACTIVATE THE SURVEY SHUTTLES!
THAT'S WHAT I SAID, ZAYNE! OUR ESCAPE IS RUINED -- AND WORSE!
IT'S JUST AS WELL -- CHANGE OF PLAN DOWN HERE, TOO.
BUT I HAVE AN IDEA...

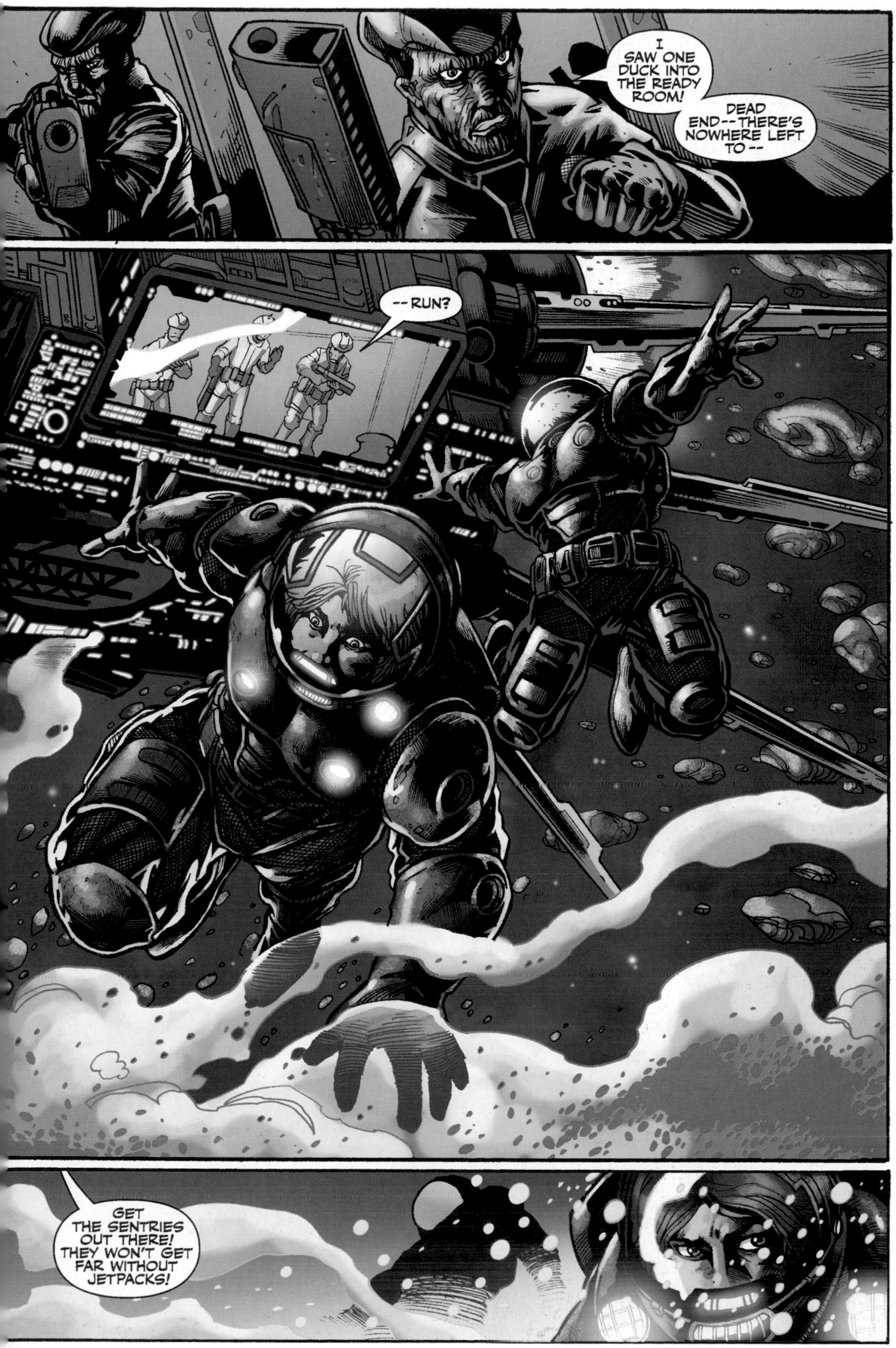

I SAW ONE DUCK INTO THE READY ROOM!
DEAD END--THERE'S NOWHERE LEFT TO--
--RUN?
GET THE SENTRIES OUT THERE! THEY WON'T GET FAR WITHOUT JETPACKS!

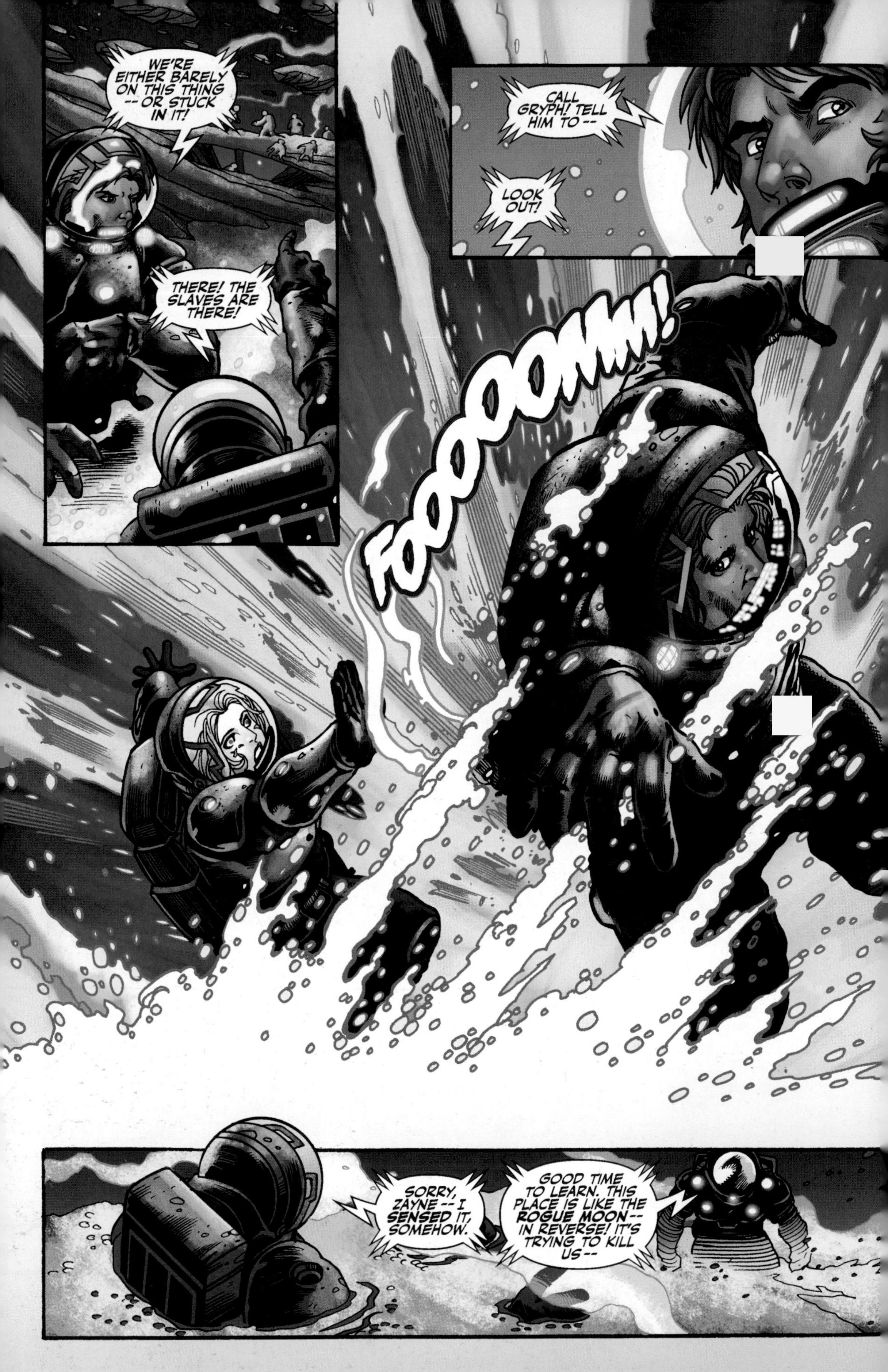
WE'RE EITHER BARELY ON THIS THING -- OR STUCK IN IT!
THERE! THE SLAVES ARE THERE!
CALL GRYPH! TELL HIM TO --
LOOK OUT!
FOOOOOMMM!
SORRY, ZAYNE -- I SENSED IT, SOMEHOW.
GOOD TIME TO LEARN. THIS PLACE IS LIKE THE ROGUE MOON -- IN REVERSE! IT'S TRYING TO KILL US --

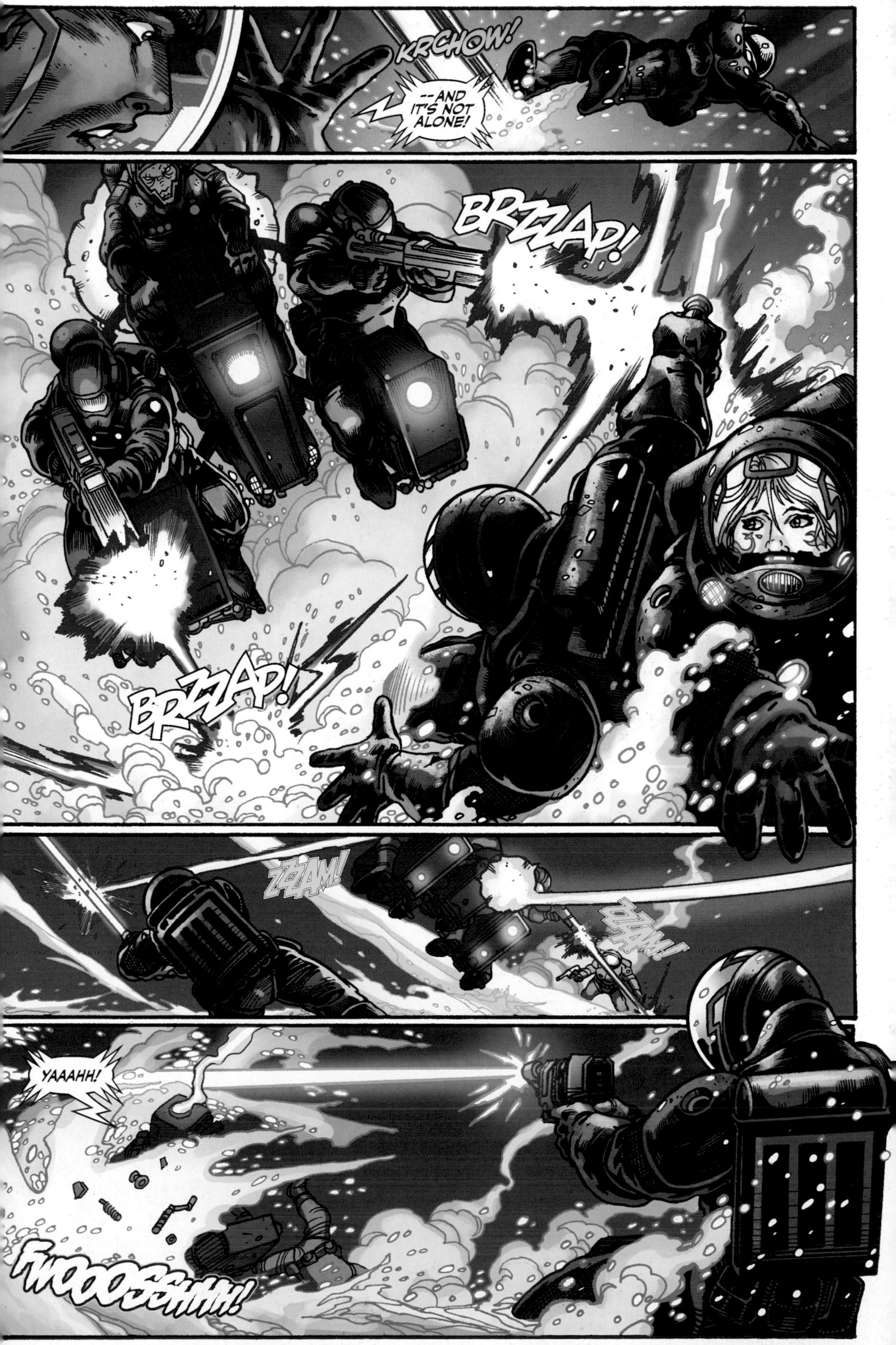
KRCHOW!
--AND IT'S NOT ALONE!
BRZZAP!
BRZZAP!
ZZZAM!
ZZZAM!
YAAAHH!
FWOOOSSHHH!

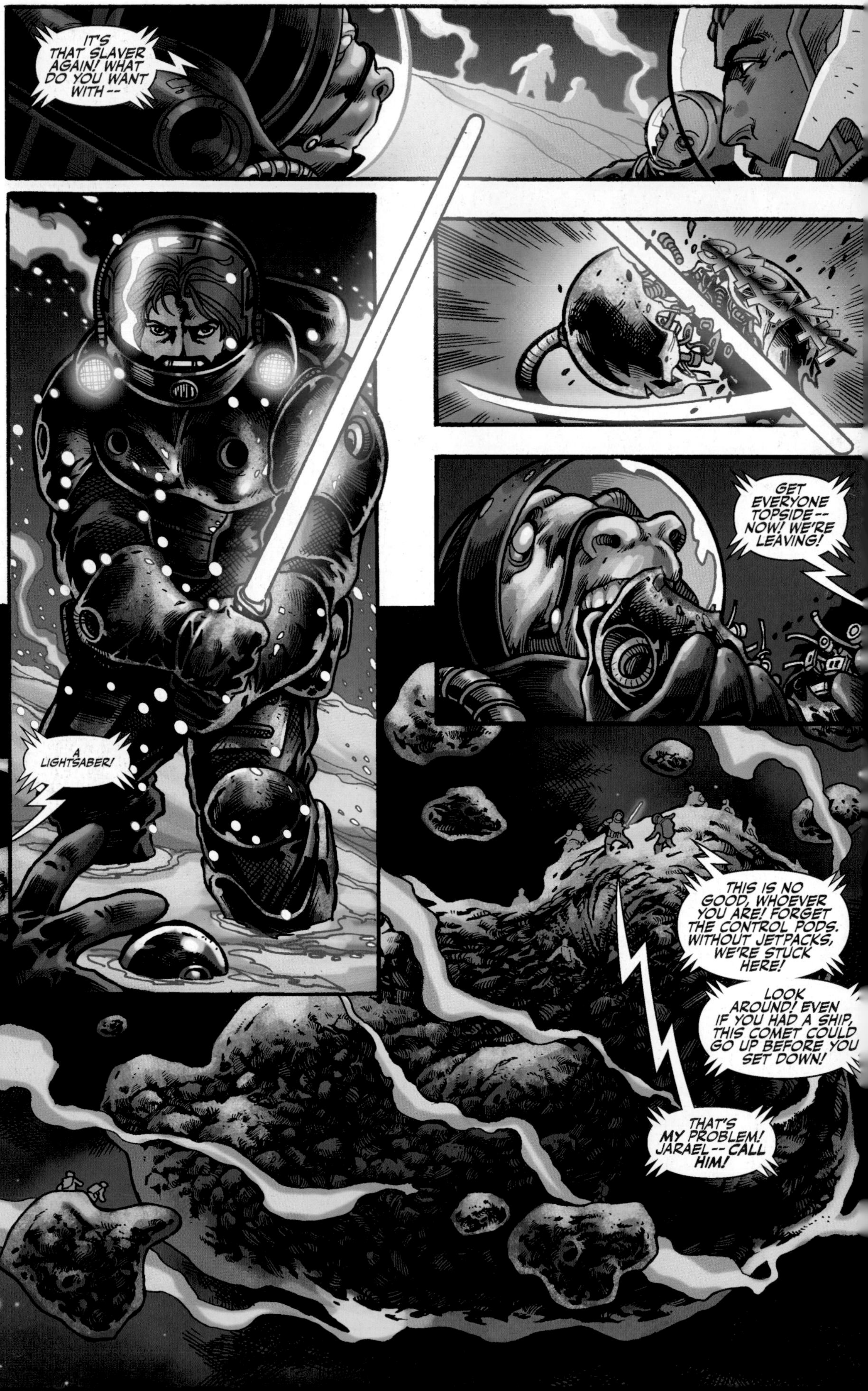
IT'S THAT SLAVER AGAIN! WHAT DO YOU WANT WITH --
A LIGHTSABER!
GET EVERYONE TOPSIDE -- NOW! WE'RE LEAVING!
THIS IS NO GOOD, WHOEVER YOU ARE! FORGET THE CONTROL PODS. WITHOUT JETPACKS, WE'RE STUCK HERE!
LOOK AROUND! EVEN IF YOU HAD A SHIP, THIS COMET COULD GO UP BEFORE YOU SET DOWN!
THAT'S MY PROBLEM! JARAEL -- CALL HIM!

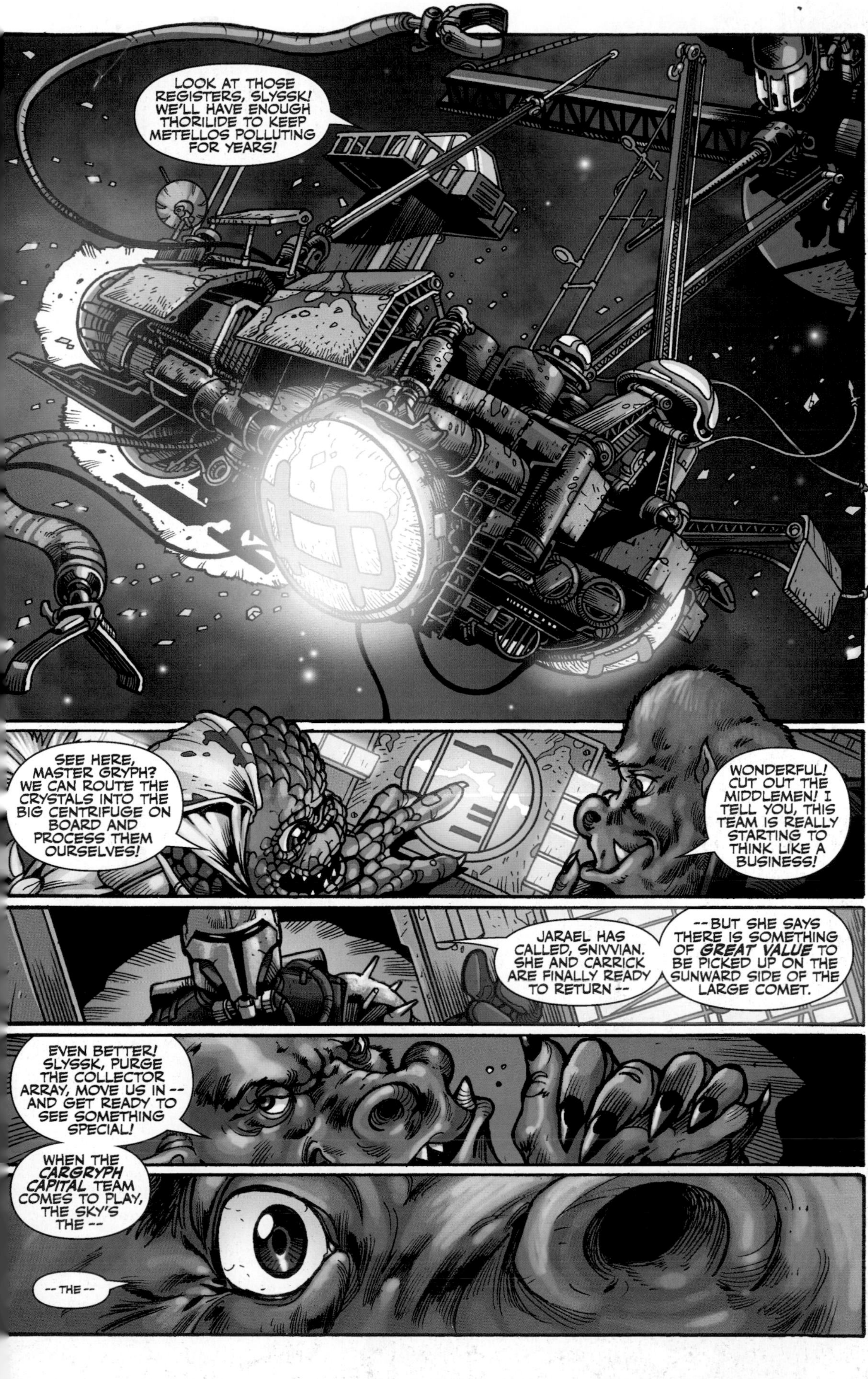
LOOK AT THOSE REGISTERS, SLYSSK! WE'LL HAVE ENOUGH THORILIDE TO KEEP METELLOS POLLUTING FOR YEARS!
SEE HERE, MASTER GRYPH? WE CAN ROUTE THE CRYSTALS INTO THE BIG CENTRIFUGE ON BOARD AND PROCESS THEM OURSELVES!
WONDERFUL! CUT OUT THE MIDDLEMEN! I TELL YOU, THIS TEAM IS REALLY STARTING TO THINK LIKE A BUSINESS!
JARAEL HAS CALLED, SNIVVIAN. SHE AND CARRICK ARE FINALLY READY TO RETURN --
-- BUT SHE SAYS THERE IS SOMETHING OF GREAT VALUE TO BE PICKED UP ON THE SUNWARD SIDE OF THE LARGE COMET.
EVEN BETTER! SLYSSK, PURGE THE COLLECTOR ARRAY, MOVE US IN -- AND GET READY TO SEE SOMETHING SPECIAL!
WHEN THE CARGRYPH CAPITAL TEAM COMES TO PLAY, THE SKY'S THE --
-- THE --

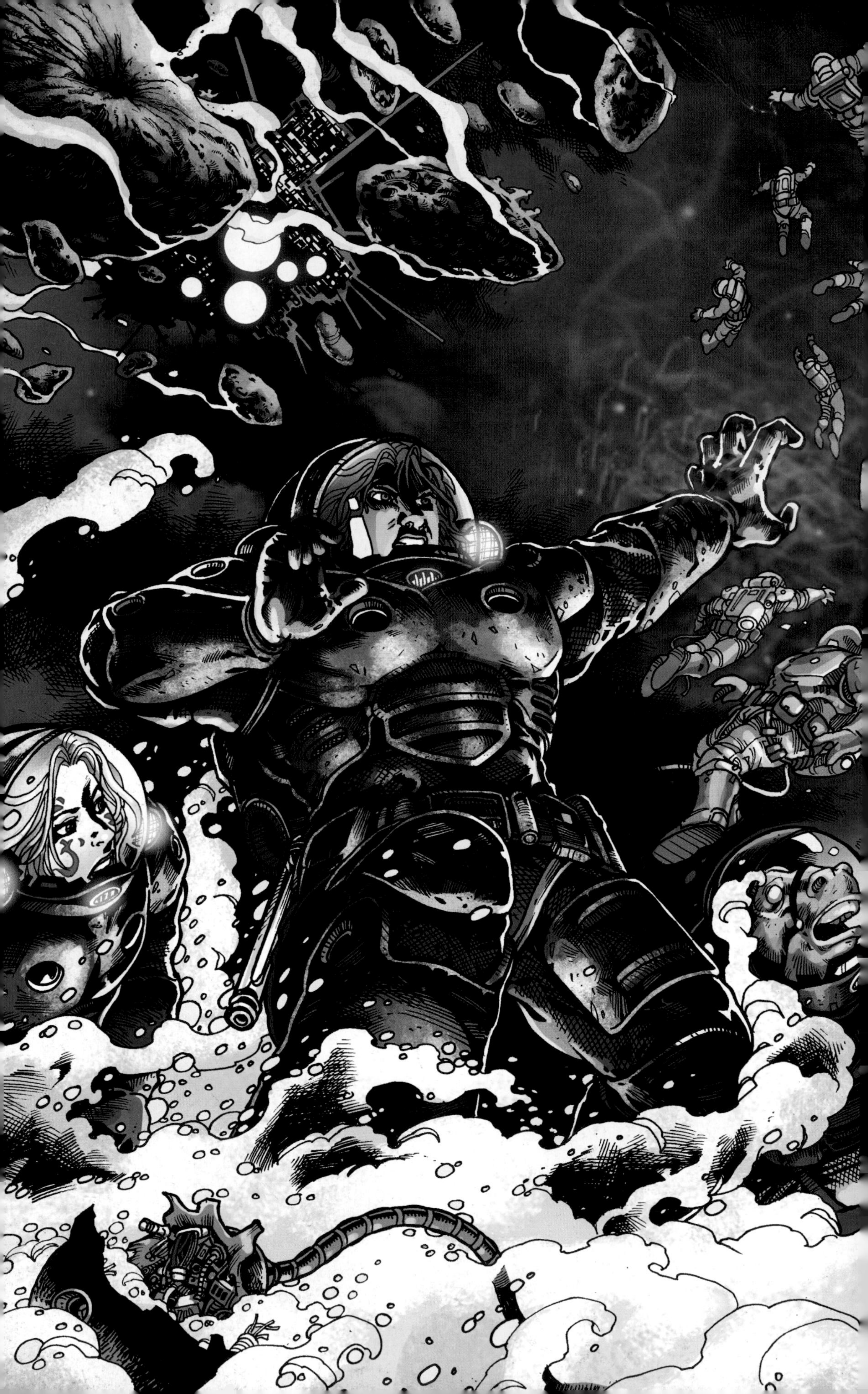

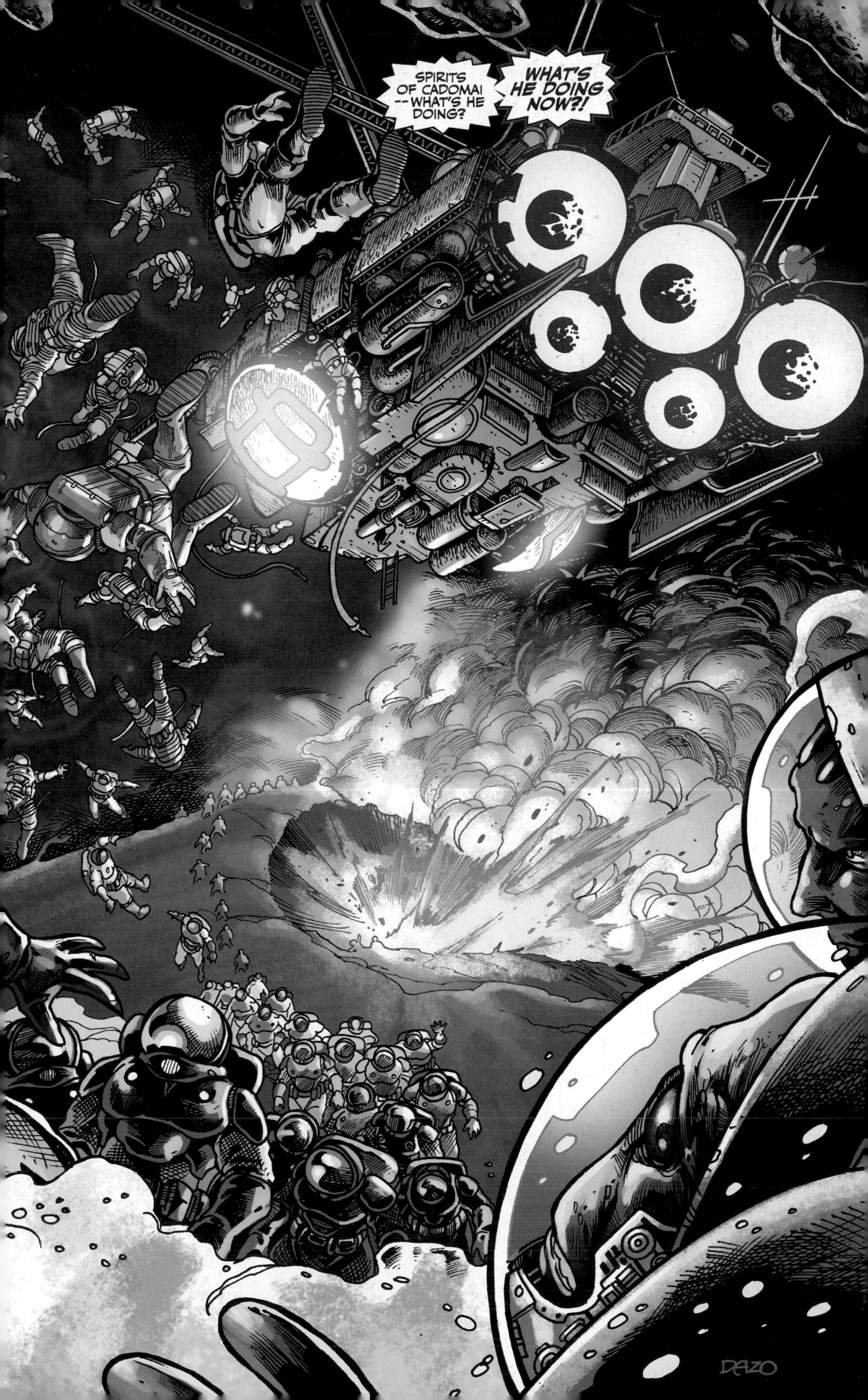
SPIRITS OF CADOMAI --WHAT'S HE DOING?
WHAT'S HE DOING NOW?!
DEZO

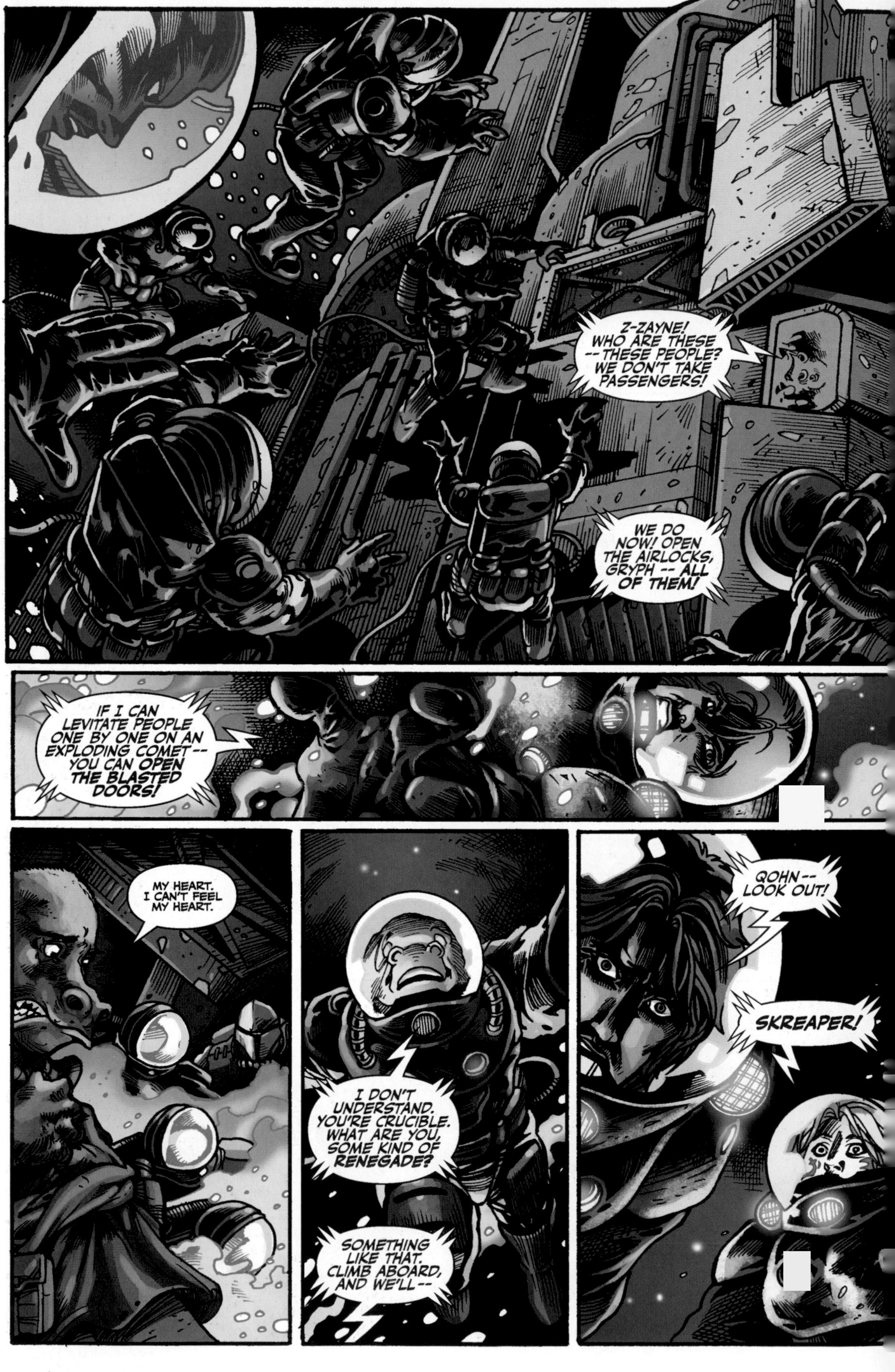
Z-ZAYNE! WHO ARE THESE --THESE PEOPLE? WE DON'T TAKE PASSENGERS!
WE DO NOW! OPEN THE AIRLOCKS, GRYPH -- ALL OF THEM!
IF I CAN LEVITATE PEOPLE ONE BY ONE ON AN EXPLODING COMET-- YOU CAN OPEN THE BLASTED DOORS!
MY HEART. I CAN'T FEEL MY HEART.
I DON'T UNDERSTAND. YOU'RE CRUCIBLE. WHAT ARE YOU, SOME KIND OF RENEGADE?
SOMETHING LIKE THAT. CLIMB ABOARD, AND WE'LL--
QOHN-- LOOK OUT!
SKREAPER!

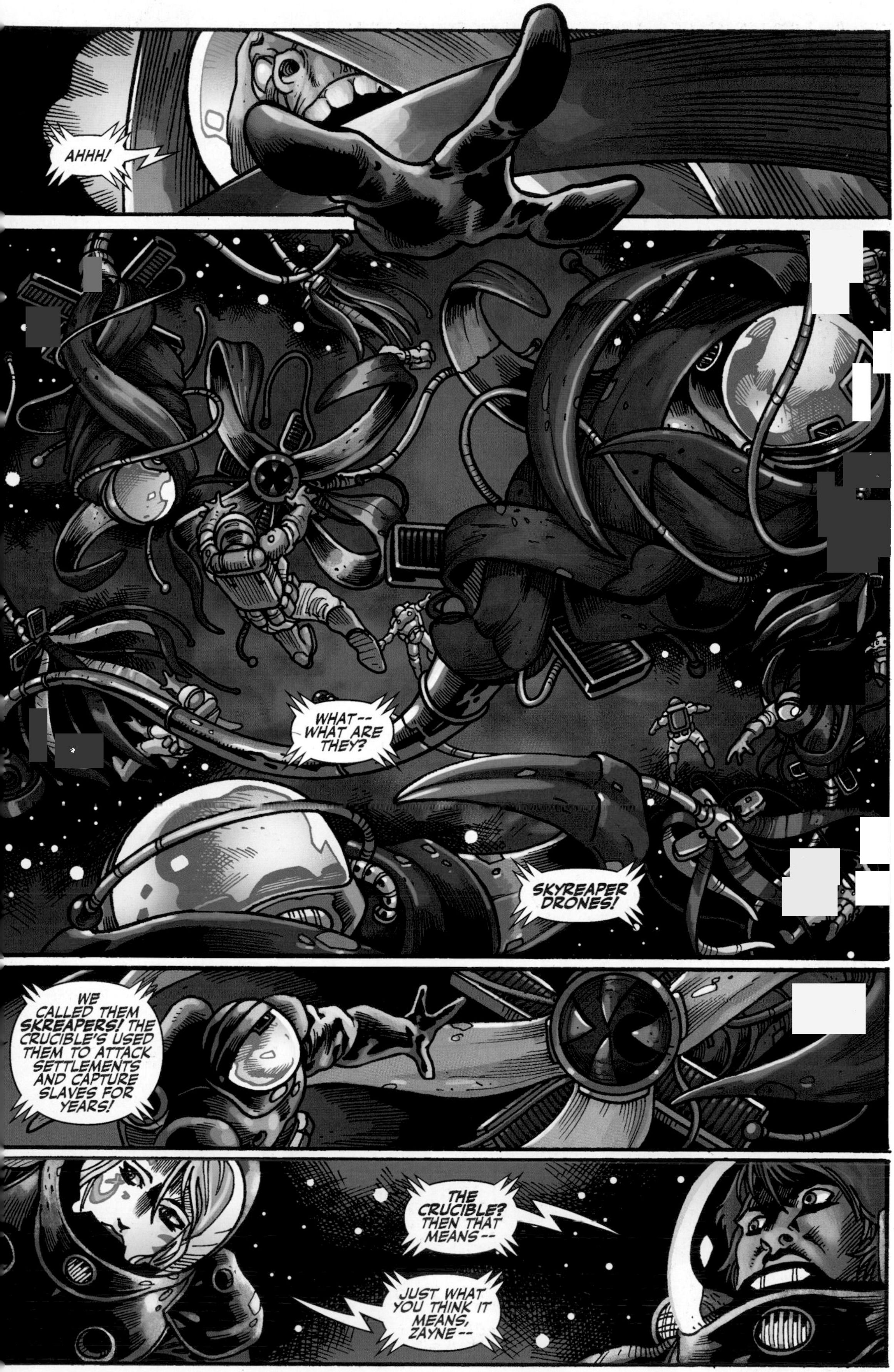
AHHH!
WHAT-- WHAT ARE THEY?
SKYREAPER DRONES!
WE CALLED THEM SKREAPERS! THE CRUCIBLE'S USED THEM TO ATTACK SETTLEMENTS AND CAPTURE SLAVES FOR YEARS!
THE CRUCIBLE? THEN THAT MEANS--
JUST WHAT YOU THINK IT MEANS, ZAYNE--

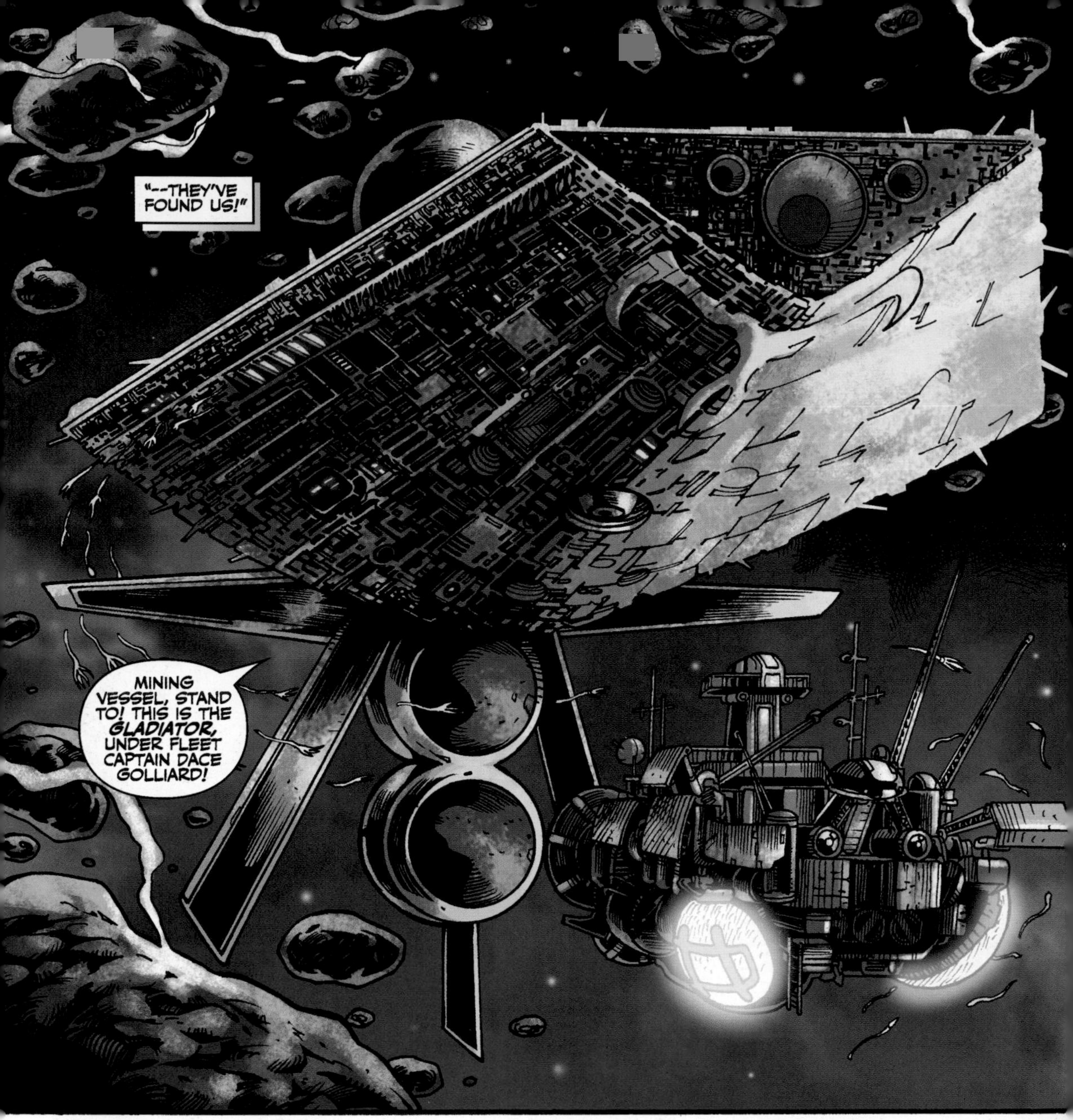
"--THEY'VE FOUND US!"
MINING VESSEL, STAND TO! THIS IS THE GLADIATOR, UNDER FLEET CAPTAIN DACE GOLLIARD!

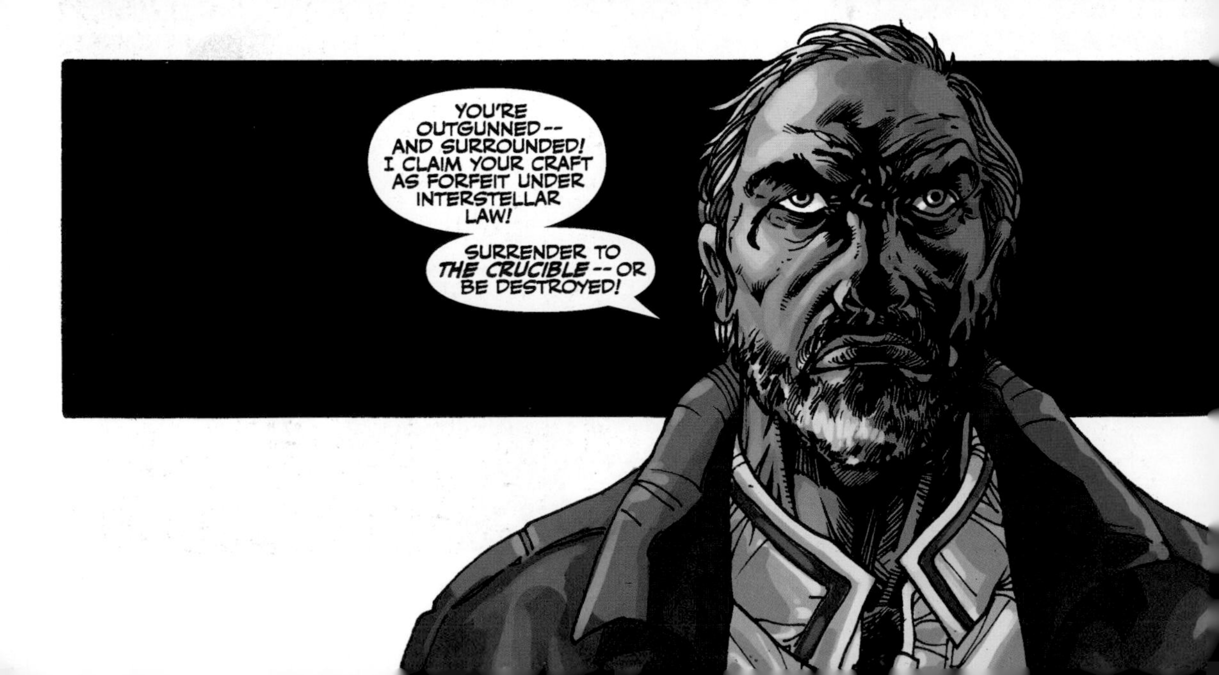
YOU'RE OUTGUNNED-- AND SURROUNDED! I CLAIM YOUR CRAFT AS FORFEIT UNDER INTERSTELLAR LAW!
SURRENDER TO THE CRUCIBLE--OR BE DESTROYED!

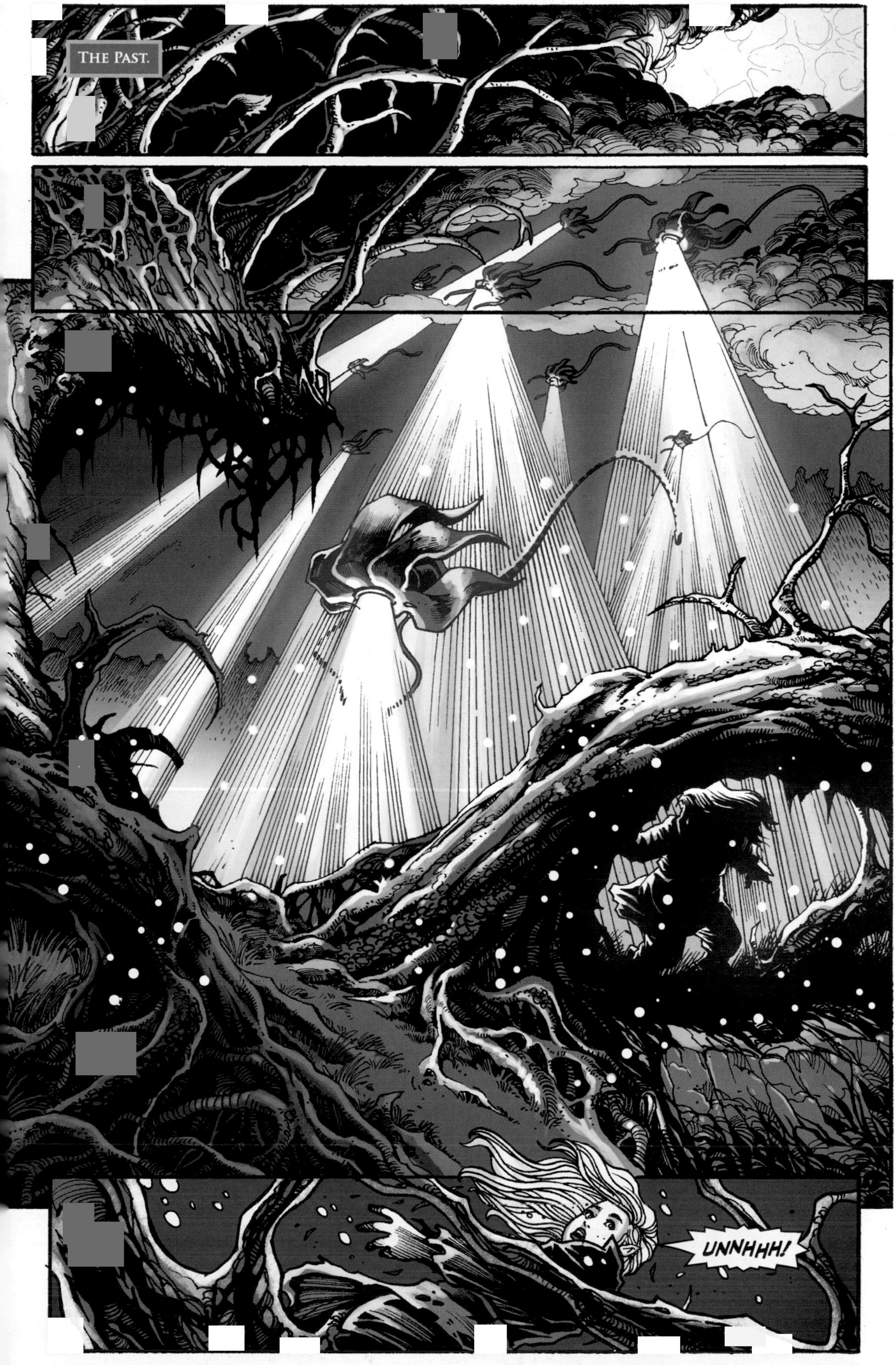
THE PAST.
UNNHHH!

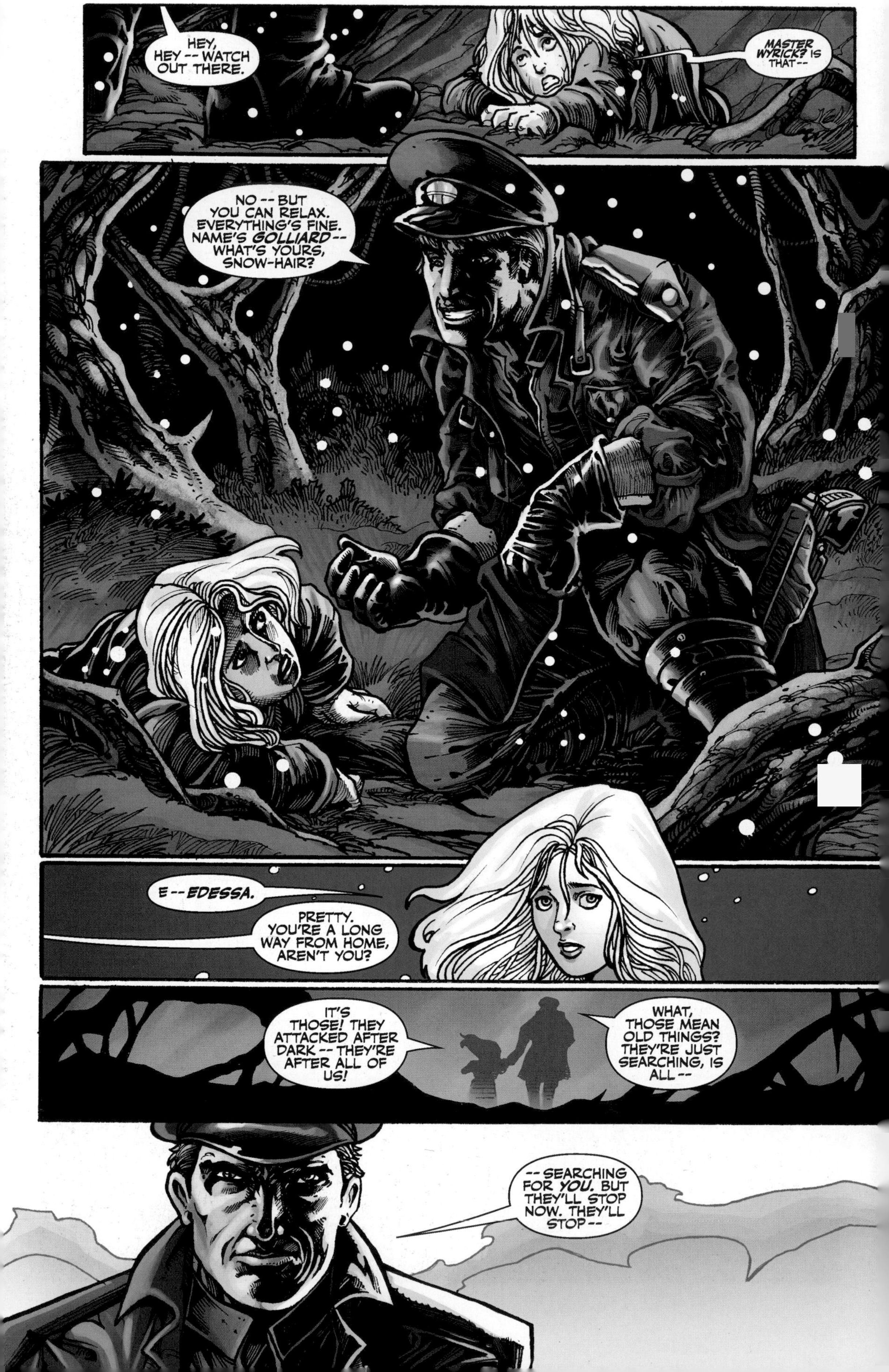
HEY, HEY -- WATCH OUT THERE.
MASTER WYRICK? IS THAT--
NO -- BUT YOU CAN RELAX. EVERYTHING'S FINE. NAME'S GOLLIARD -- WHAT'S YOURS, SNOW-HAIR?
E -- EDESSA.
PRETTY. YOU'RE A LONG WAY FROM HOME, AREN'T YOU?
IT'S THOSE! THEY ATTACKED AFTER DARK -- THEY'RE AFTER ALL OF US!
WHAT, THOSE MEAN OLD THINGS? THEY'RE JUST SEARCHING, IS ALL --
-- SEARCHING FOR YOU. BUT THEY'LL STOP NOW. THEY'LL STOP --

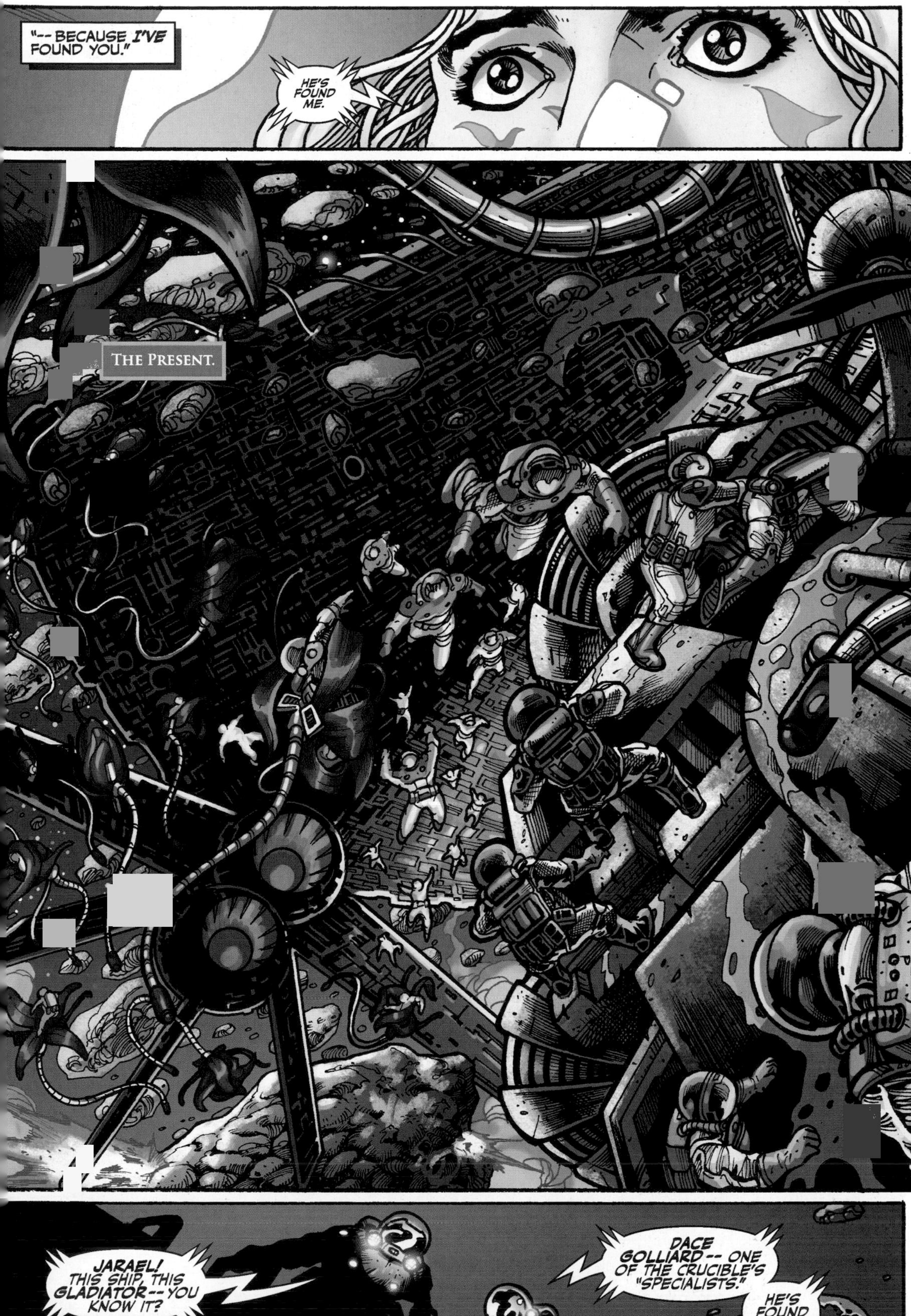
"-- BECAUSE I'VE FOUND YOU."
HE'S FOUND ME.
THE PRESENT.
JARAEL! THIS SHIP, THIS GLADIATOR-- YOU KNOW IT?
DACE GOLLIARD -- ONE OF THE CRUCIBLE'S "SPECIALISTS."
HE'S FOUND ME--

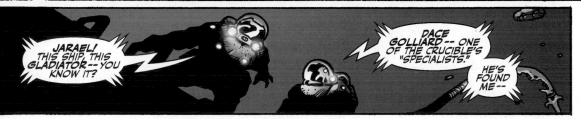

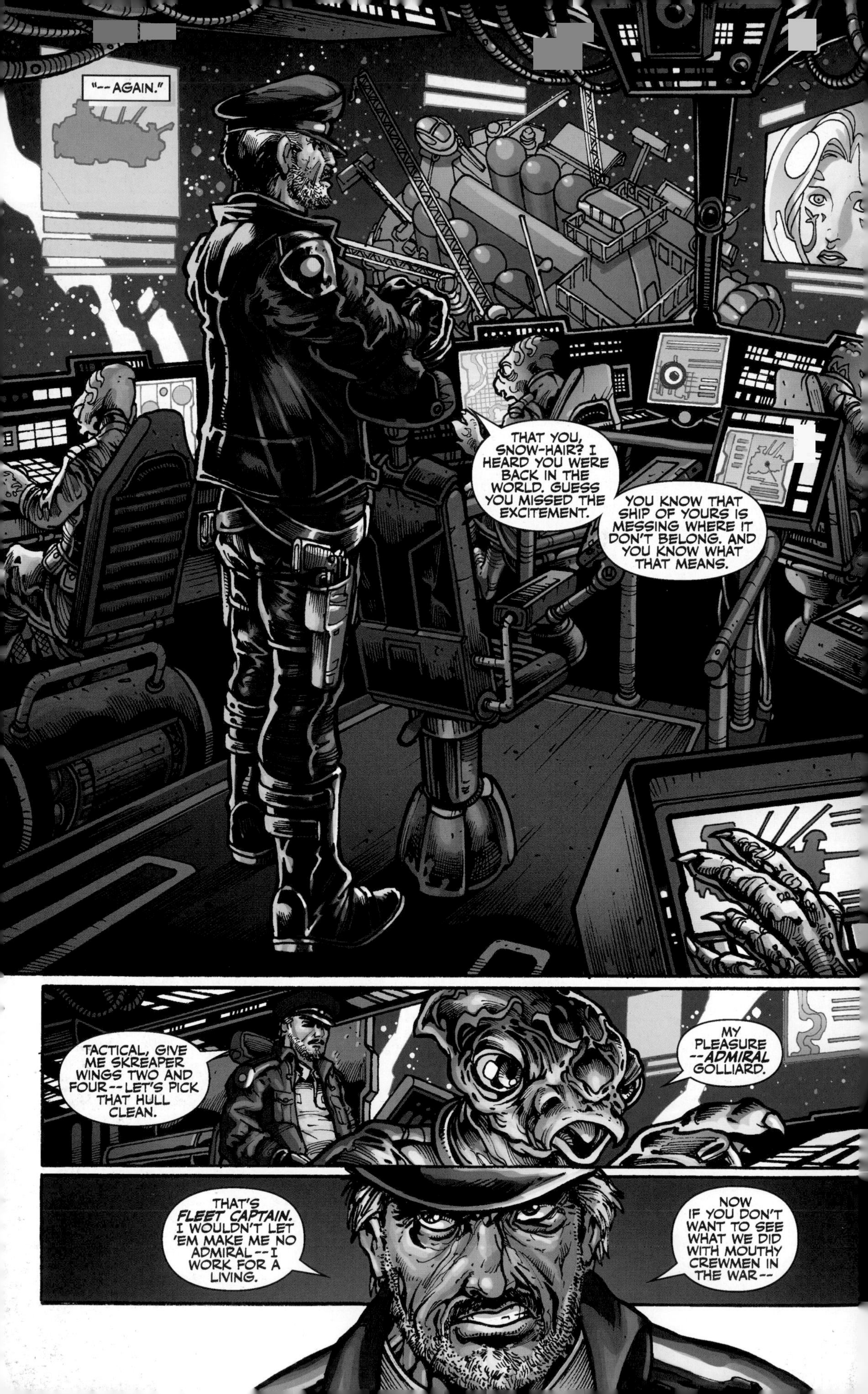
"--AGAIN."
THAT YOU, SNOW-HAIR? I HEARD YOU WERE BACK IN THE WORLD. GUESS YOU MISSED THE EXCITEMENT.
YOU KNOW THAT SHIP OF YOURS IS MESSING WHERE IT DON'T BELONG. AND YOU KNOW WHAT THAT MEANS.
TACTICAL, GIVE ME SKREAPER WINGS TWO AND FOUR--LET'S PICK THAT HULL CLEAN.
MY PLEASURE --ADMIRAL GOLLIARD.
THAT'S FLEET CAPTAIN. I WOULDN'T LET 'EM MAKE ME NO ADMIRAL--I WORK FOR A LIVING.
NOW IF YOU DON'T WANT TO SEE WHAT WE DID WITH MOUTHY CREWMEN IN THE WAR--

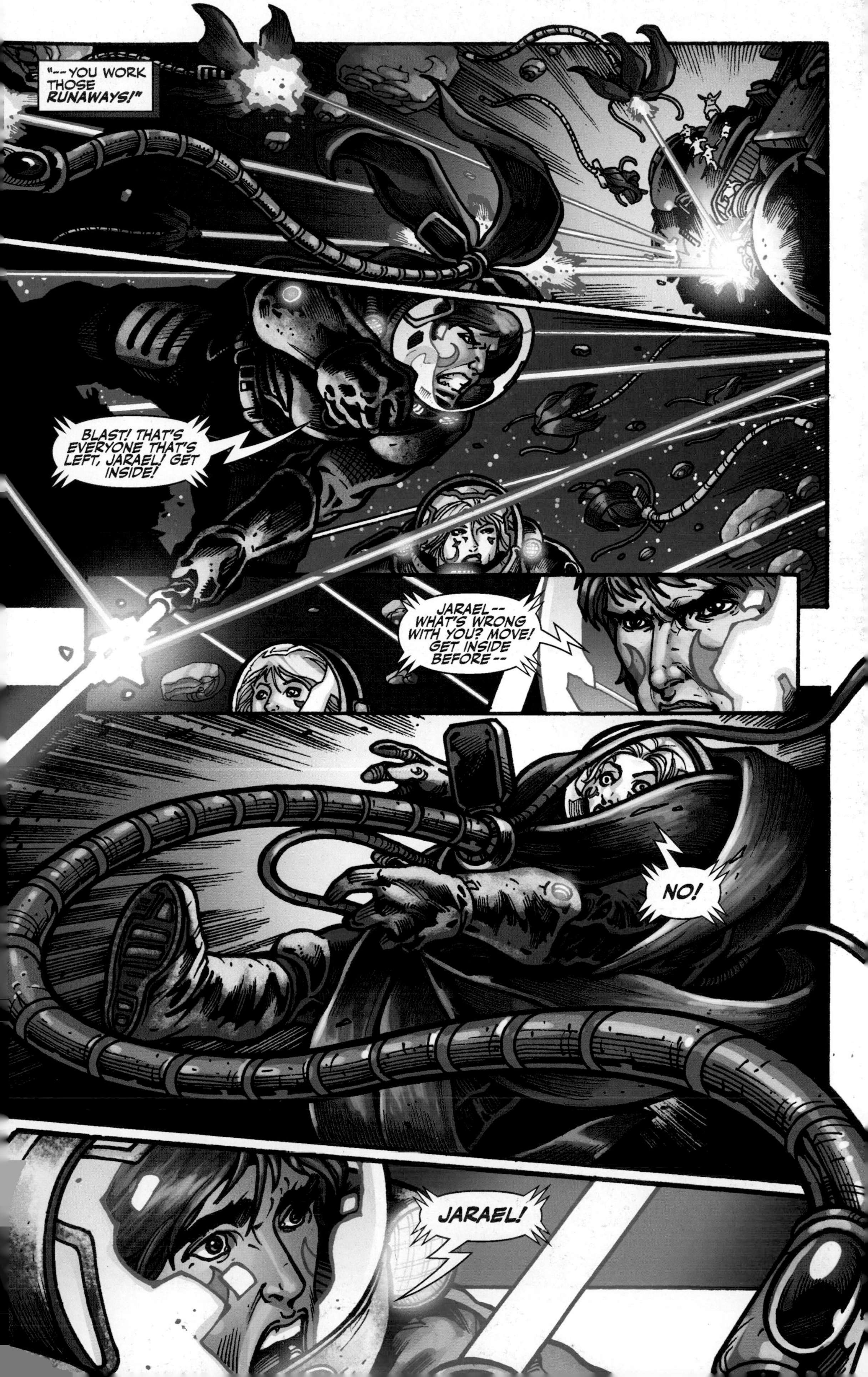
"--YOU WORK THOSE RUNAWAYS!"
BLAST! THAT'S EVERYONE THAT'S LEFT, JARAEL! GET INSIDE!
JARAEL-- WHAT'S WRONG WITH YOU? MOVE! GET INSIDE BEFORE--
NO!
JARAEL!

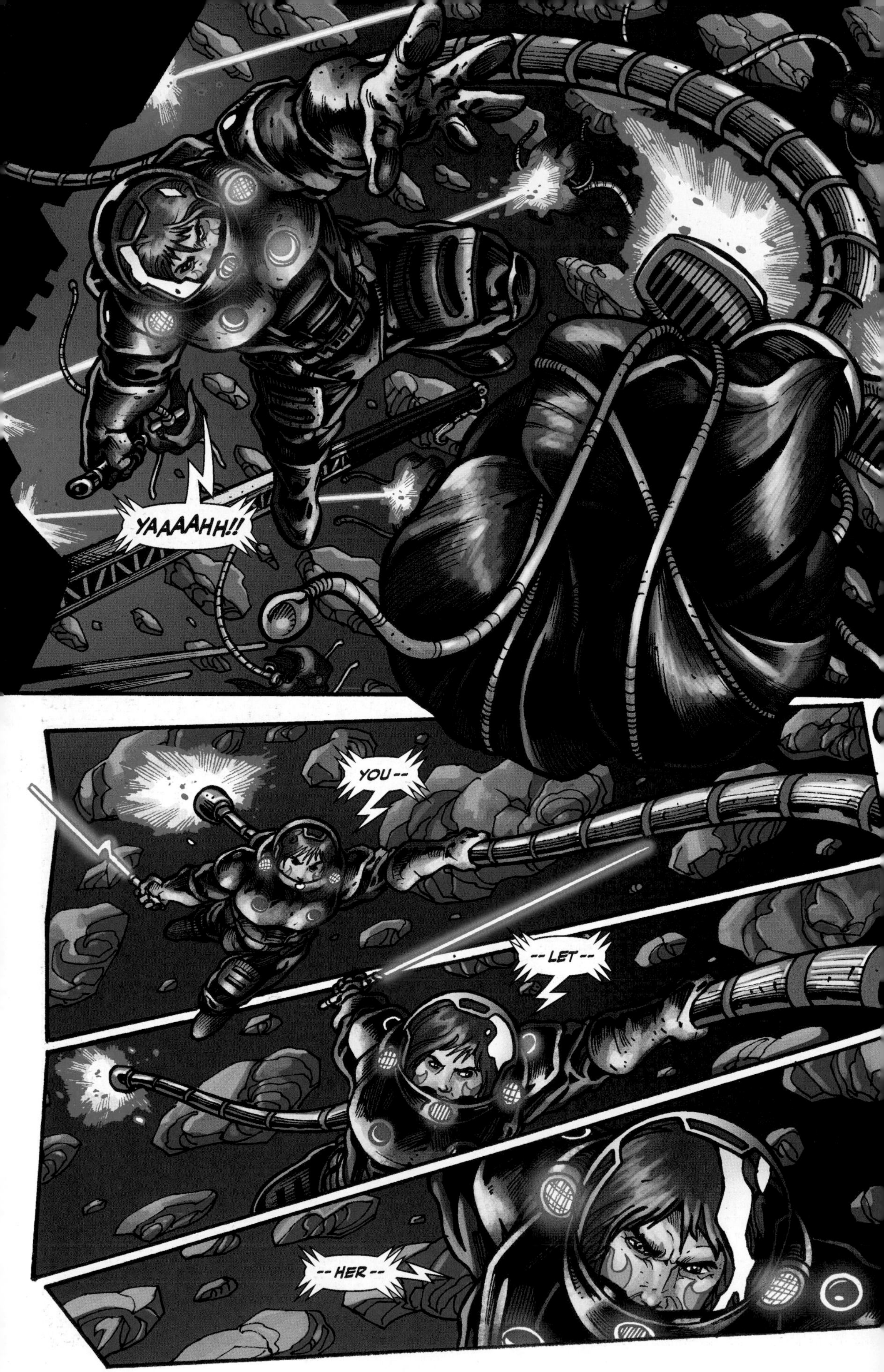
YAAAAHH!!
YOU--
--LET--
--HER--

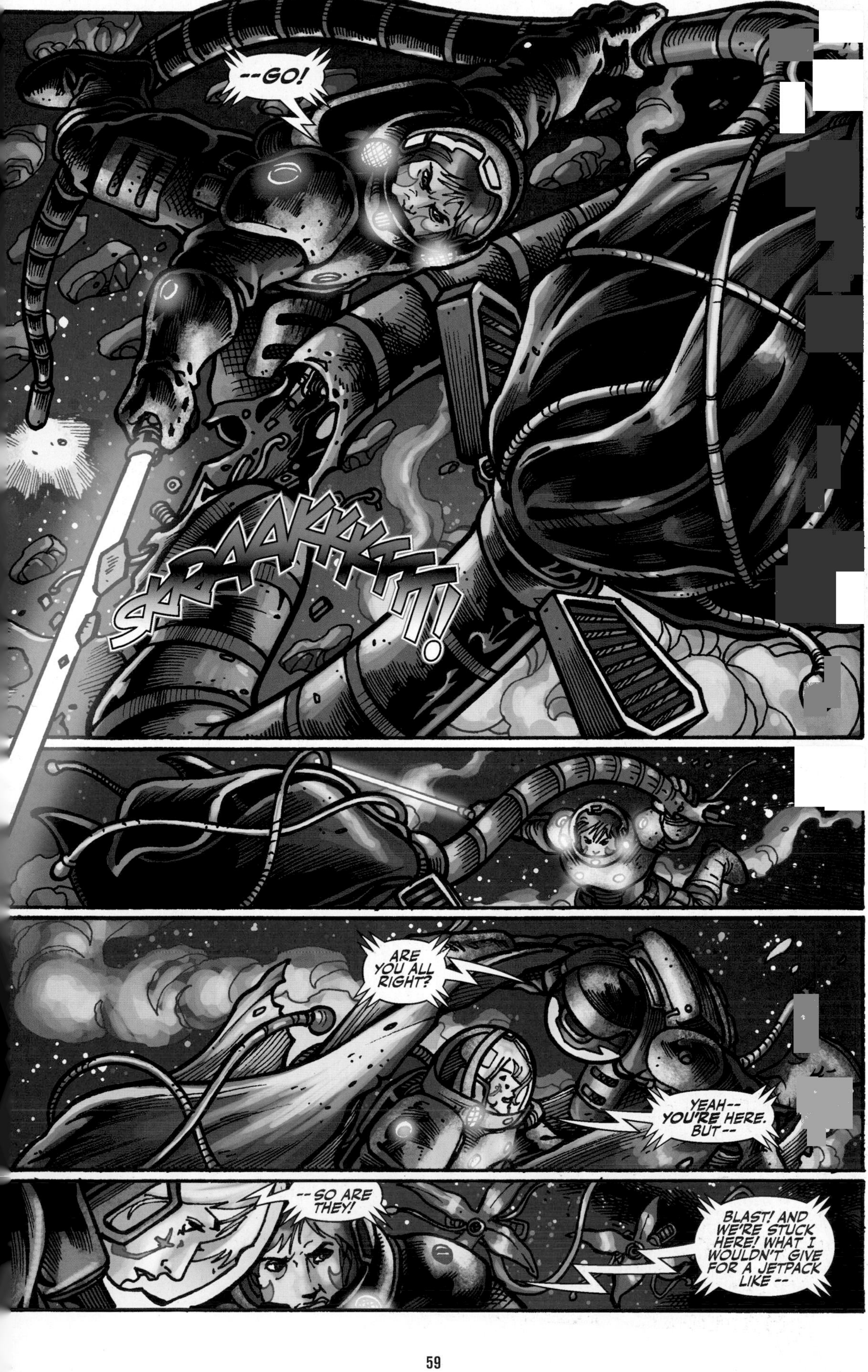
--GO!
ARE YOU ALL RIGHT?
YEAH-- YOU'RE HERE. BUT --
--SO ARE THEY!
BLAST! AND WE'RE STUCK HERE! WHAT I WOULDN'T GIVE FOR A JETPACK LIKE --

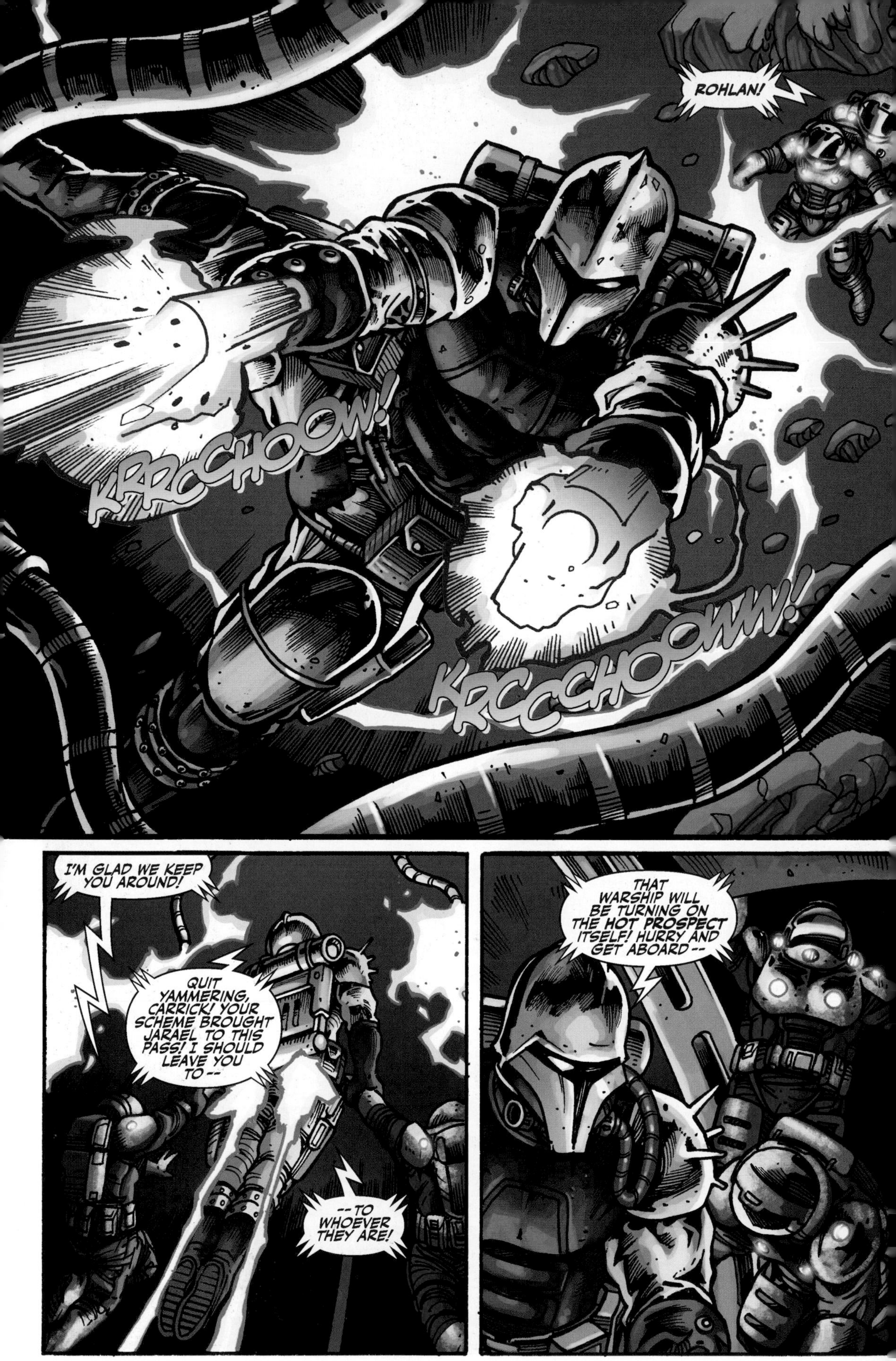
ROHLAN!
KRRCCHOOW!
KRCCCHOOWW!
I'M GLAD WE KEEP YOU AROUND!
QUIT YAMMERING, CARRICK! YOUR SCHEME BROUGHT JARAEL TO THIS PASS! I SHOULD LEAVE YOU TO --
-- TO WHOEVER THEY ARE!
THAT WARSHIP WILL BE TURNING ON THE HOT PROSPECT ITSELF! HURRY AND GET ABOARD --

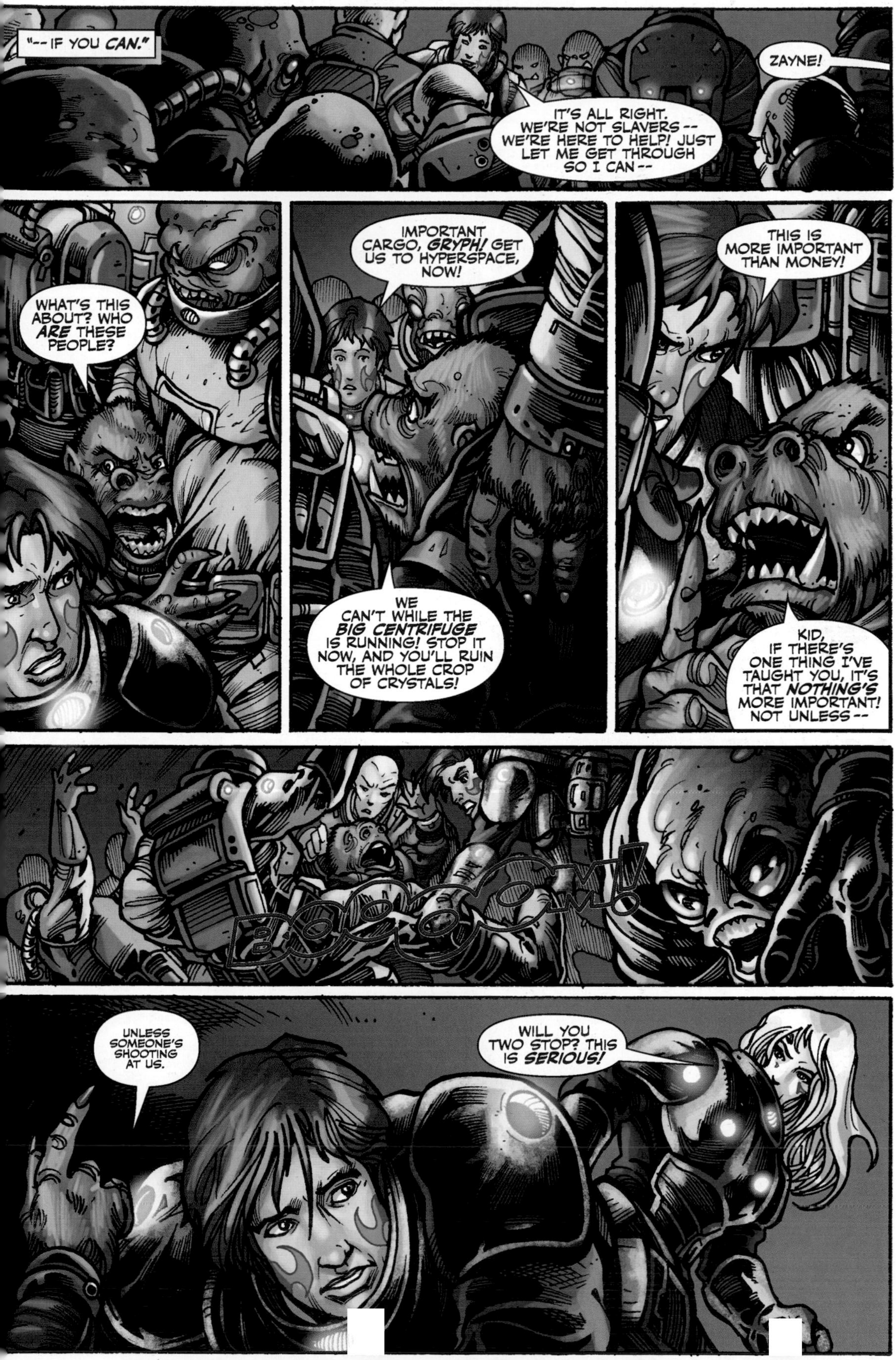
"-- IF YOU CAN."
ZAYNE!
IT'S ALL RIGHT. WE'RE NOT SLAVERS -- WE'RE HERE TO HELP! JUST LET ME GET THROUGH SO I CAN --
WHAT'S THIS ABOUT? WHO ARE THESE PEOPLE?
IMPORTANT CARGO, GRYPH! GET US TO HYPERSPACE, NOW!
WE CAN'T WHILE THE BIG CENTRIFUGE IS RUNNING! STOP IT NOW, AND YOU'LL RUIN THE WHOLE CROP OF CRYSTALS!
THIS IS MORE IMPORTANT THAN MONEY!
KID, IF THERE'S ONE THING I'VE TAUGHT YOU, IT'S THAT NOTHING'S MORE IMPORTANT! NOT UNLESS --
BOOOOOM!
UNLESS SOMEONE'S SHOOTING AT US.
WILL YOU TWO STOP? THIS IS SERIOUS!

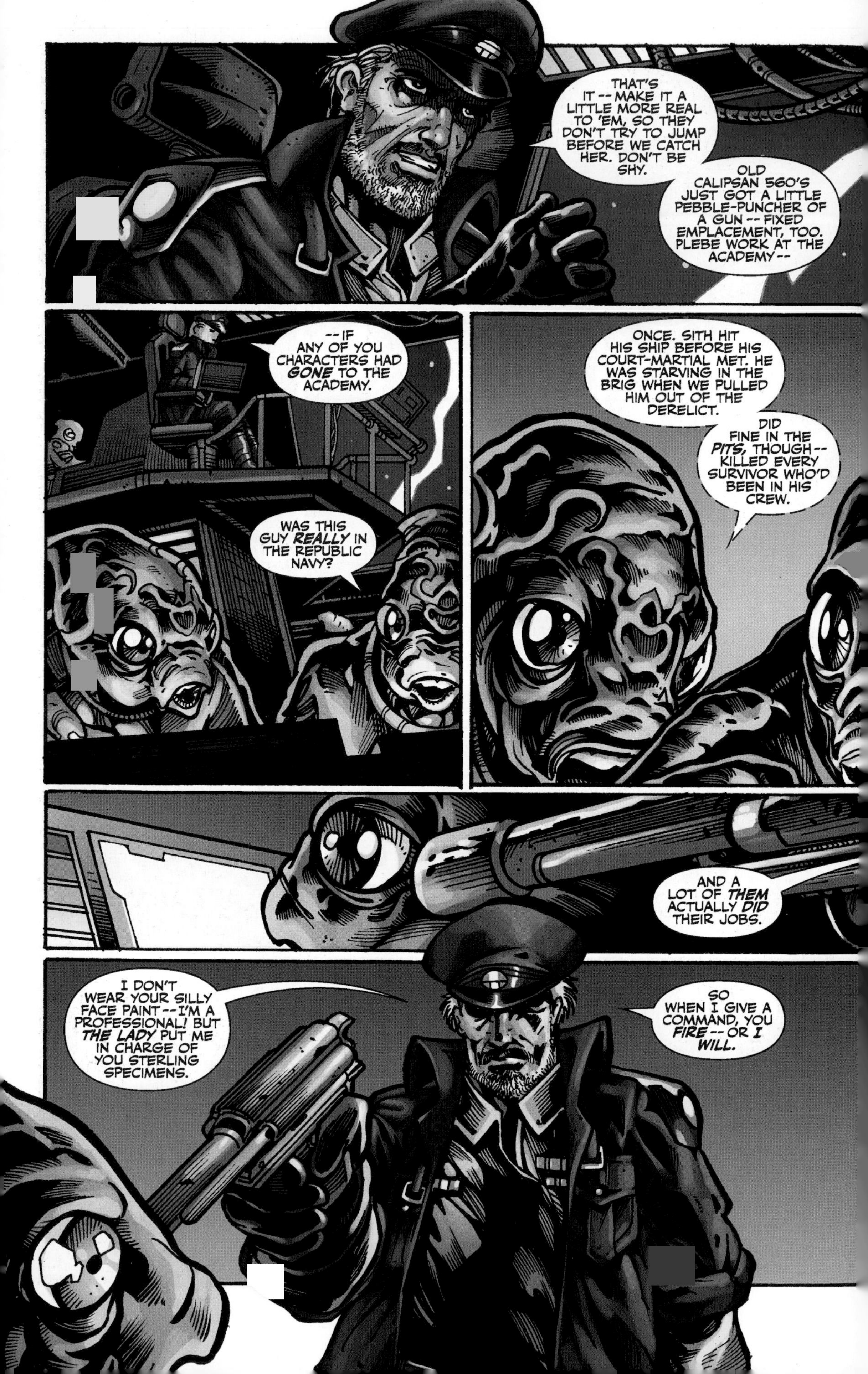
THAT'S IT -- MAKE IT A LITTLE MORE REAL TO 'EM, SO THEY DON'T TRY TO JUMP BEFORE WE CATCH HER. DON'T BE SHY.
OLD CALIPSAN 560'S JUST GOT A LITTLE PEBBLE-PUNCHER OF A GUN -- FIXED EMPLACEMENT, TOO. PLEBE WORK AT THE ACADEMY--
--IF ANY OF YOU CHARACTERS HAD *GONE* TO THE ACADEMY.
WAS THIS GUY *REALLY* IN THE REPUBLIC NAVY?
ONCE. SITH HIT HIS SHIP BEFORE HIS COURT-MARTIAL MET. HE WAS STARVING IN THE BRIG WHEN WE PULLED HIM OUT OF THE DERELICT.
DID FINE IN THE *PITS,* THOUGH--KILLED EVERY SURVIVOR WHO'D BEEN IN HIS CREW.
AND A LOT OF *THEM* ACTUALLY *DID* THEIR JOBS.
I DON'T WEAR YOUR SILLY FACE PAINT--I'M A PROFESSIONAL! BUT *THE LADY* PUT ME IN CHARGE OF YOU STERLING SPECIMENS.
SO WHEN I GIVE A COMMAND, YOU *FIRE*--OR *I WILL.*

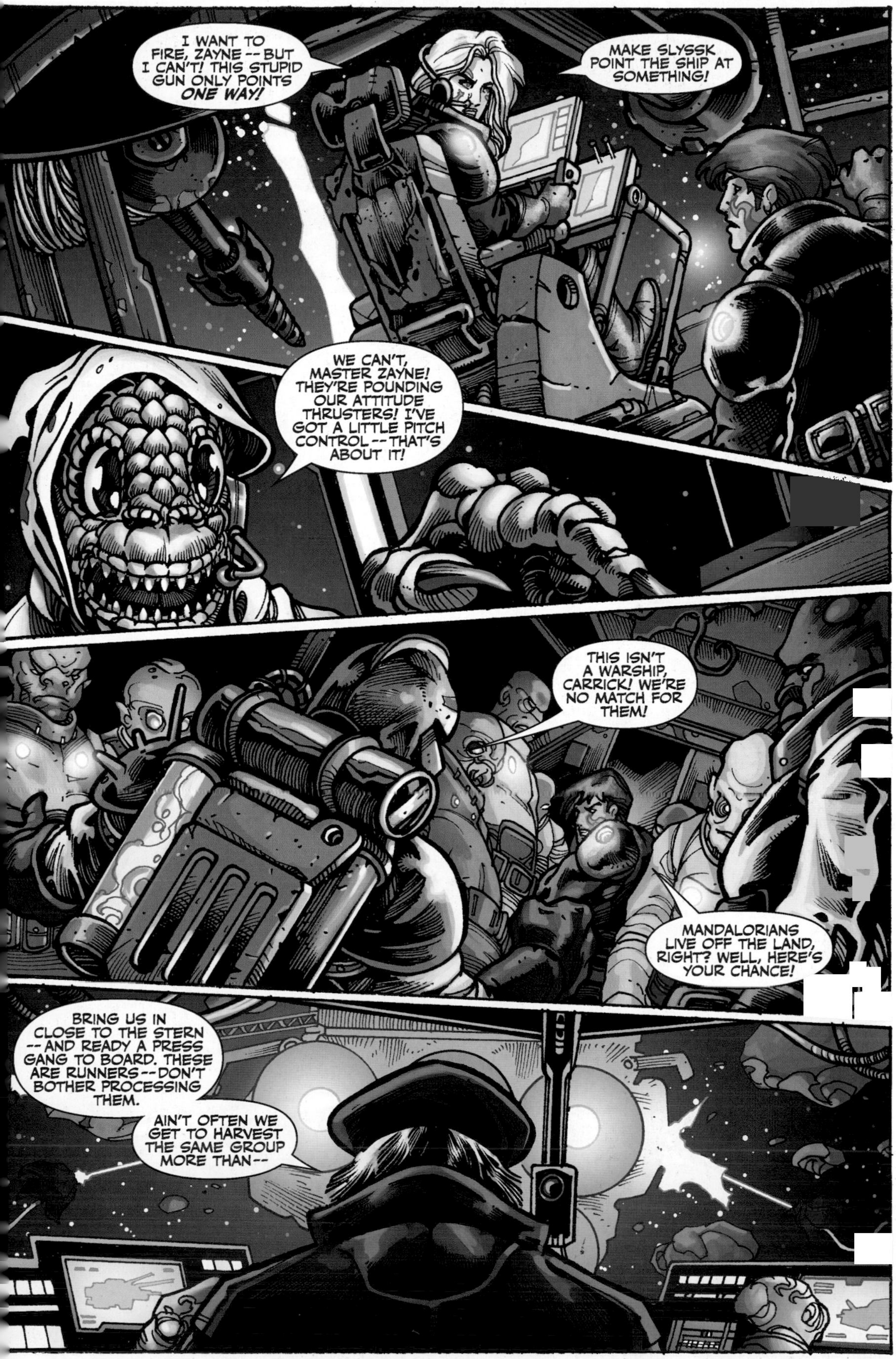
I WANT TO FIRE, ZAYNE -- BUT I CAN'T! THIS STUPID GUN ONLY POINTS *ONE WAY!*
MAKE SLYSSK POINT THE SHIP AT SOMETHING!
WE CAN'T, MASTER ZAYNE! THEY'RE POUNDING OUR ATTITUDE THRUSTERS! I'VE GOT A LITTLE PITCH CONTROL -- THAT'S ABOUT IT!
THIS ISN'T A WARSHIP, CARRICK! WE'RE NO MATCH FOR THEM!
MANDALORIANS LIVE OFF THE LAND, RIGHT? WELL, HERE'S YOUR CHANCE!
BRING US IN CLOSE TO THE STERN -- AND READY A PRESS GANG TO BOARD. THESE ARE RUNNERS -- DON'T BOTHER PROCESSING THEM.
AIN'T OFTEN WE GET TO HARVEST THE SAME GROUP MORE THAN--

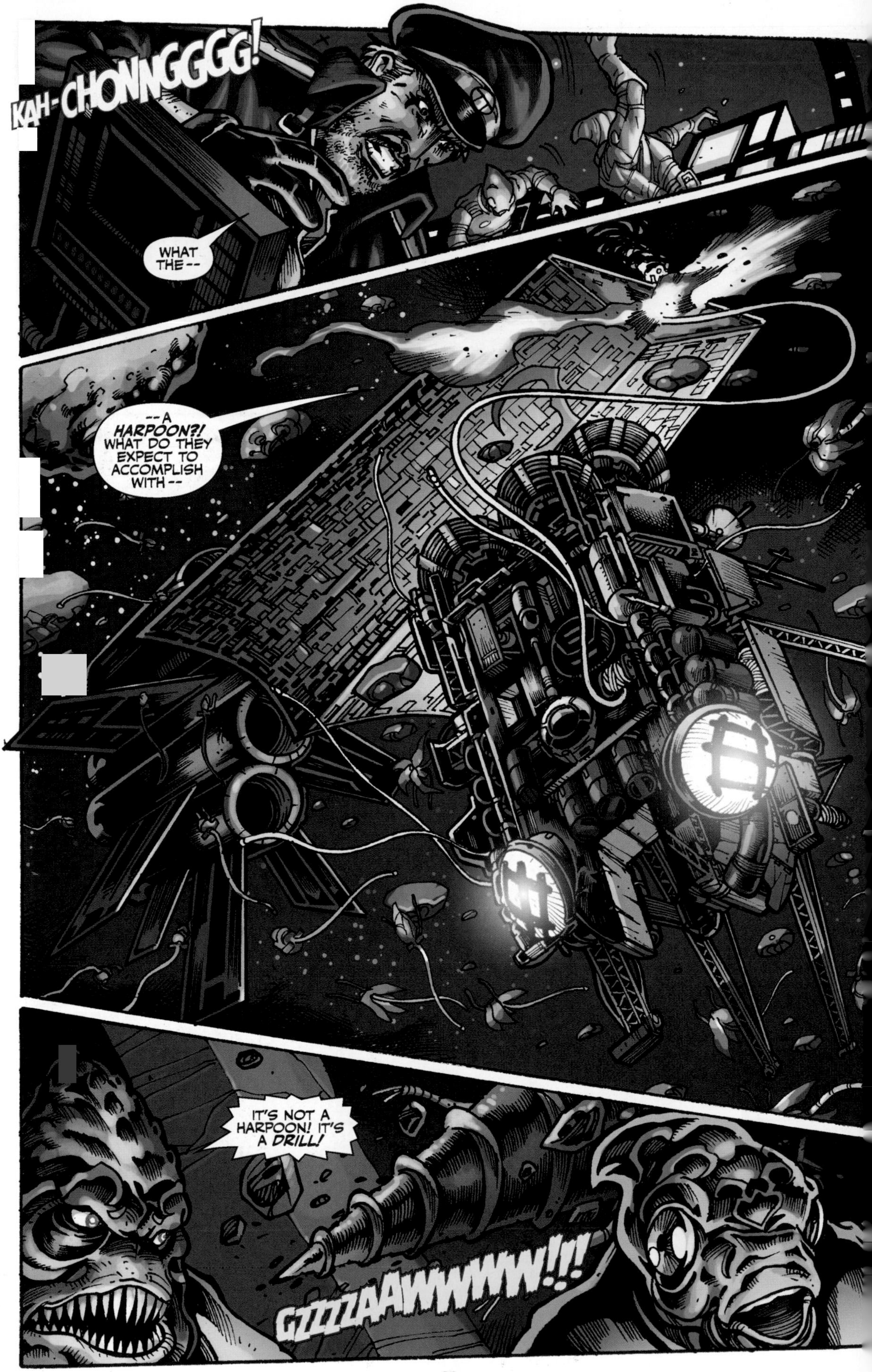
KAH-CHONNGGGG!
WHAT THE --
-- A HARPOON?! WHAT DO THEY EXPECT TO ACCOMPLISH WITH --
IT'S NOT A HARPOON! IT'S A DRILL!
GZZZZAAWWWWW!!!

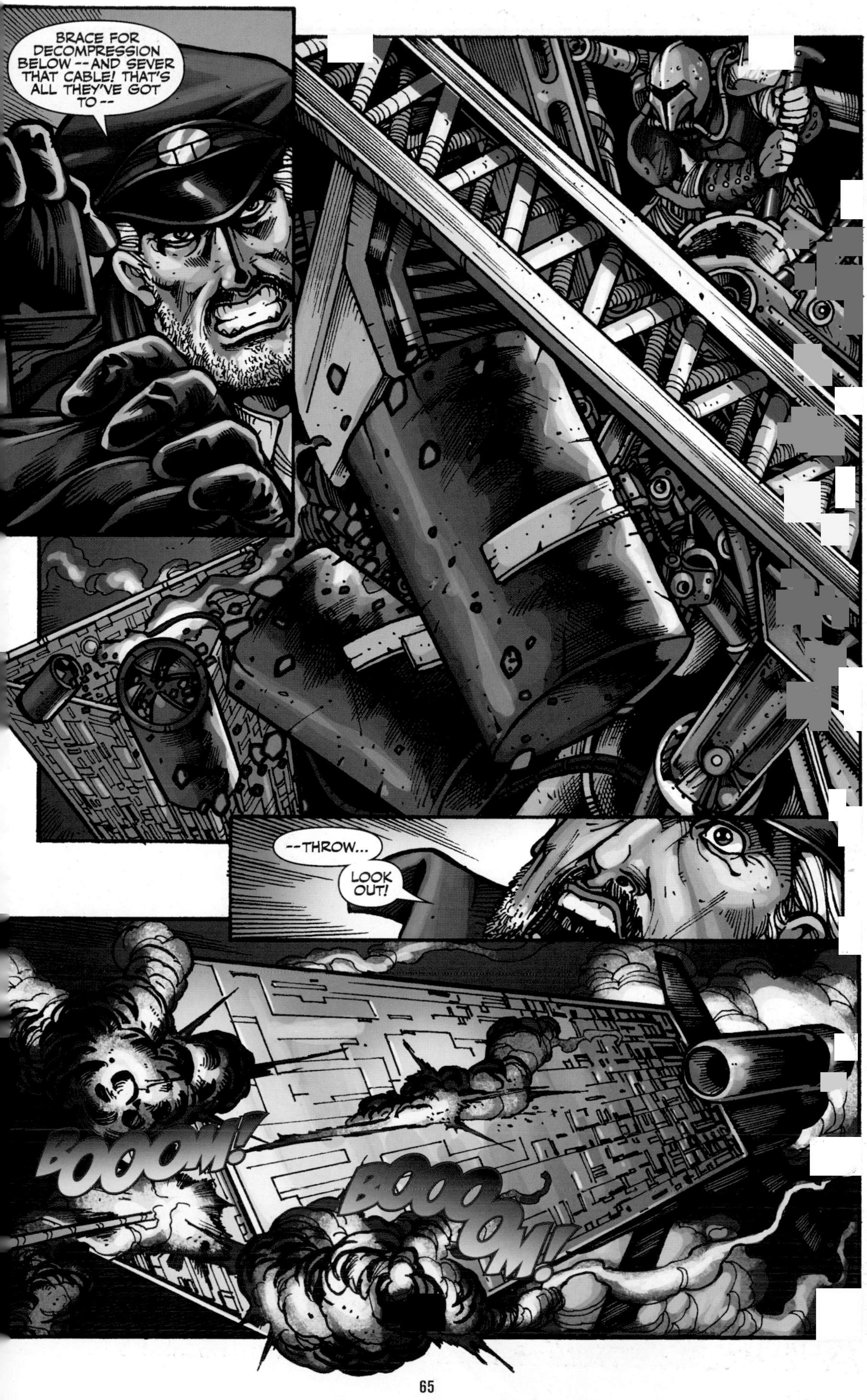
BRACE FOR DECOMPRESSION BELOW--AND SEVER THAT CABLE! THAT'S ALL THEY'VE GOT TO--
--THROW...
LOOK OUT!
BOOOM!
BOOOOM!

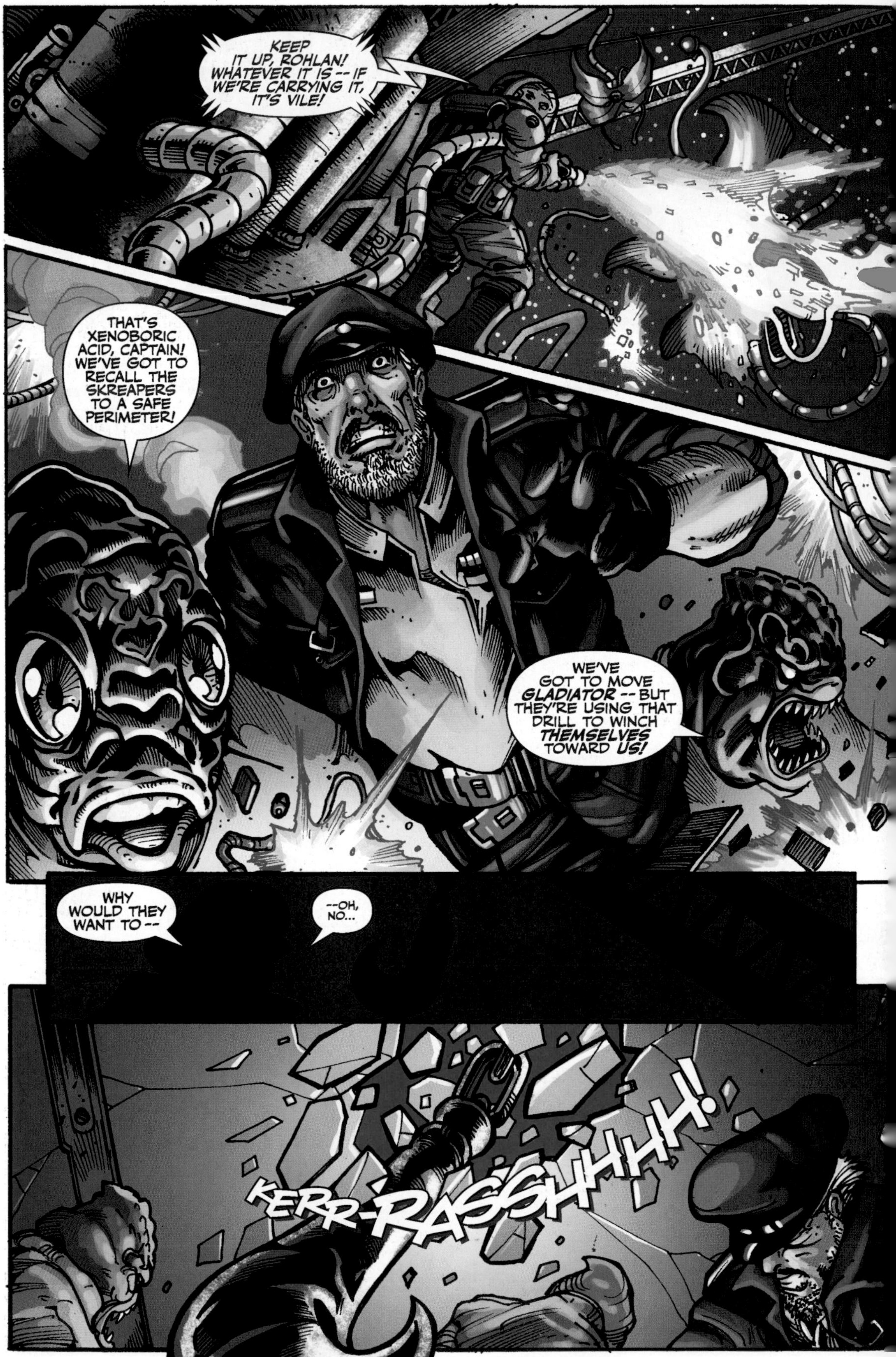
KEEP IT UP, ROHLAN! WHATEVER IT IS -- IF WE'RE CARRYING IT, IT'S VILE!
THAT'S XENOBORIC ACID, CAPTAIN! WE'VE GOT TO RECALL THE SKREAPERS TO A SAFE PERIMETER!
WE'VE GOT TO MOVE GLADIATOR -- BUT THEY'RE USING THAT DRILL TO WINCH THEMSELVES TOWARD US!
WHY WOULD THEY WANT TO --
--OH, NO...
KERR-RASSHHHH!

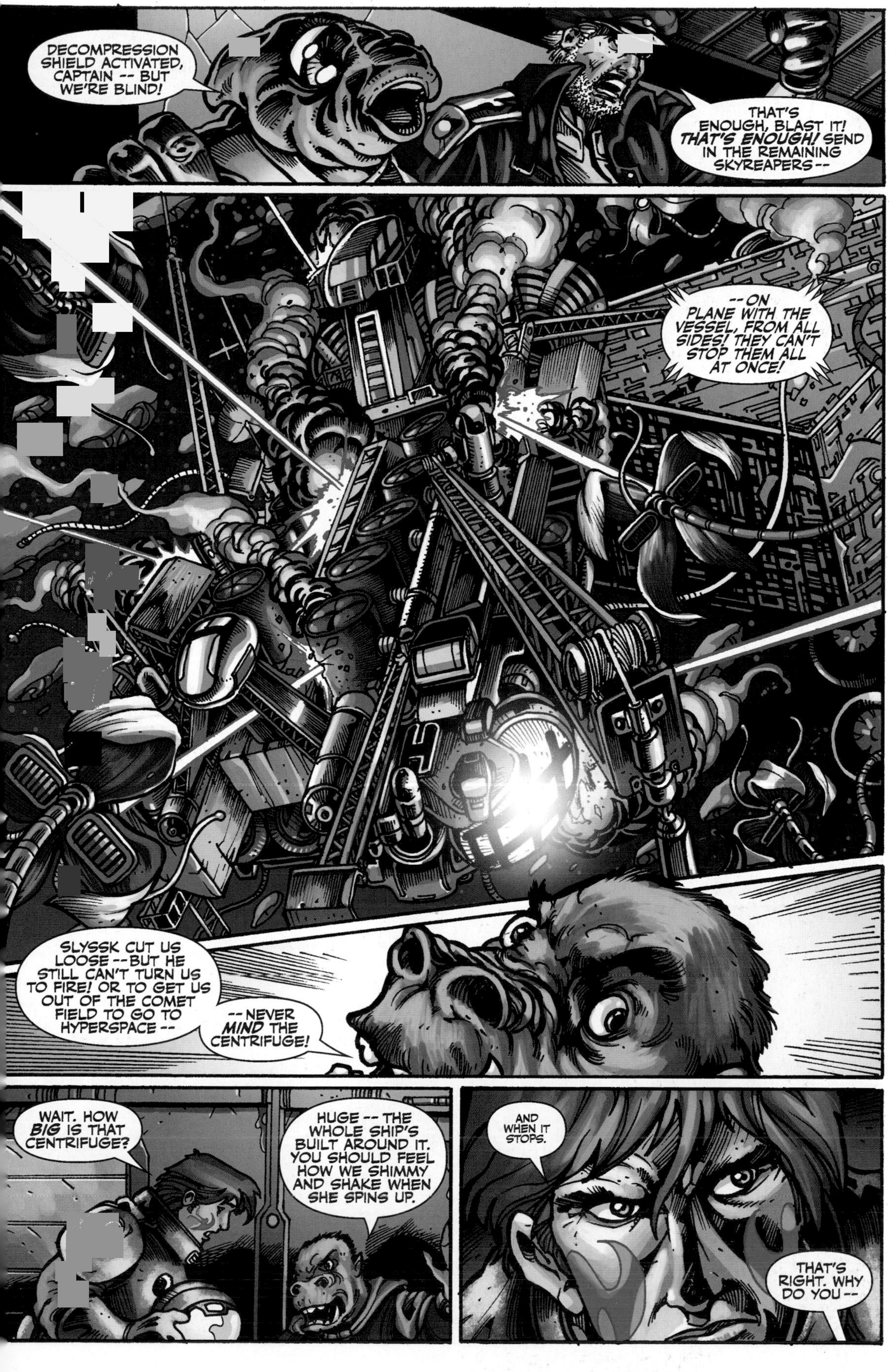
DECOMPRESSION SHIELD ACTIVATED, CAPTAIN -- BUT WE'RE BLIND!
THAT'S ENOUGH, BLAST IT! *THAT'S ENOUGH!* SEND IN THE REMAINING SKYREAPERS --
-- ON PLANE WITH THE VESSEL, FROM ALL SIDES! THEY CAN'T STOP THEM ALL AT ONCE!
SLYSSK CUT US LOOSE -- BUT HE STILL CAN'T TURN US TO FIRE! OR TO GET US OUT OF THE COMET FIELD TO GO TO HYPERSPACE --
-- NEVER *MIND* THE CENTRIFUGE!
WAIT. HOW *BIG* IS THAT CENTRIFUGE?
HUGE -- THE WHOLE SHIP'S BUILT AROUND IT. YOU SHOULD FEEL HOW WE SHIMMY AND SHAKE WHEN SHE SPINS UP.
AND WHEN IT STOPS.
THAT'S RIGHT. WHY DO YOU --

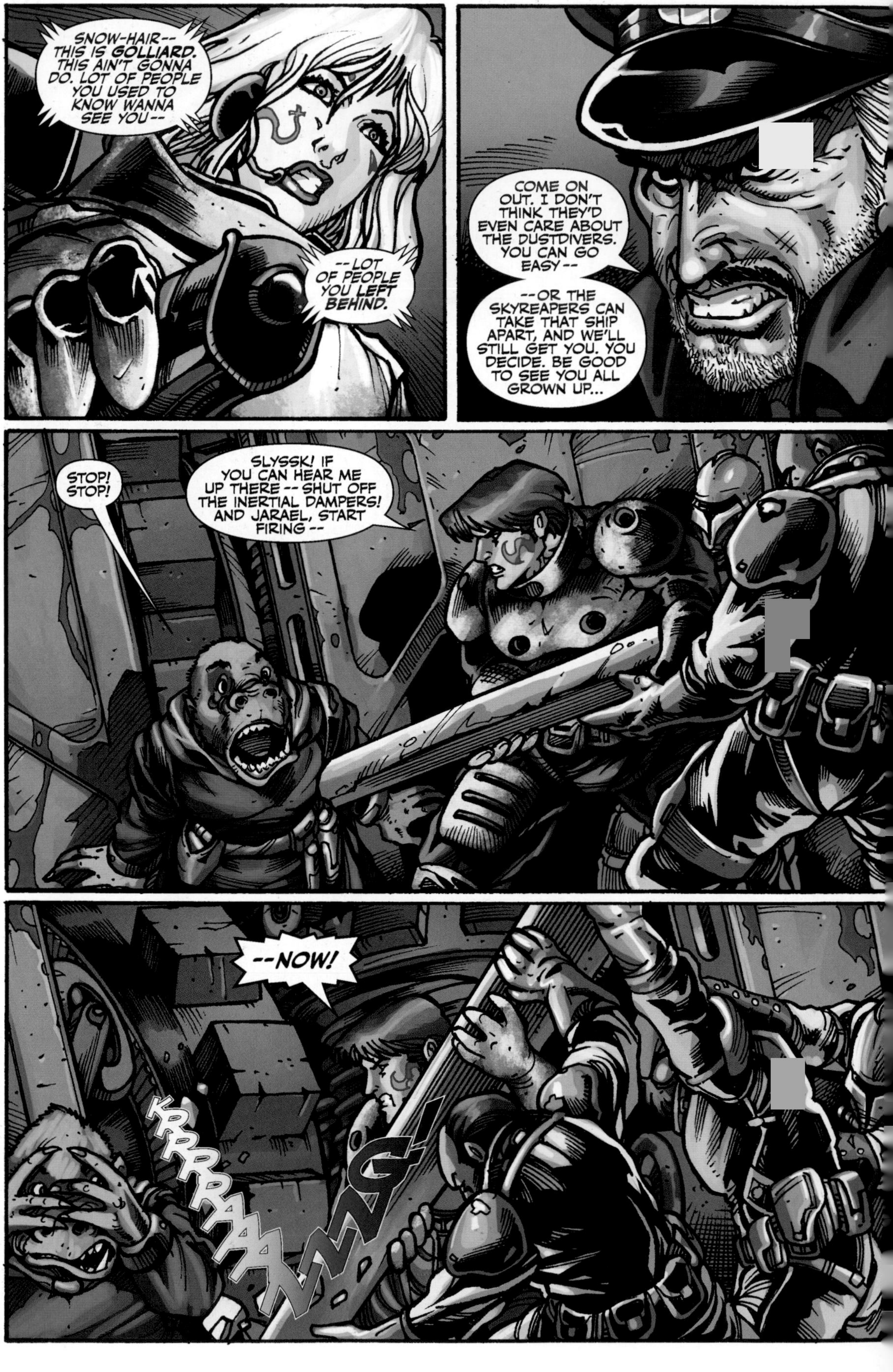
SNOW-HAIR-- THIS IS GOLLIARD. THIS AIN'T GONNA DO. LOT OF PEOPLE YOU USED TO KNOW WANNA SEE YOU--
--LOT OF PEOPLE YOU LEFT BEHIND.
COME ON OUT. I DON'T THINK THEY'D EVEN CARE ABOUT THE DUSTDIVERS. YOU CAN GO EASY--
--OR THE SKYREAPERS CAN TAKE THAT SHIP APART, AND WE'LL STILL GET YOU. YOU DECIDE. BE GOOD TO SEE YOU ALL GROWN UP...
STOP! STOP!
SLYSSK! IF YOU CAN HEAR ME UP THERE -- SHUT OFF THE INERTIAL DAMPERS! AND JARAEL, START FIRING --
--NOW!
KRRRRAAANNG!

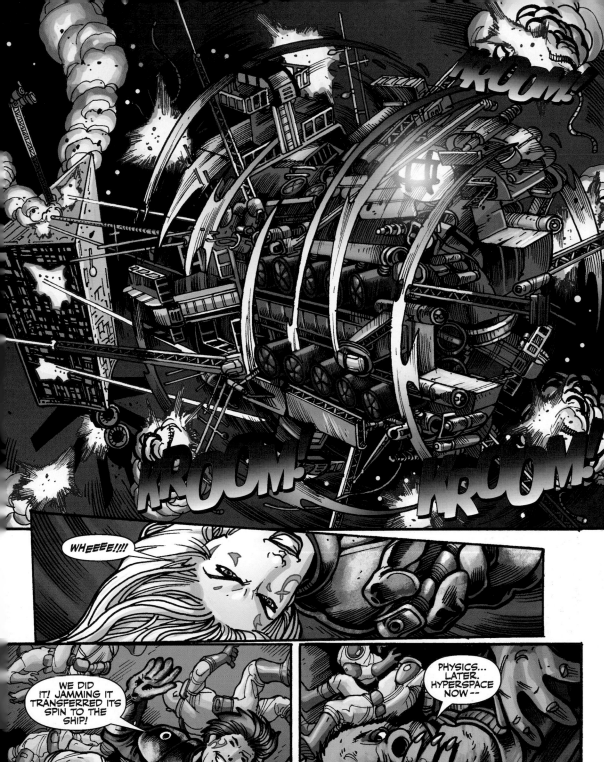

KROOM!

KROOM! KROOM!

WHEEEE!!!!

WE DID IT! JAMMING IT TRANSFERRED ITS SPIN TO THE SHIP!

PHYSICS... LATER. HYPERSPACE NOW --

-- AND FIND ME A PLACE TO BE SICK!

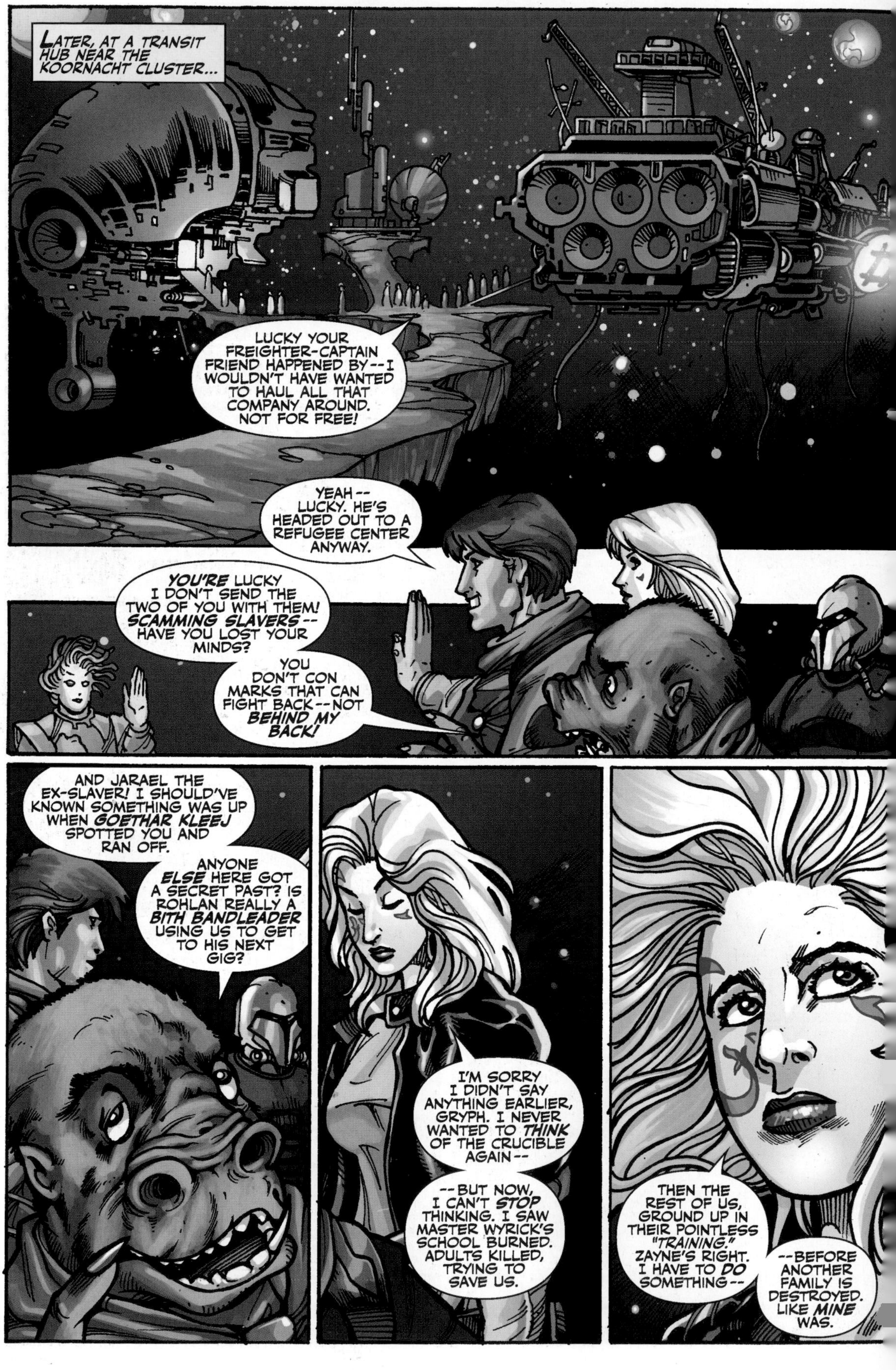
LATER, AT A TRANSIT HUB NEAR THE KOORNACHT CLUSTER...
LUCKY YOUR FREIGHTER-CAPTAIN FRIEND HAPPENED BY--I WOULDN'T HAVE WANTED TO HAUL ALL THAT COMPANY AROUND. NOT FOR FREE!
YEAH--LUCKY. HE'S HEADED OUT TO A REFUGEE CENTER ANYWAY.
YOU'RE LUCKY I DON'T SEND THE TWO OF YOU WITH THEM! SCAMMING SLAVERS--HAVE YOU LOST YOUR MINDS?
YOU DON'T CON MARKS THAT CAN FIGHT BACK--NOT BEHIND MY BACK!
AND JARAEL THE EX-SLAVER! I SHOULD'VE KNOWN SOMETHING WAS UP WHEN GOETHAR KLEEJ SPOTTED YOU AND RAN OFF.
ANYONE ELSE HERE GOT A SECRET PAST? IS ROHLAN REALLY A BITH BANDLEADER USING US TO GET TO HIS NEXT GIG?
I'M SORRY I DIDN'T SAY ANYTHING EARLIER, GRYPH. I NEVER WANTED TO THINK OF THE CRUCIBLE AGAIN--
--BUT NOW, I CAN'T STOP THINKING. I SAW MASTER WYRICK'S SCHOOL BURNED. ADULTS KILLED, TRYING TO SAVE US.
THEN THE REST OF US, GROUND UP IN THEIR POINTLESS "TRAINING." ZAYNE'S RIGHT. I HAVE TO DO SOMETHING--
--BEFORE ANOTHER FAMILY IS DESTROYED. LIKE MINE WAS.

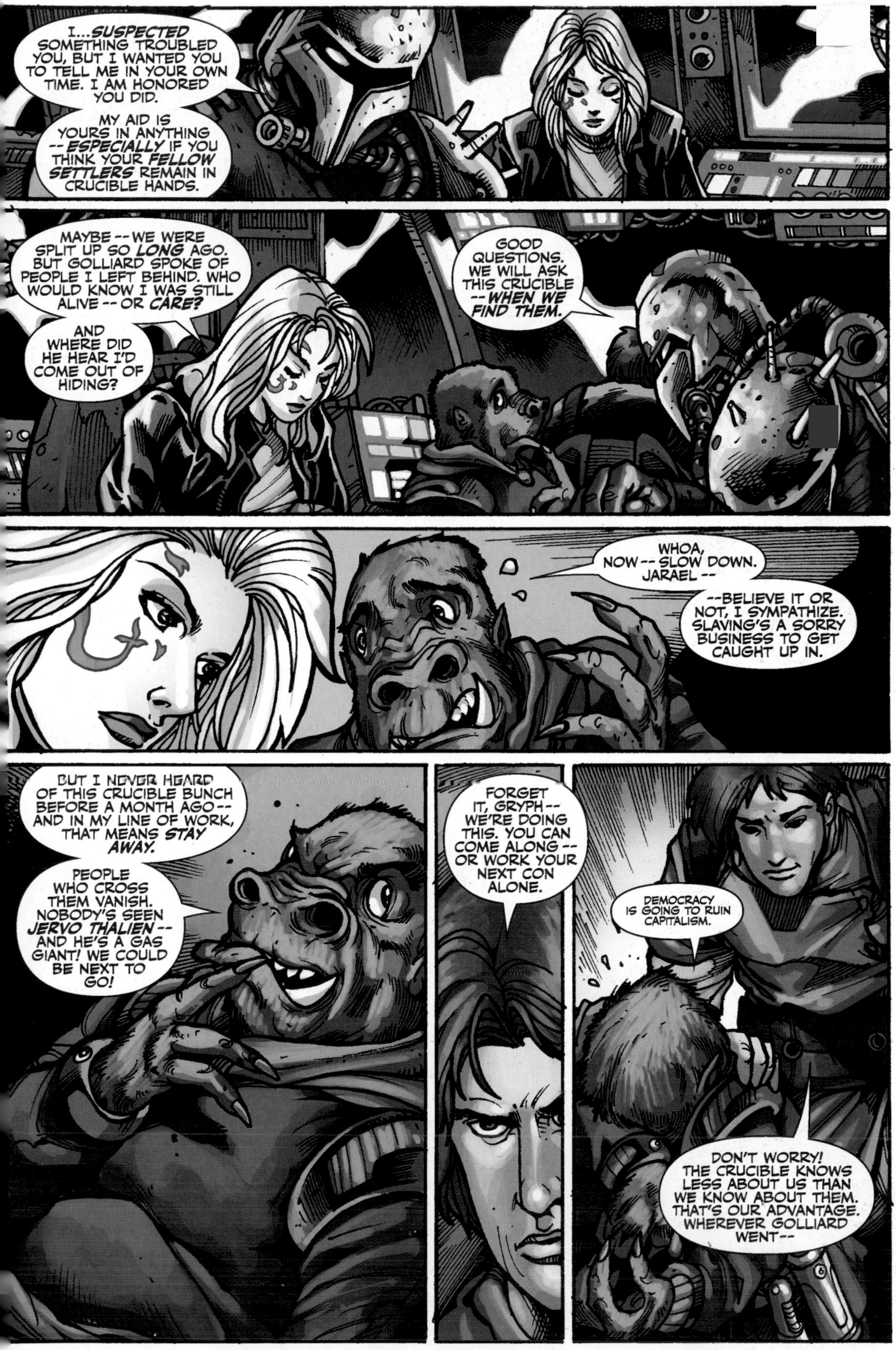
I...SUSPECTED SOMETHING TROUBLED YOU, BUT I WANTED YOU TO TELL ME IN YOUR OWN TIME. I AM HONORED YOU DID.
MY AID IS YOURS IN ANYTHING --ESPECIALLY IF YOU THINK YOUR FELLOW SETTLERS REMAIN IN CRUCIBLE HANDS.
MAYBE--WE WERE SPLIT UP SO LONG AGO. BUT GOLLIARD SPOKE OF PEOPLE I LEFT BEHIND. WHO WOULD KNOW I WAS STILL ALIVE--OR CARE?
AND WHERE DID HE HEAR I'D COME OUT OF HIDING?
GOOD QUESTIONS. WE WILL ASK THIS CRUCIBLE --WHEN WE FIND THEM.
WHOA, NOW--SLOW DOWN. JARAEL--
--BELIEVE IT OR NOT, I SYMPATHIZE. SLAVING'S A SORRY BUSINESS TO GET CAUGHT UP IN.
BUT I NEVER HEARD OF THIS CRUCIBLE BUNCH BEFORE A MONTH AGO--AND IN MY LINE OF WORK, THAT MEANS STAY AWAY.
PEOPLE WHO CROSS THEM VANISH. NOBODY'S SEEN JERVO THALIEN--AND HE'S A GAS GIANT! WE COULD BE NEXT TO GO!
FORGET IT, GRYPH--WE'RE DOING THIS. YOU CAN COME ALONG--OR WORK YOUR NEXT CON ALONE.
DEMOCRACY IS GOING TO RUIN CAPITALISM.
DON'T WORRY! THE CRUCIBLE KNOWS LESS ABOUT US THAN WE KNOW ABOUT THEM. THAT'S OUR ADVANTAGE. WHEREVER GOLLIARD WENT--

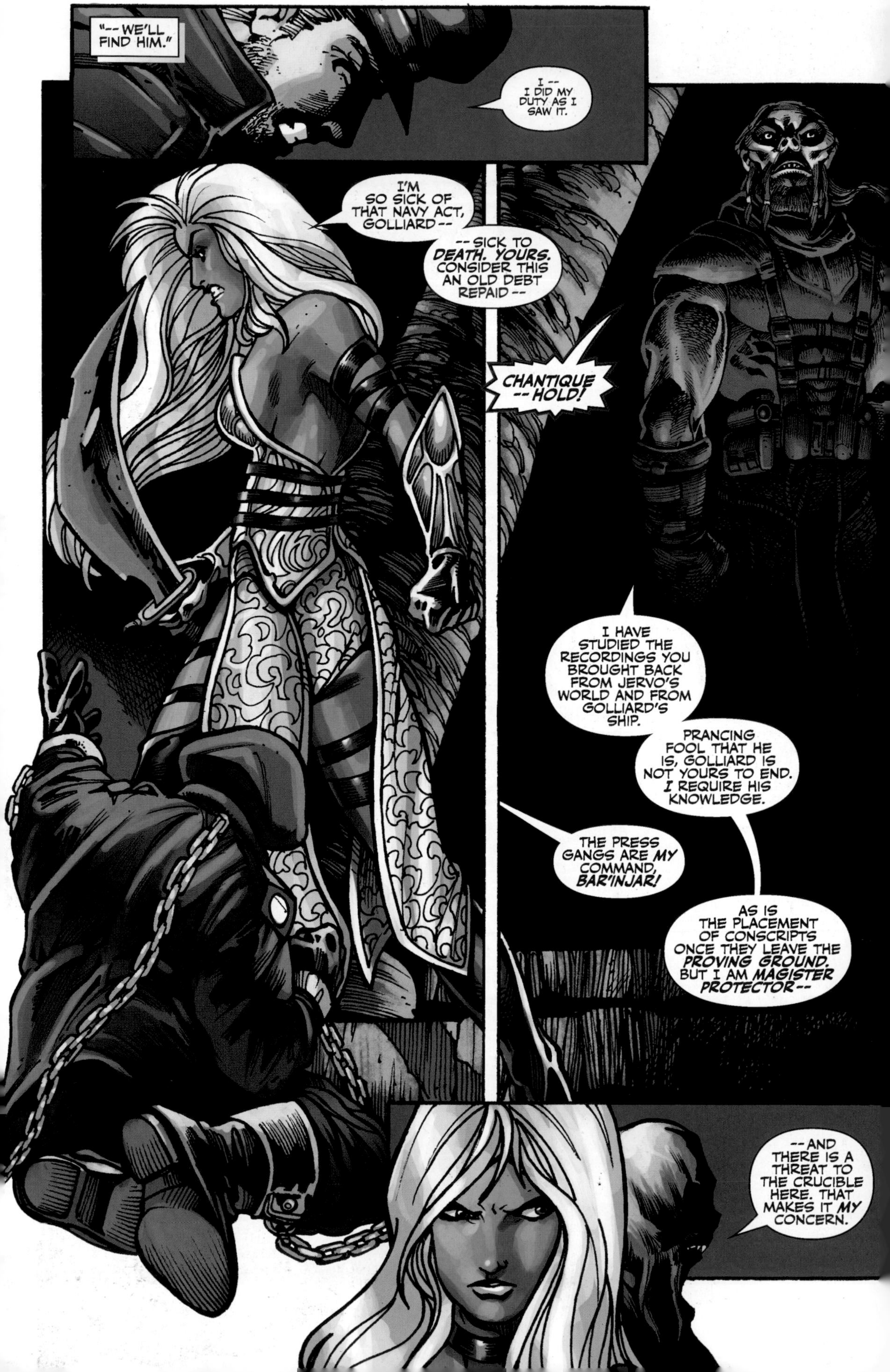
"--WE'LL FIND HIM."
I -- I DID MY DUTY AS I SAW IT.
I'M SO SICK OF THAT NAVY ACT, GOLLIARD--
--SICK TO DEATH. YOURS. CONSIDER THIS AN OLD DEBT REPAID--
CHANTIQUE --HOLD!
I HAVE STUDIED THE RECORDINGS YOU BROUGHT BACK FROM JERVO'S WORLD AND FROM GOLLIARD'S SHIP.
PRANCING FOOL THAT HE IS, GOLLIARD IS NOT YOURS TO END. I REQUIRE HIS KNOWLEDGE.
THE PRESS GANGS ARE MY COMMAND, BAR'INJAR!
AS IS THE PLACEMENT OF CONSCRIPTS ONCE THEY LEAVE THE PROVING GROUND. BUT I AM MAGISTER PROTECTOR--
--AND THERE IS A THREAT TO THE CRUCIBLE HERE. THAT MAKES IT MY CONCERN.

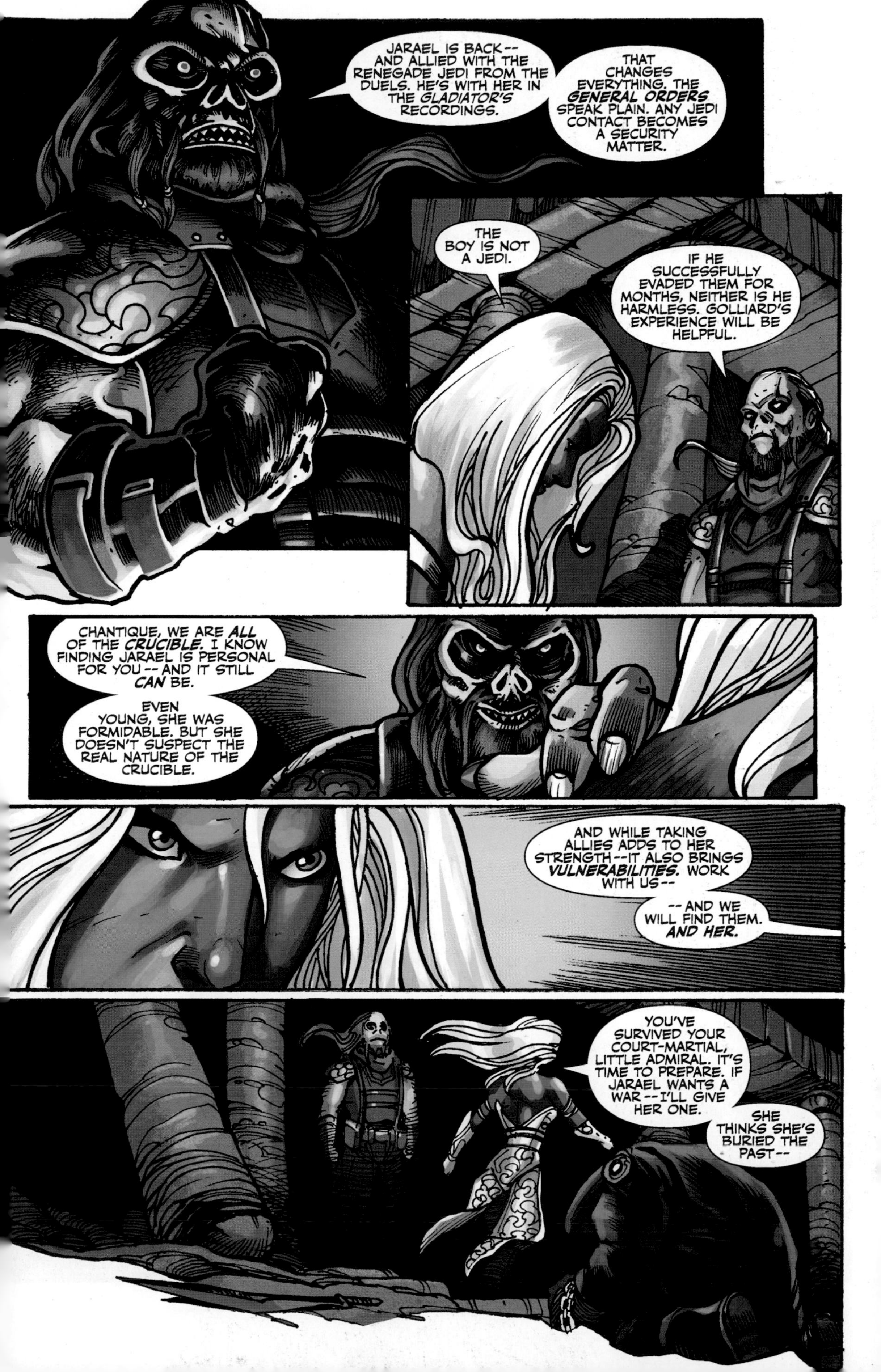
JARAEL IS BACK-- AND ALLIED WITH THE RENEGADE JEDI FROM THE DUELS. HE'S WITH HER IN THE *GLADIATOR'S* RECORDINGS.
THAT CHANGES EVERYTHING. THE ***GENERAL ORDERS*** SPEAK PLAIN. ANY JEDI CONTACT BECOMES A SECURITY MATTER.
THE BOY IS NOT A JEDI.
IF HE SUCCESSFULLY EVADED THEM FOR MONTHS, NEITHER IS HE HARMLESS. GOLLIARD'S EXPERIENCE WILL BE HELPFUL.
CHANTIQUE, WE ARE ***ALL*** OF THE ***CRUCIBLE.*** I KNOW FINDING JARAEL IS PERSONAL FOR YOU--AND IT STILL ***CAN*** BE.
EVEN YOUNG, SHE WAS FORMIDABLE. BUT SHE DOESN'T SUSPECT THE REAL NATURE OF THE CRUCIBLE.
AND WHILE TAKING ALLIES ADDS TO HER STRENGTH--IT ALSO BRINGS ***VULNERABILITIES.*** WORK WITH US--
--AND WE WILL FIND THEM. ***AND HER.***
YOU'VE SURVIVED YOUR COURT-MARTIAL, LITTLE ADMIRAL. IT'S TIME TO PREPARE. IF JARAEL WANTS A WAR--I'LL GIVE HER ONE.
SHE THINKS SHE'S BURIED THE PAST--

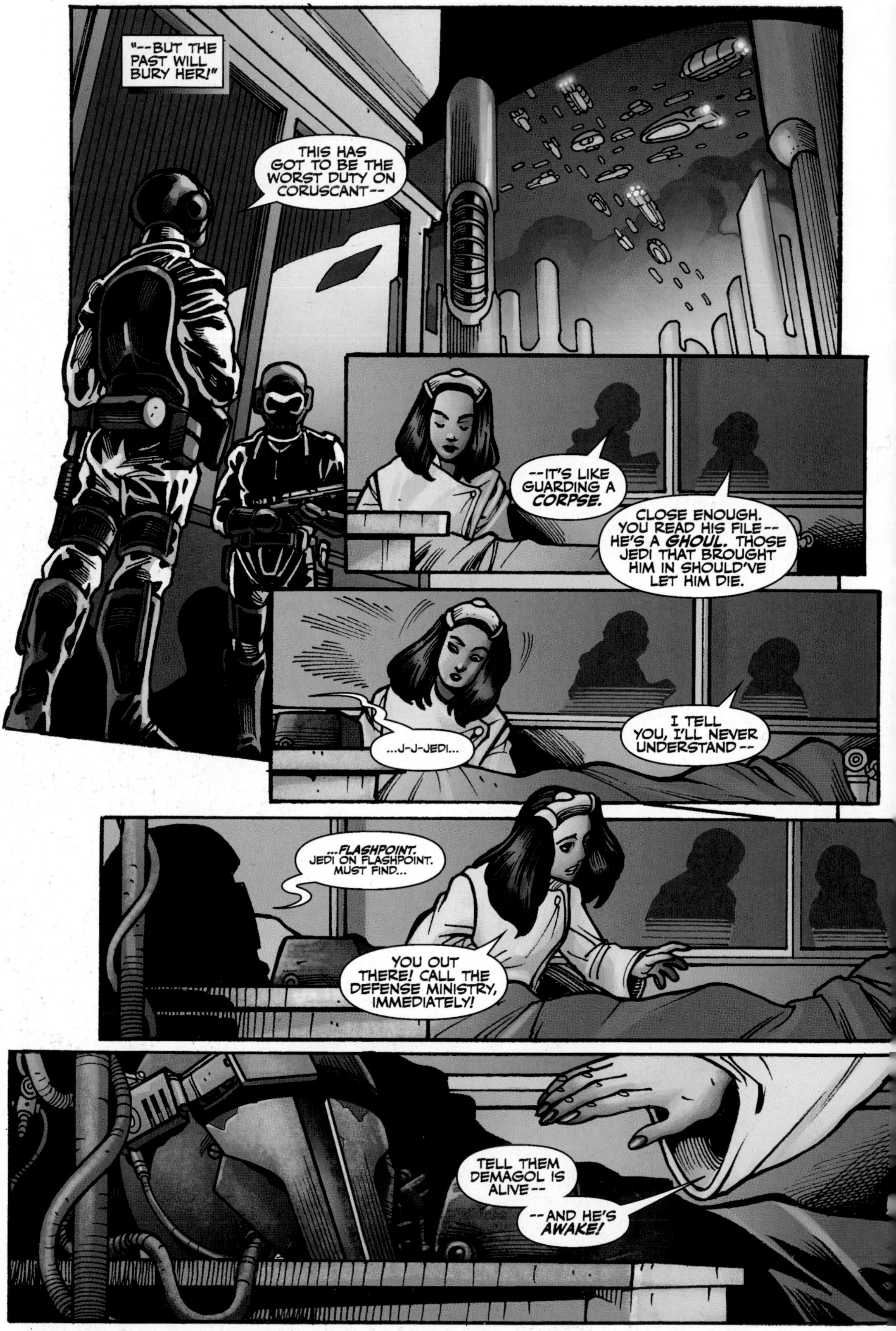
"--BUT THE PAST WILL BURY HER!"
THIS HAS GOT TO BE THE WORST DUTY ON CORUSCANT--
--IT'S LIKE GUARDING A CORPSE.
CLOSE ENOUGH. YOU READ HIS FILE-- HE'S A GHOUL. THOSE JEDI THAT BROUGHT HIM IN SHOULD'VE LET HIM DIE.
...J-J-JEDI...
I TELL YOU, I'LL NEVER UNDERSTAND--
...FLASHPOINT. JEDI ON FLASHPOINT. MUST FIND...
YOU OUT THERE! CALL THE DEFENSE MINISTRY, IMMEDIATELY!
TELL THEM DEMAGOL IS ALIVE--
--AND HE'S AWAKE!

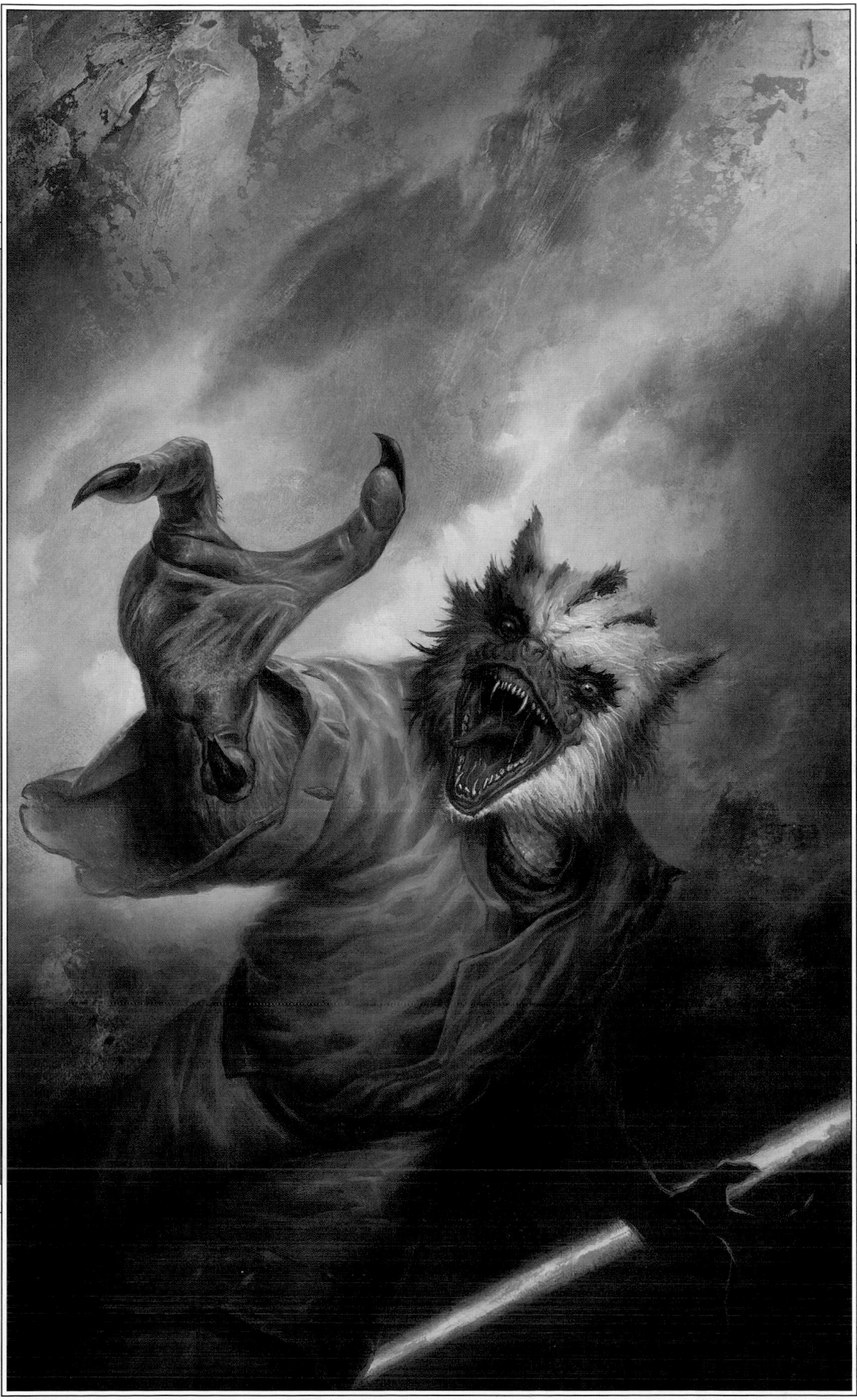

ILLUSTRATION BY JIM PAVELEC

DESTROYER

art by Brian Ching

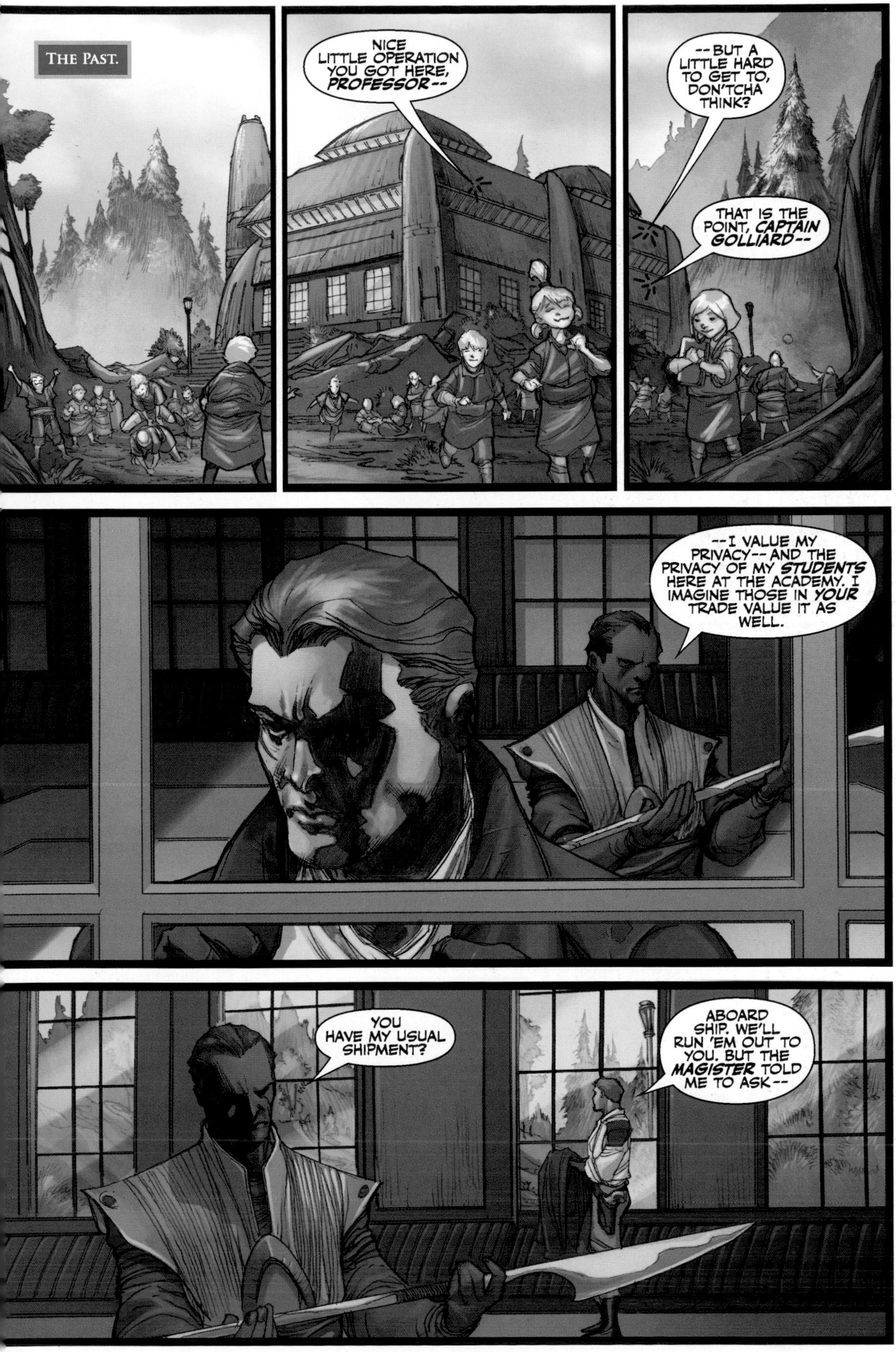
THE PAST.
NICE LITTLE OPERATION YOU GOT HERE, PROFESSOR--
--BUT A LITTLE HARD TO GET TO, DON'TCHA THINK?
THAT IS THE POINT, CAPTAIN GOLLIARD--
--I VALUE MY PRIVACY--AND THE PRIVACY OF MY STUDENTS HERE AT THE ACADEMY. I IMAGINE THOSE IN YOUR TRADE VALUE IT AS WELL.
YOU HAVE MY USUAL SHIPMENT?
ABOARD SHIP. WE'LL RUN 'EM OUT TO YOU. BUT THE MAGISTER TOLD ME TO ASK--

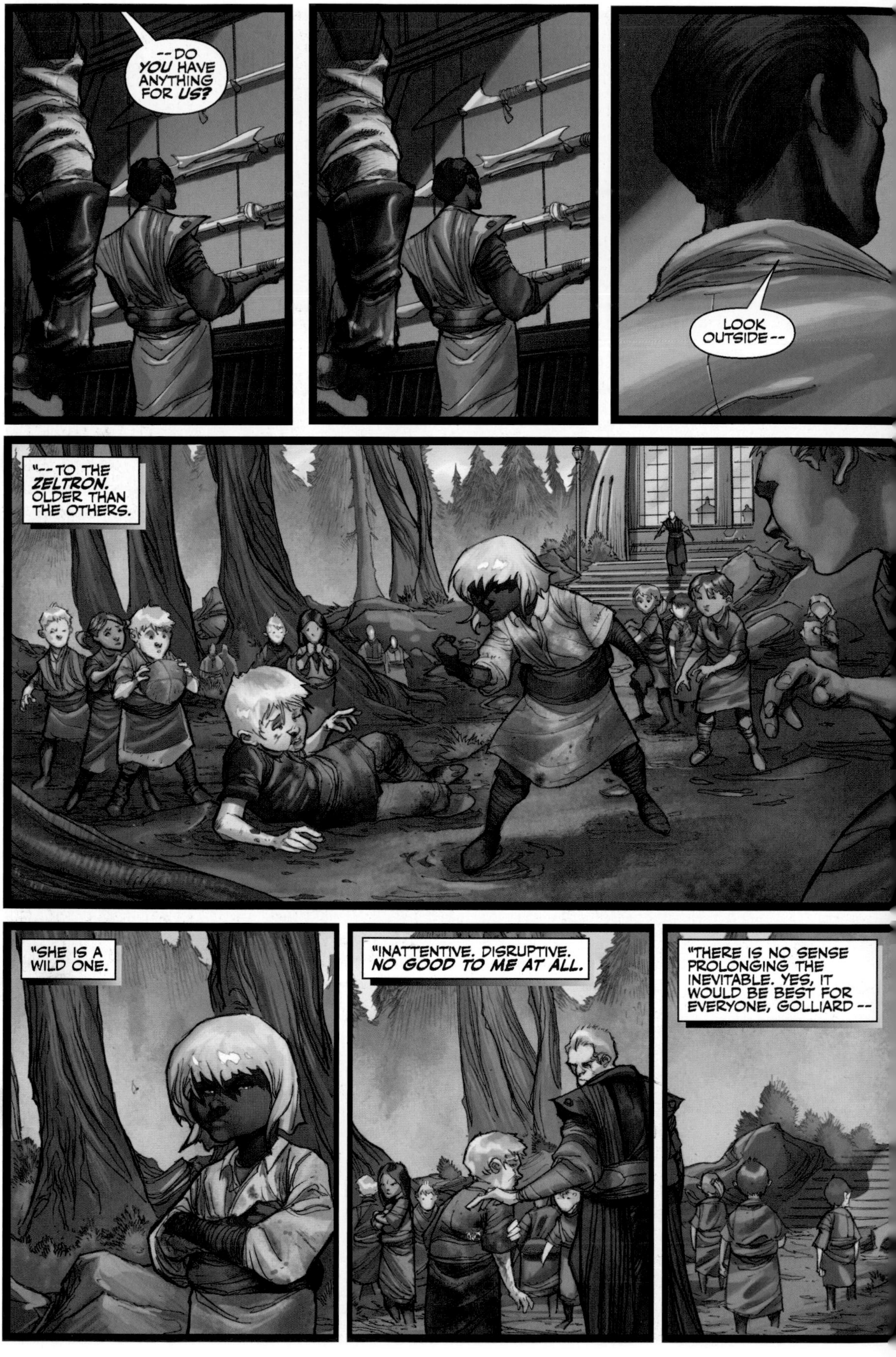

--DO YOU HAVE ANYTHING FOR US?
LOOK OUTSIDE--
"--TO THE ZELTRON. OLDER THAN THE OTHERS.
"SHE IS A WILD ONE.
"INATTENTIVE. DISRUPTIVE. NO GOOD TO ME AT ALL.
"THERE IS NO SENSE PROLONGING THE INEVITABLE. YES, IT WOULD BE BEST FOR EVERYONE, GOLLIARD--

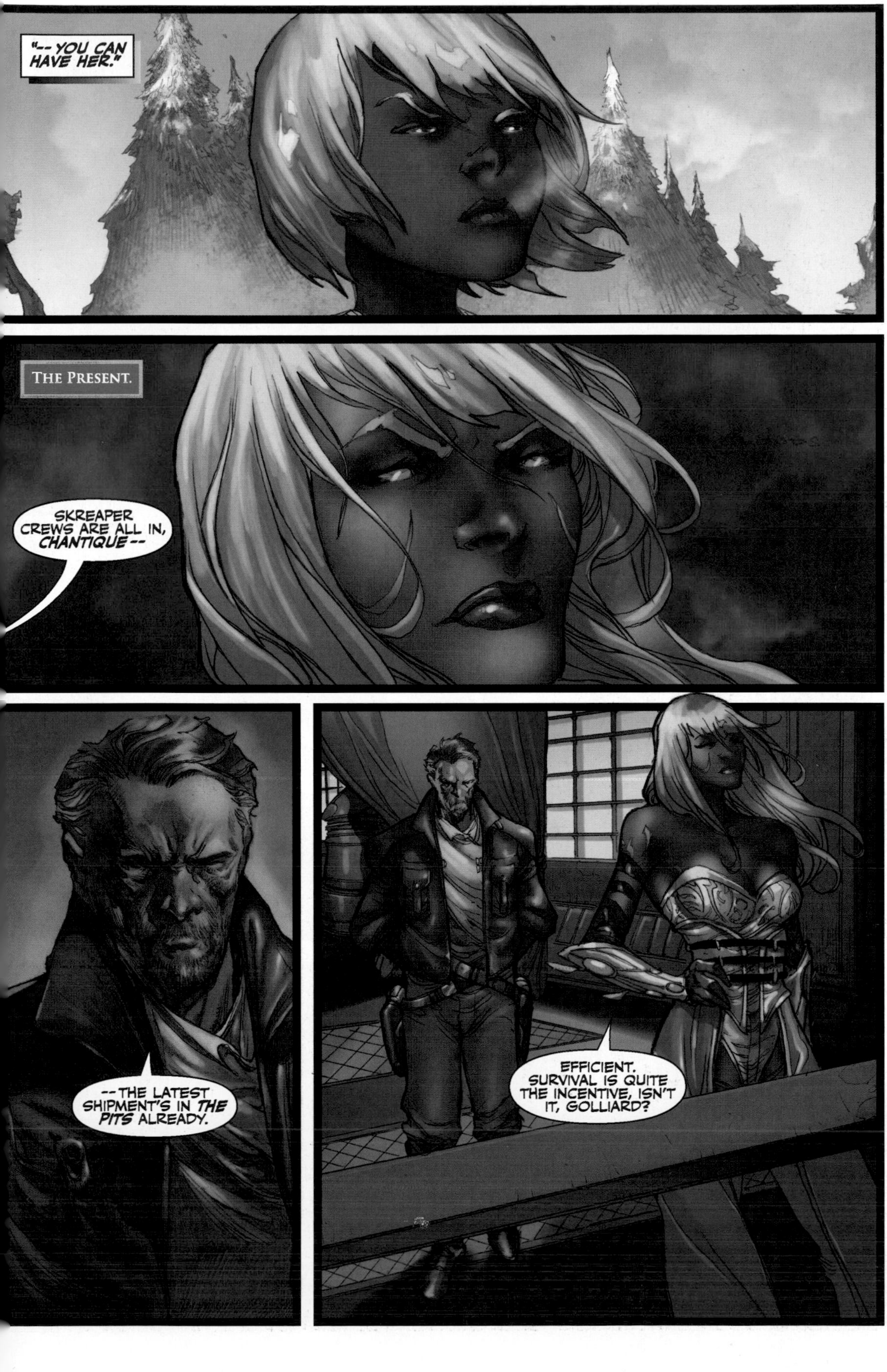
"--YOU CAN HAVE HER."
THE PRESENT.
SKREAPER CREWS ARE ALL IN, CHANTIQUE--
--THE LATEST SHIPMENT'S IN THE PITS ALREADY.
EFFICIENT. SURVIVAL IS QUITE THE INCENTIVE, ISN'T IT, GOLLIARD?

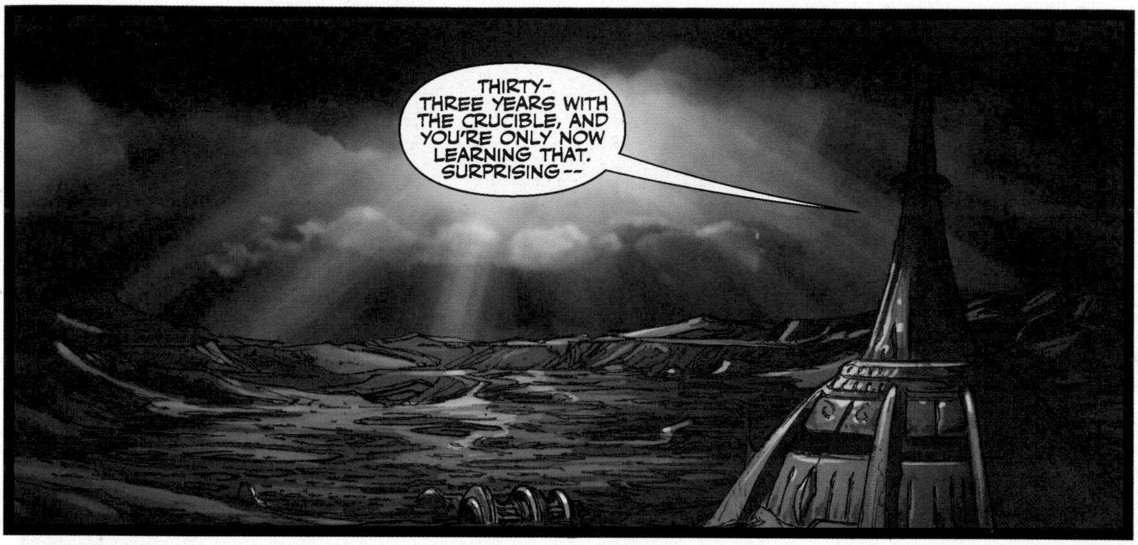
THIRTY-THREE YEARS WITH THE CRUCIBLE, AND YOU'RE ONLY NOW LEARNING THAT. SURPRISING--

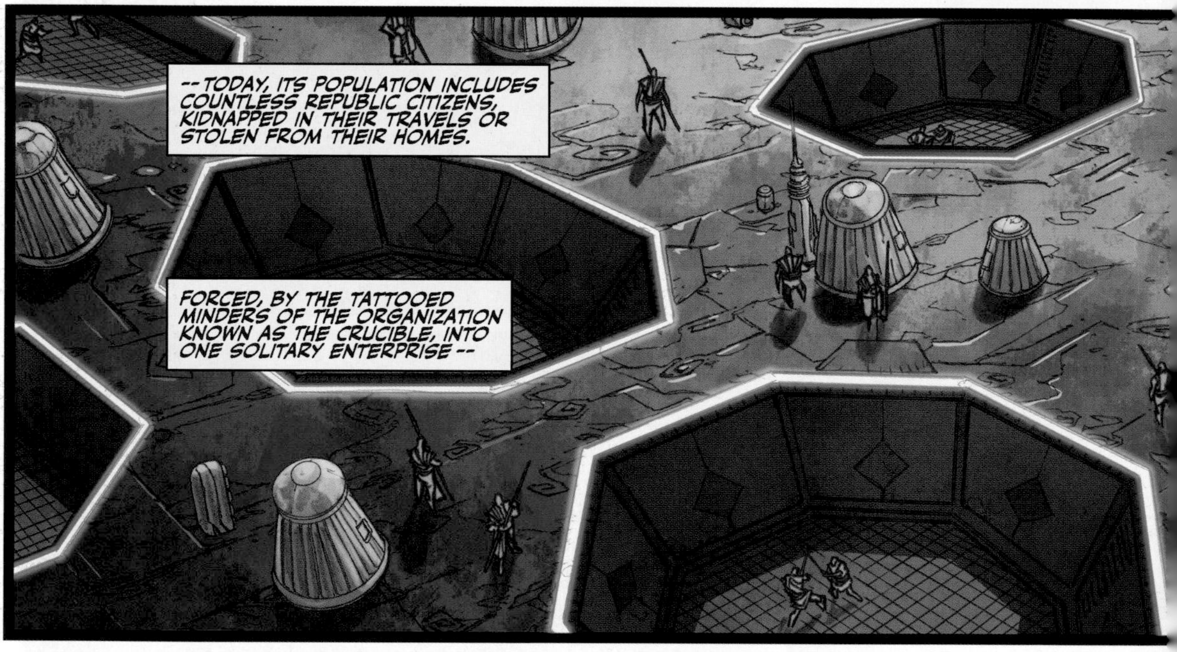
--TODAY, ITS POPULATION INCLUDES COUNTLESS REPUBLIC CITIZENS, KIDNAPPED IN THEIR TRAVELS OR STOLEN FROM THEIR HOMES.
FORCED, BY THE TATTOOED MINDERS OF THE ORGANIZATION KNOWN AS THE CRUCIBLE, INTO ONE SOLITARY ENTERPRISE--

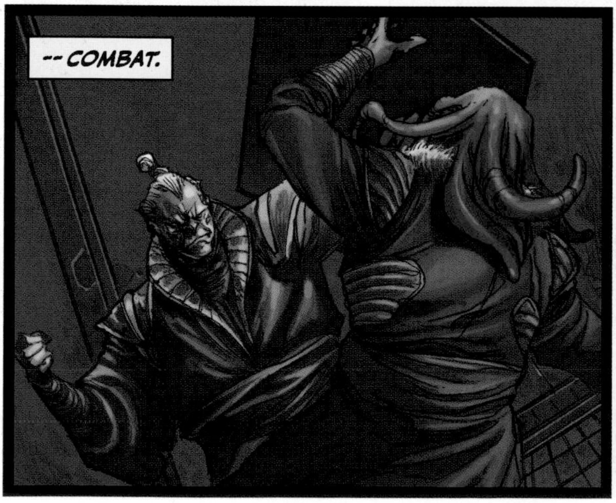
--COMBAT.

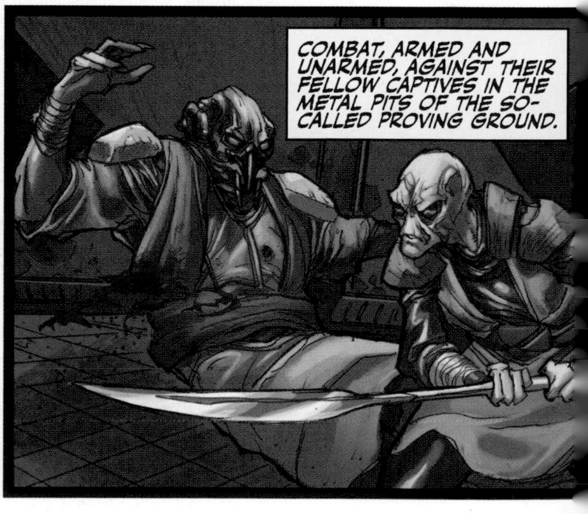
COMBAT, ARMED AND UNARMED, AGAINST THEIR FELLOW CAPTIVES IN THE METAL PITS OF THE SO-CALLED PROVING GROUND.

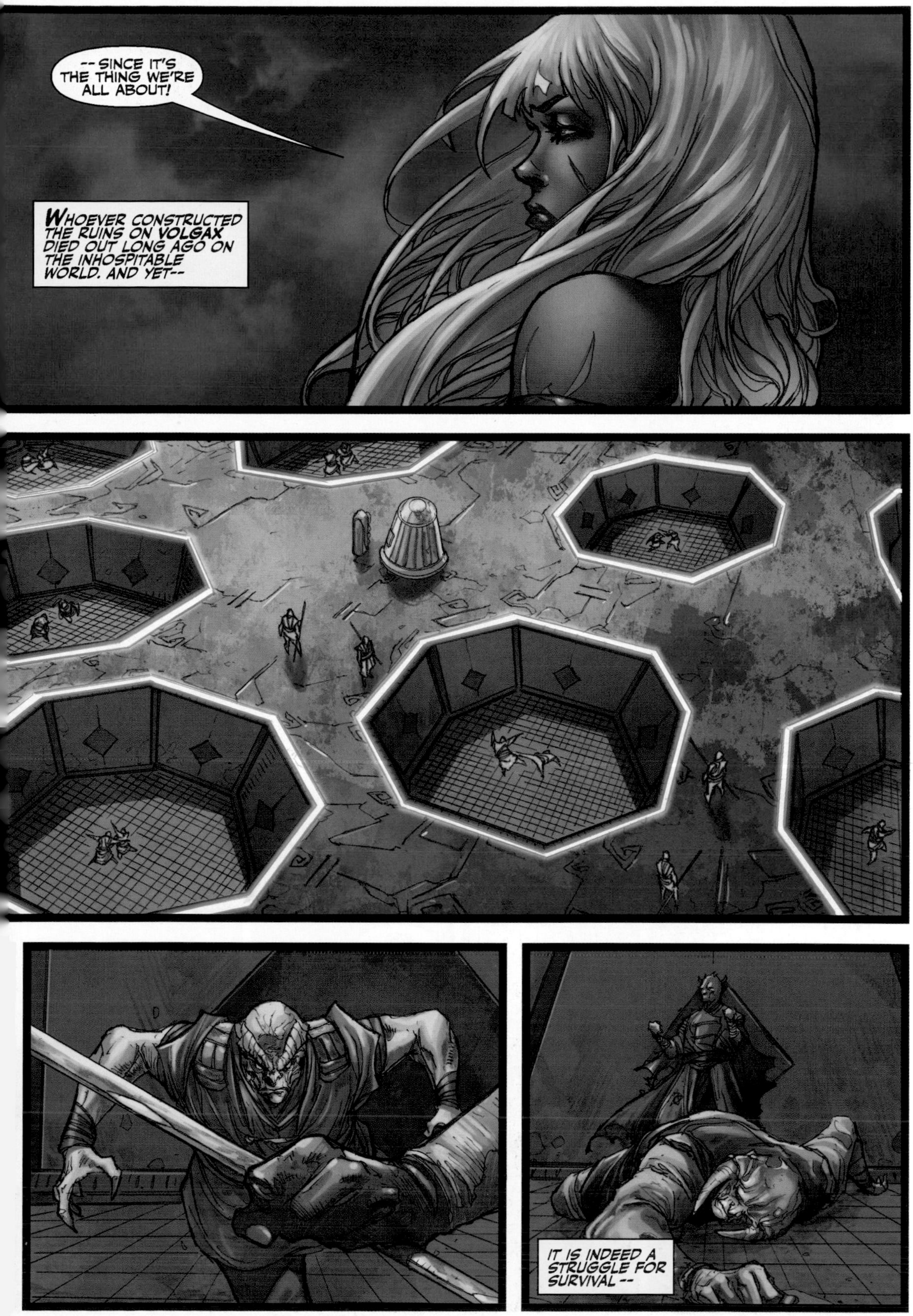
-- SINCE IT'S THE THING WE'RE ALL ABOUT!
WHOEVER CONSTRUCTED THE RUINS ON VOLGAX DIED OUT LONG AGO ON THE INHOSPITABLE WORLD. AND YET--
IT IS INDEED A STRUGGLE FOR SURVIVAL --

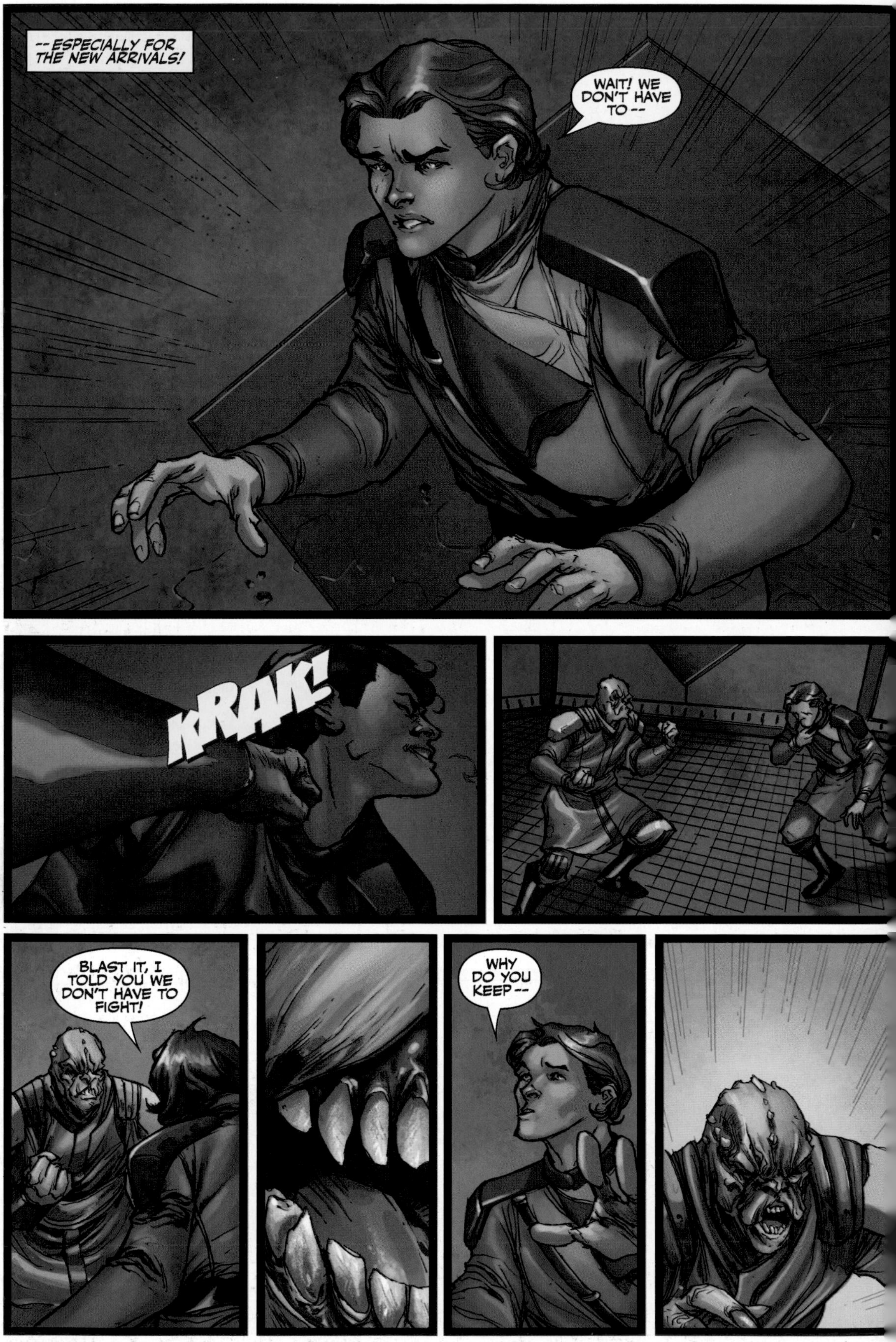
--ESPECIALLY FOR THE NEW ARRIVALS!
WAIT! WE DON'T HAVE TO--
KRAK!
BLAST IT, I TOLD YOU WE DON'T HAVE TO FIGHT!
WHY DO YOU KEEP--

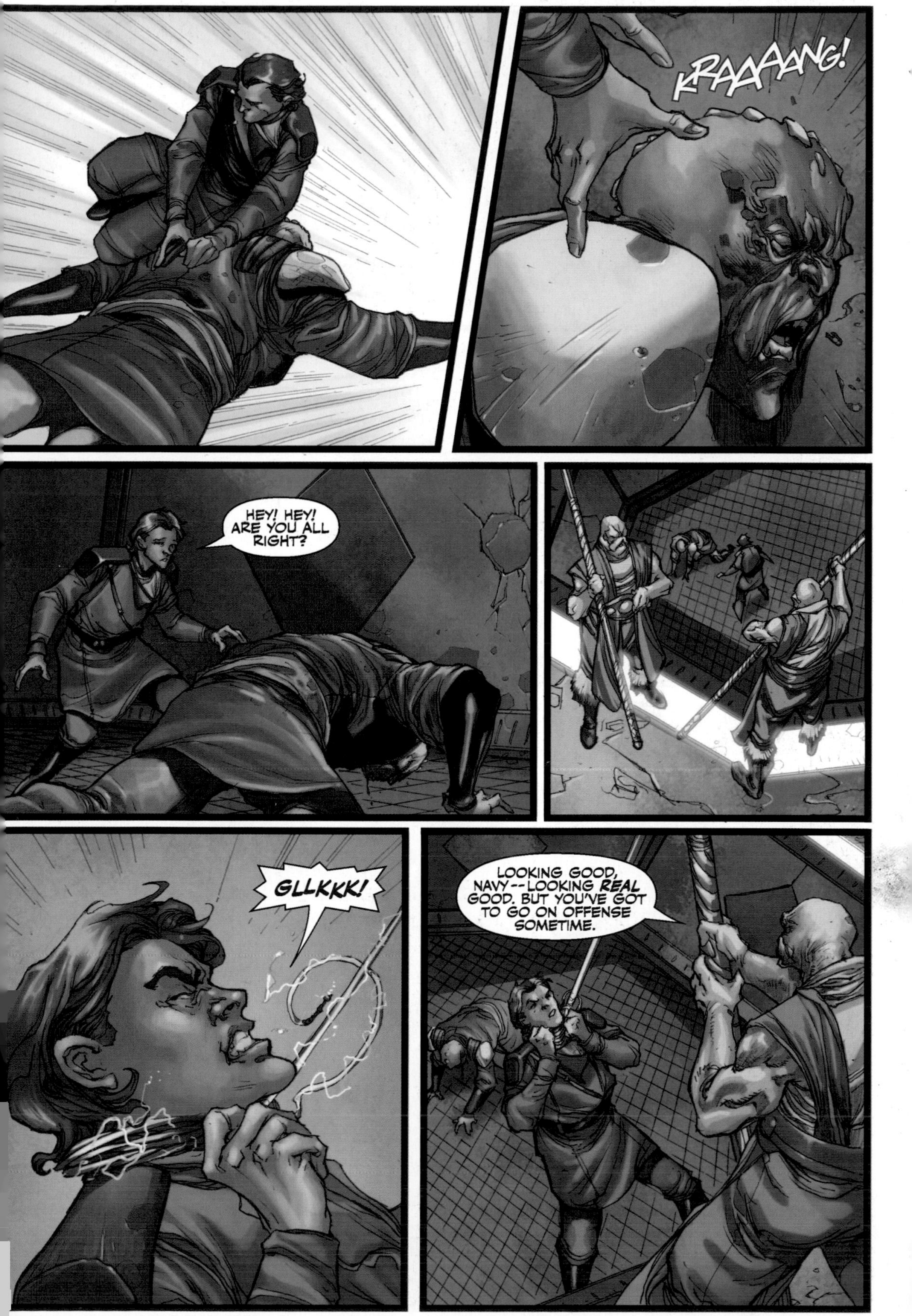
KRAAAANG!
HEY! HEY! ARE YOU ALL RIGHT?
GLLKKK!
LOOKING GOOD, NAVY--LOOKING *REAL* GOOD. BUT YOU'VE GOT TO GO ON OFFENSE SOMETIME.

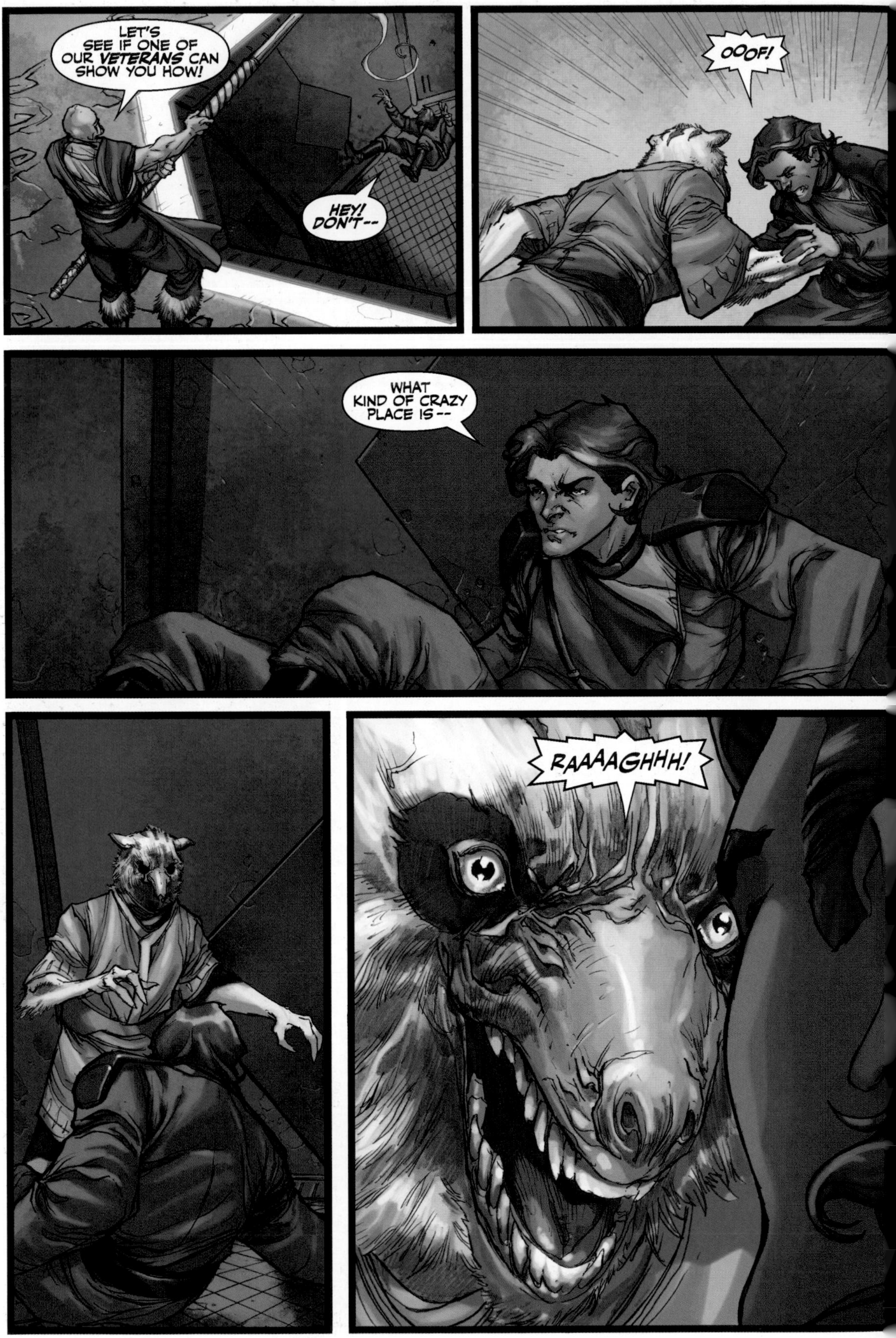
LET'S SEE IF ONE OF OUR VETERANS CAN SHOW YOU HOW!
HEY! DON'T--
OOOF!
WHAT KIND OF CRAZY PLACE IS--
RAAAAGHHH!

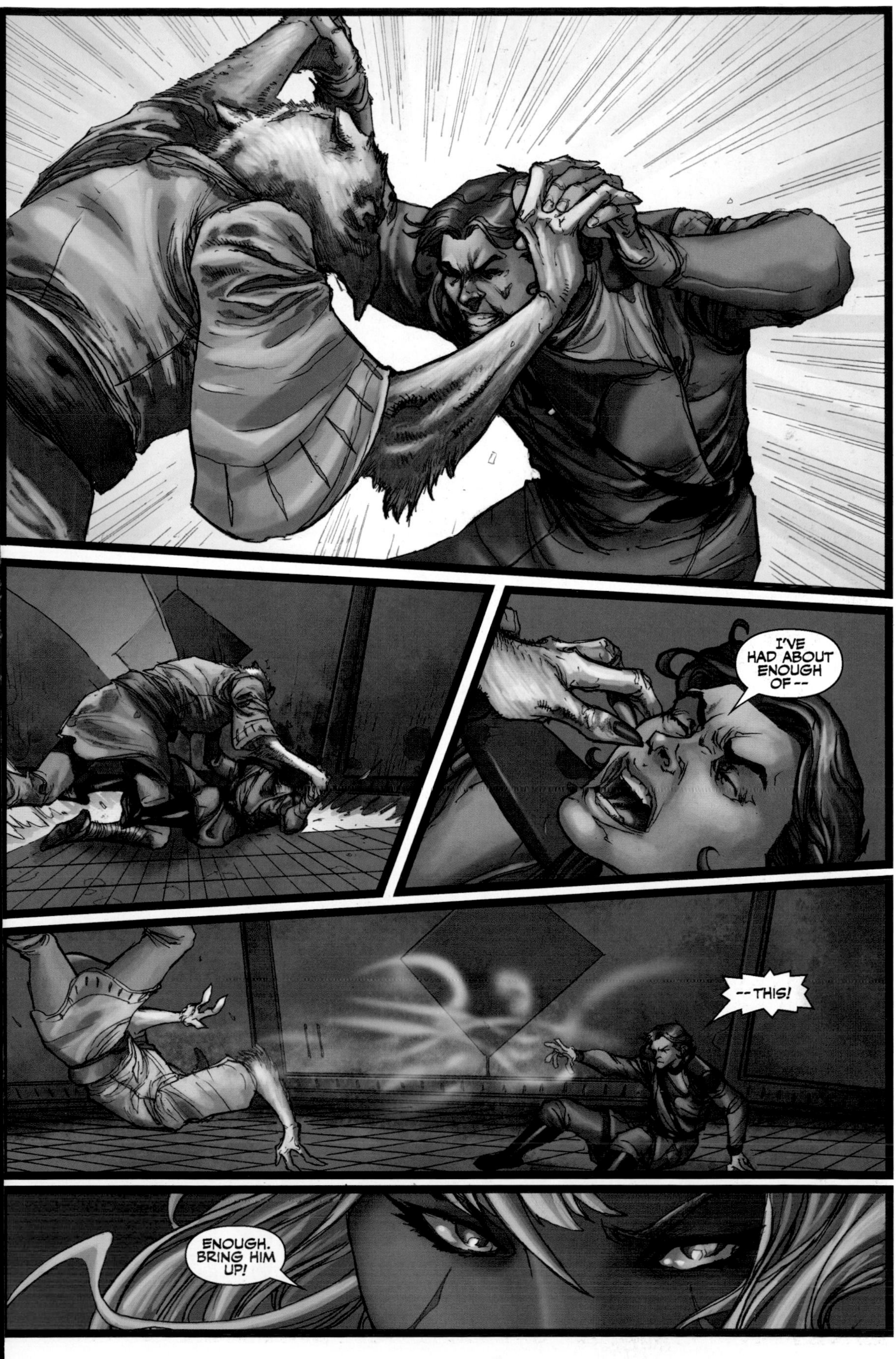
I'VE HAD ABOUT ENOUGH OF --
-- THIS!
ENOUGH. BRING HIM UP!

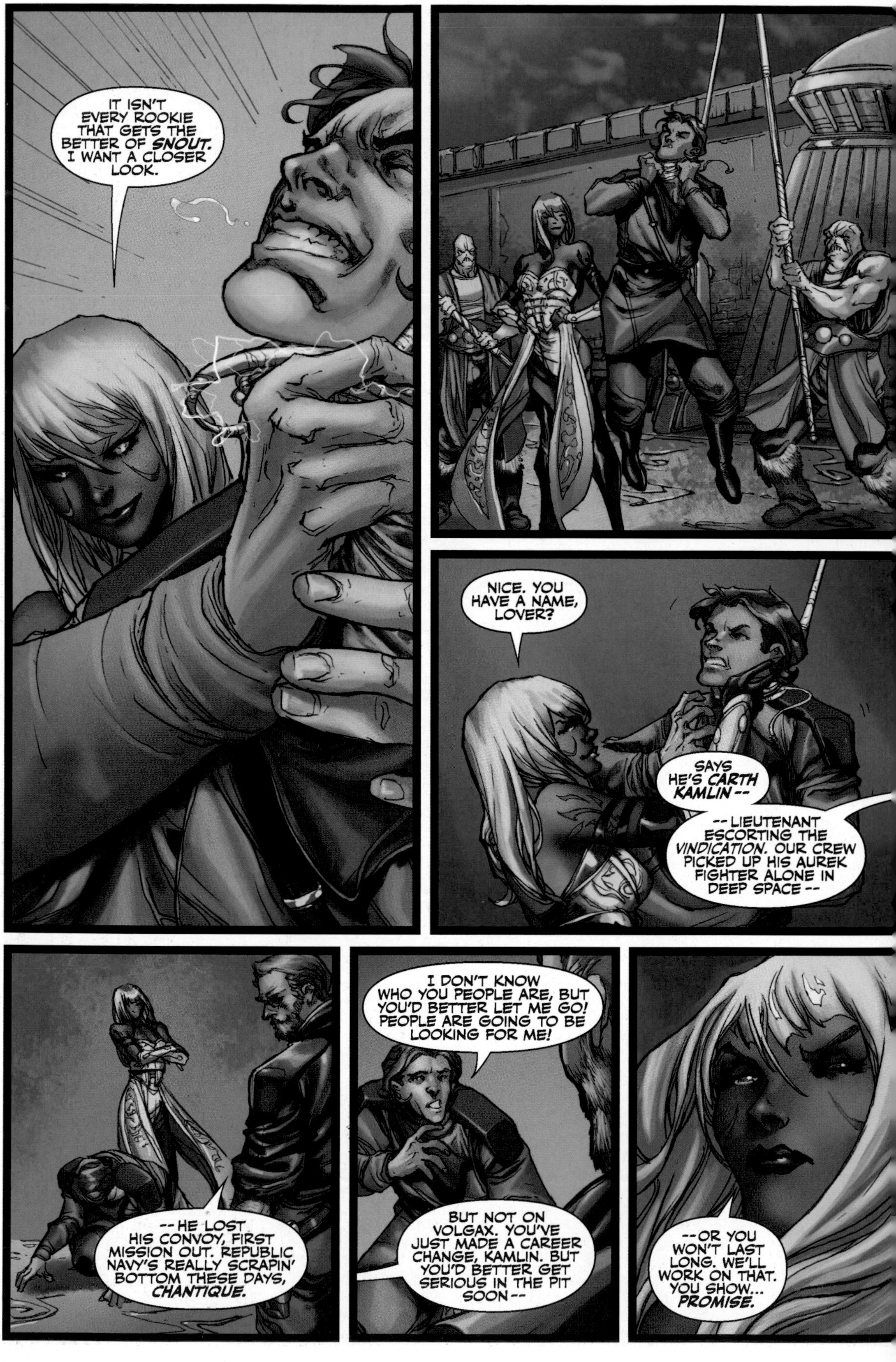
IT ISN'T EVERY ROOKIE THAT GETS THE BETTER OF SNOUT. I WANT A CLOSER LOOK.
NICE. YOU HAVE A NAME, LOVER?
SAYS HE'S CARTH KAMLIN--
--LIEUTENANT ESCORTING THE VINDICATION. OUR CREW PICKED UP HIS AUREK FIGHTER ALONE IN DEEP SPACE--
--HE LOST HIS CONVOY, FIRST MISSION OUT. REPUBLIC NAVY'S REALLY SCRAPIN' BOTTOM THESE DAYS, CHANTIQUE.
I DON'T KNOW WHO YOU PEOPLE ARE, BUT YOU'D BETTER LET ME GO! PEOPLE ARE GOING TO BE LOOKING FOR ME!
BUT NOT ON VOLGAX. YOU'VE JUST MADE A CAREER CHANGE, KAMLIN. BUT YOU'D BETTER GET SERIOUS IN THE PIT SOON--
--OR YOU WON'T LAST LONG. WE'LL WORK ON THAT. YOU SHOW... PROMISE.

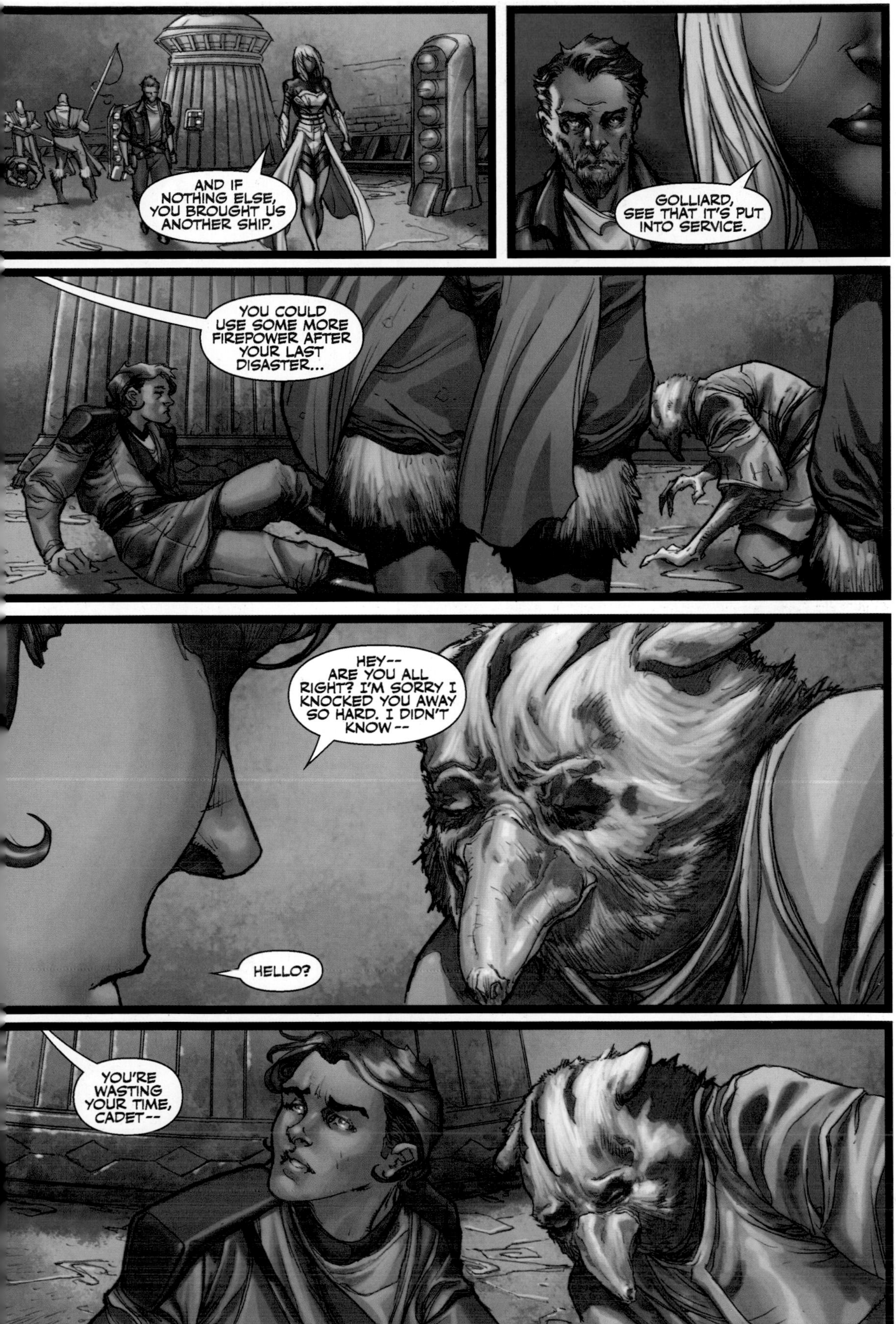
AND IF NOTHING ELSE, YOU BROUGHT US ANOTHER SHIP.
GOLLIARD, SEE THAT IT'S PUT INTO SERVICE.
YOU COULD USE SOME MORE FIREPOWER AFTER YOUR LAST DISASTER...
HEY-- ARE YOU ALL RIGHT? I'M SORRY I KNOCKED YOU AWAY SO HARD. I DIDN'T KNOW --
HELLO?
YOU'RE WASTING YOUR TIME, CADET --

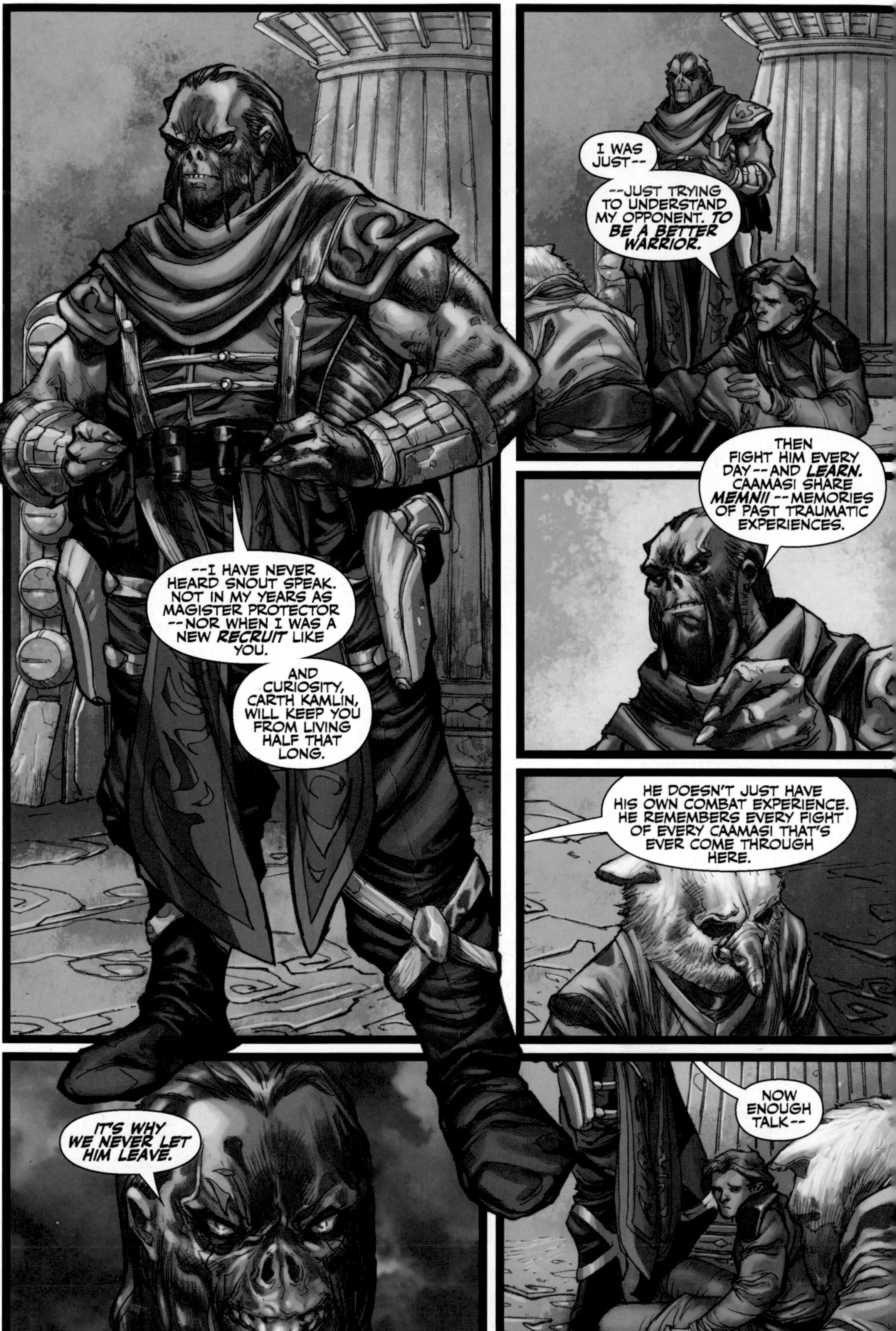
--I HAVE NEVER HEARD SNOUT SPEAK. NOT IN MY YEARS AS MAGISTER PROTECTOR --NOR WHEN I WAS A NEW RECRUIT LIKE YOU.
AND CURIOSITY, CARTH KAMLIN, WILL KEEP YOU FROM LIVING HALF THAT LONG.
I WAS JUST--
--JUST TRYING TO UNDERSTAND MY OPPONENT. TO BE A BETTER WARRIOR.
THEN FIGHT HIM EVERY DAY--AND LEARN. CAAMASI SHARE MEMNII--MEMORIES OF PAST TRAUMATIC EXPERIENCES.
HE DOESN'T JUST HAVE HIS OWN COMBAT EXPERIENCE. HE REMEMBERS EVERY FIGHT OF EVERY CAAMASI THAT'S EVER COME THROUGH HERE.
IT'S WHY WE NEVER LET HIM LEAVE.
NOW ENOUGH TALK--

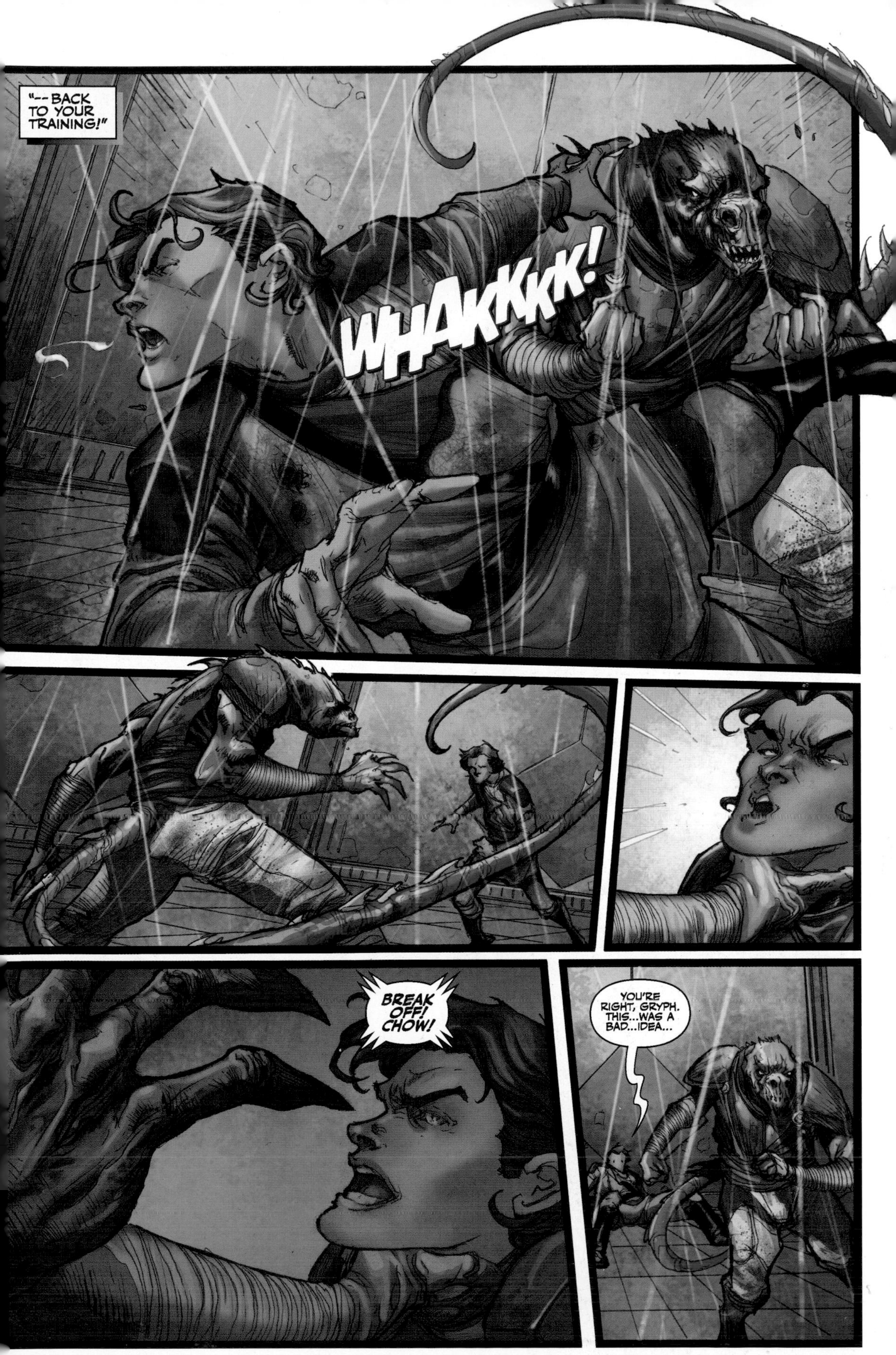
"--BACK TO YOUR TRAINING!"
WHAKKKK!
BREAK OFF! CHOW!
YOU'RE RIGHT, GRYPH. THIS...WAS A BAD...IDEA...

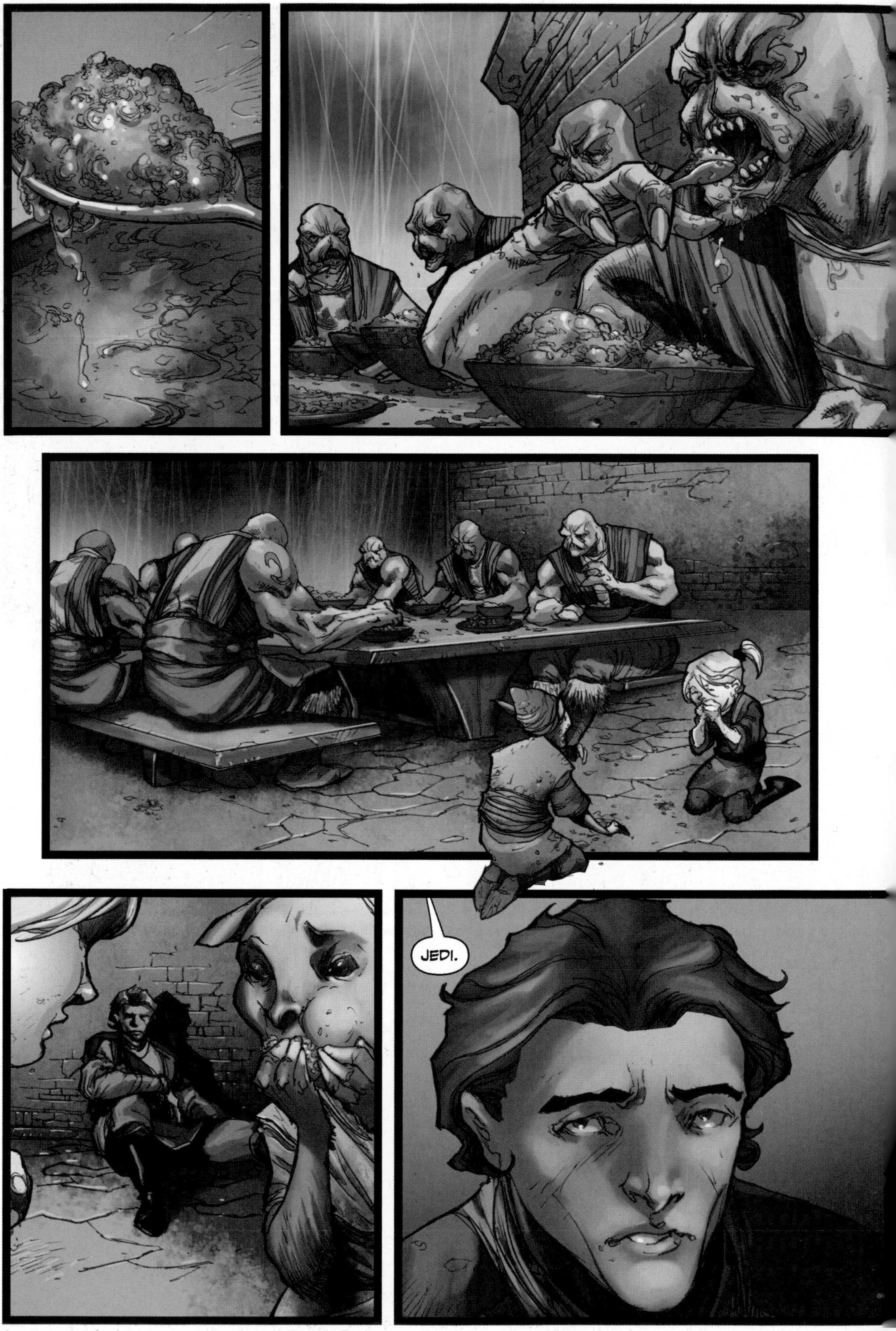
JEDI.

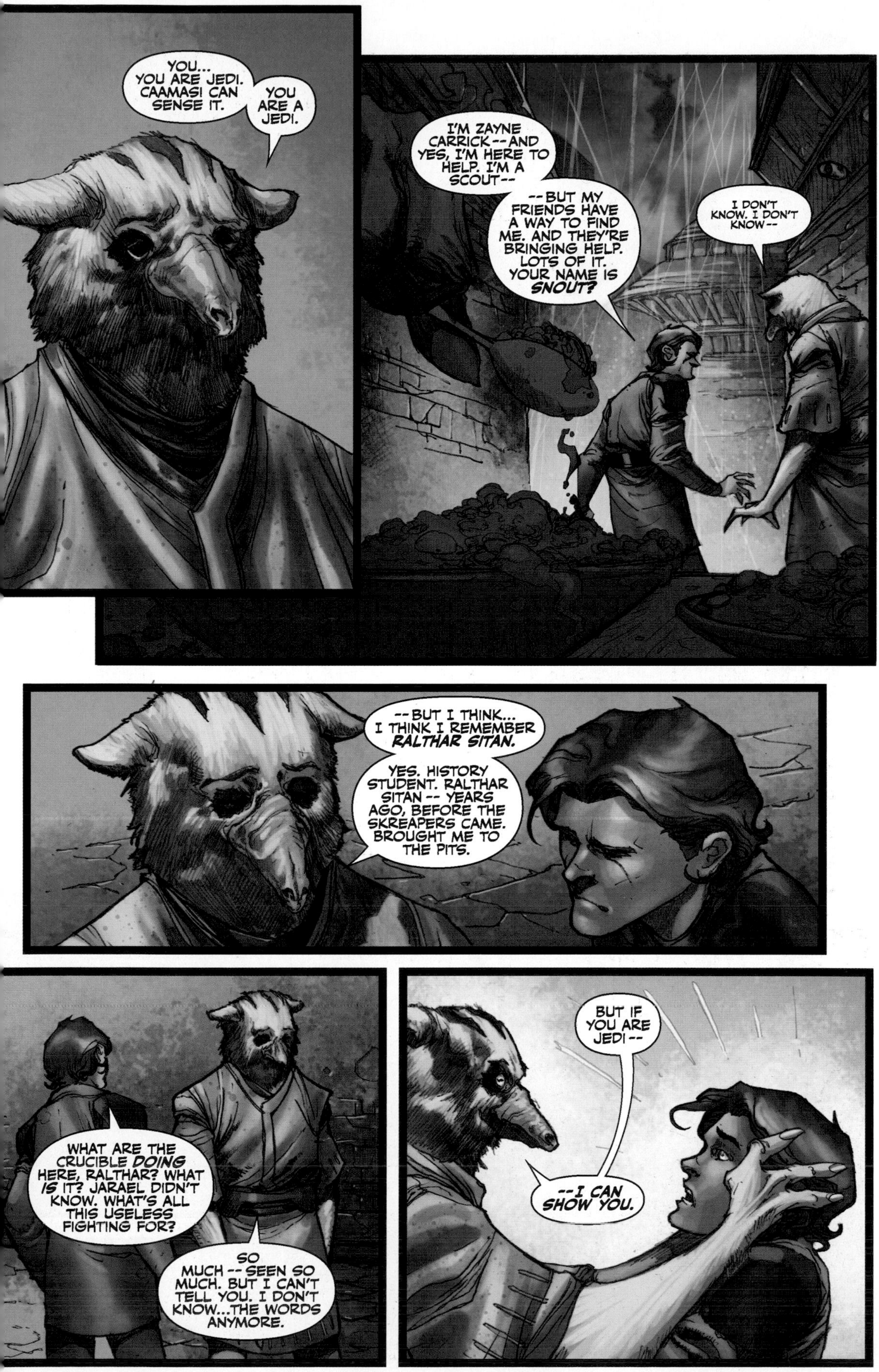
YOU... YOU ARE JEDI. CAAMASI CAN SENSE IT.
YOU ARE A JEDI.
I'M ZAYNE CARRICK--AND YES, I'M HERE TO HELP. I'M A SCOUT--
--BUT MY FRIENDS HAVE A WAY TO FIND ME. AND THEY'RE BRINGING HELP. LOTS OF IT. YOUR NAME IS *SNOUT?*
I DON'T KNOW. I DON'T KNOW--
--BUT I THINK... I THINK I REMEMBER *RALTHAR SITAN.*
YES. HISTORY STUDENT. RALTHAR SITAN -- YEARS AGO, BEFORE THE SKREAPERS CAME. BROUGHT ME TO THE PITS.
WHAT ARE THE CRUCIBLE *DOING* HERE, RALTHAR? WHAT *IS* IT? JARAEL DIDN'T KNOW. WHAT'S ALL THIS USELESS FIGHTING FOR?
SO MUCH -- SEEN SO MUCH. BUT I CAN'T TELL YOU. I DON'T KNOW...THE WORDS ANYMORE.
BUT IF YOU ARE JEDI --
--I CAN SHOW YOU.

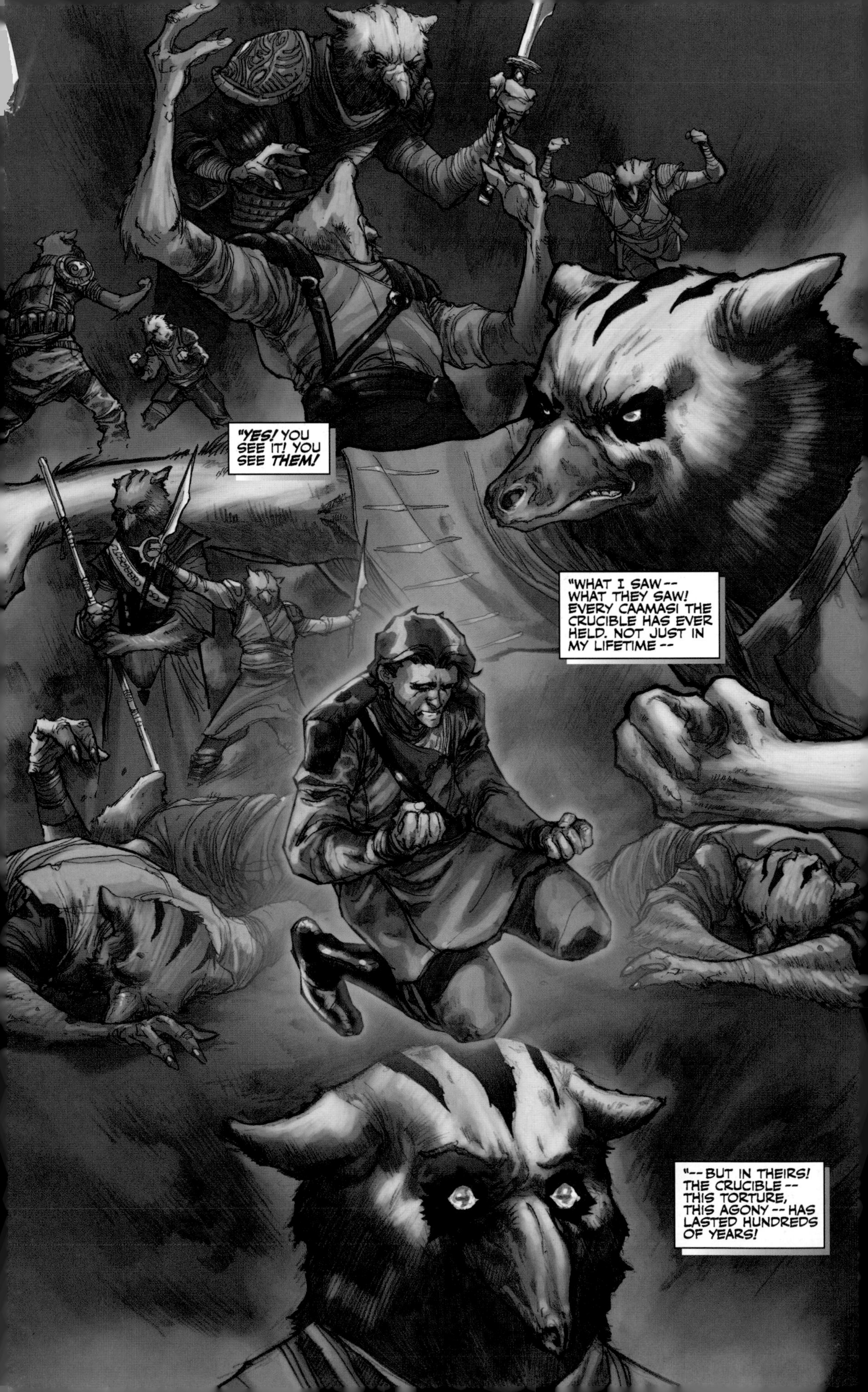
"YES! YOU SEE IT! YOU SEE THEM!
"WHAT I SAW -- WHAT THEY SAW! EVERY CAAMASI THE CRUCIBLE HAS EVER HELD. NOT JUST IN MY LIFETIME --
"-- BUT IN THEIRS! THE CRUCIBLE -- THIS TORTURE, THIS AGONY -- HAS LASTED HUNDREDS OF YEARS!

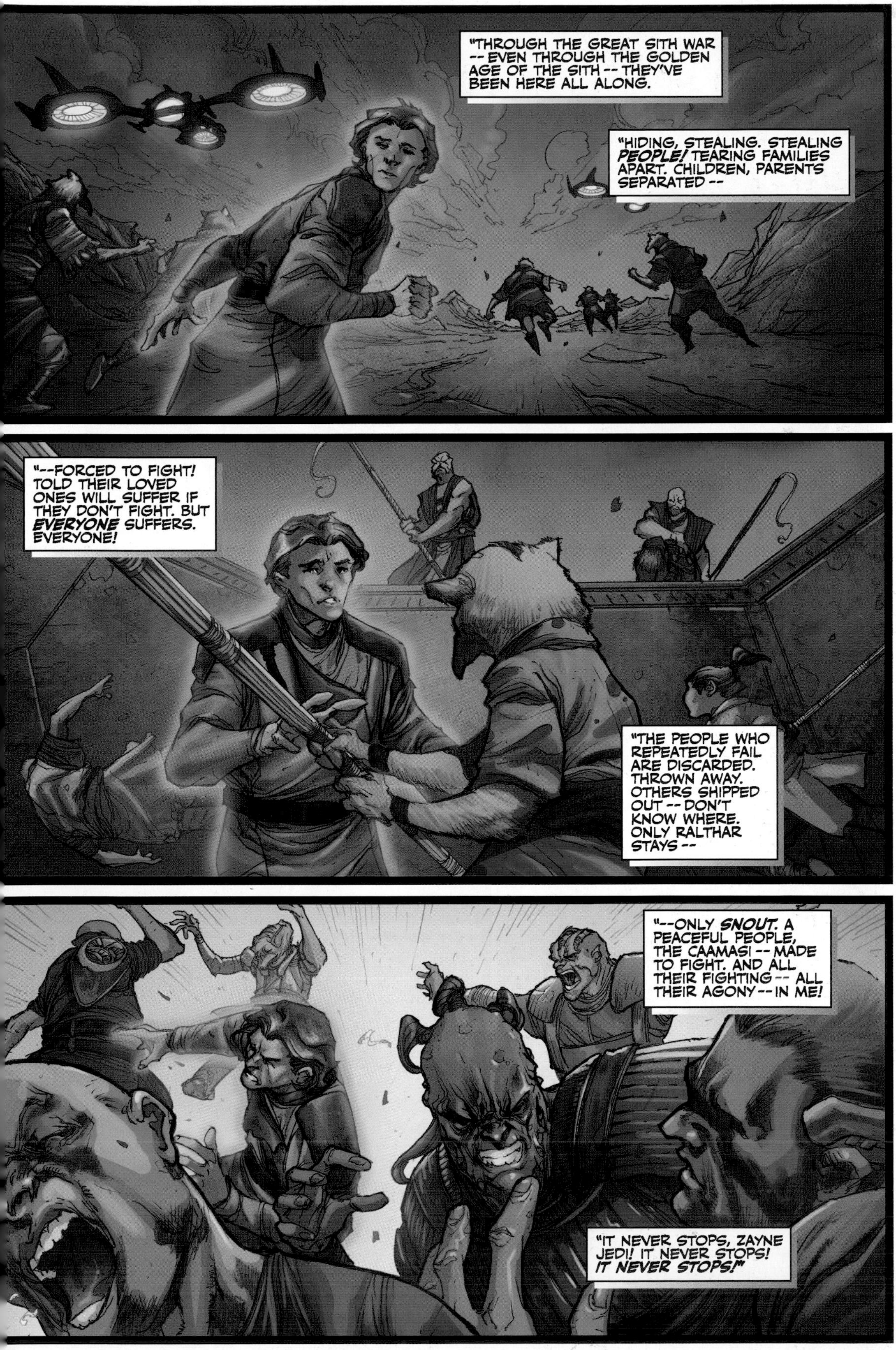
"THROUGH THE GREAT SITH WAR -- EVEN THROUGH THE GOLDEN AGE OF THE SITH -- THEY'VE BEEN HERE ALL ALONG.
"HIDING, STEALING. STEALING *PEOPLE!* TEARING FAMILIES APART. CHILDREN, PARENTS SEPARATED --
"--FORCED TO FIGHT! TOLD THEIR LOVED ONES WILL SUFFER IF THEY DON'T FIGHT. BUT *EVERYONE* SUFFERS. EVERYONE!
"THE PEOPLE WHO REPEATEDLY FAIL ARE DISCARDED. THROWN AWAY. OTHERS SHIPPED OUT -- DON'T KNOW WHERE. ONLY RALTHAR STAYS --
"--ONLY *SNOUT.* A PEACEFUL PEOPLE, THE CAAMASI -- MADE TO FIGHT. AND ALL THEIR FIGHTING -- ALL THEIR AGONY -- IN ME!
"IT NEVER STOPS, ZAYNE JEDI! IT NEVER STOPS! *IT NEVER STOPS!*"

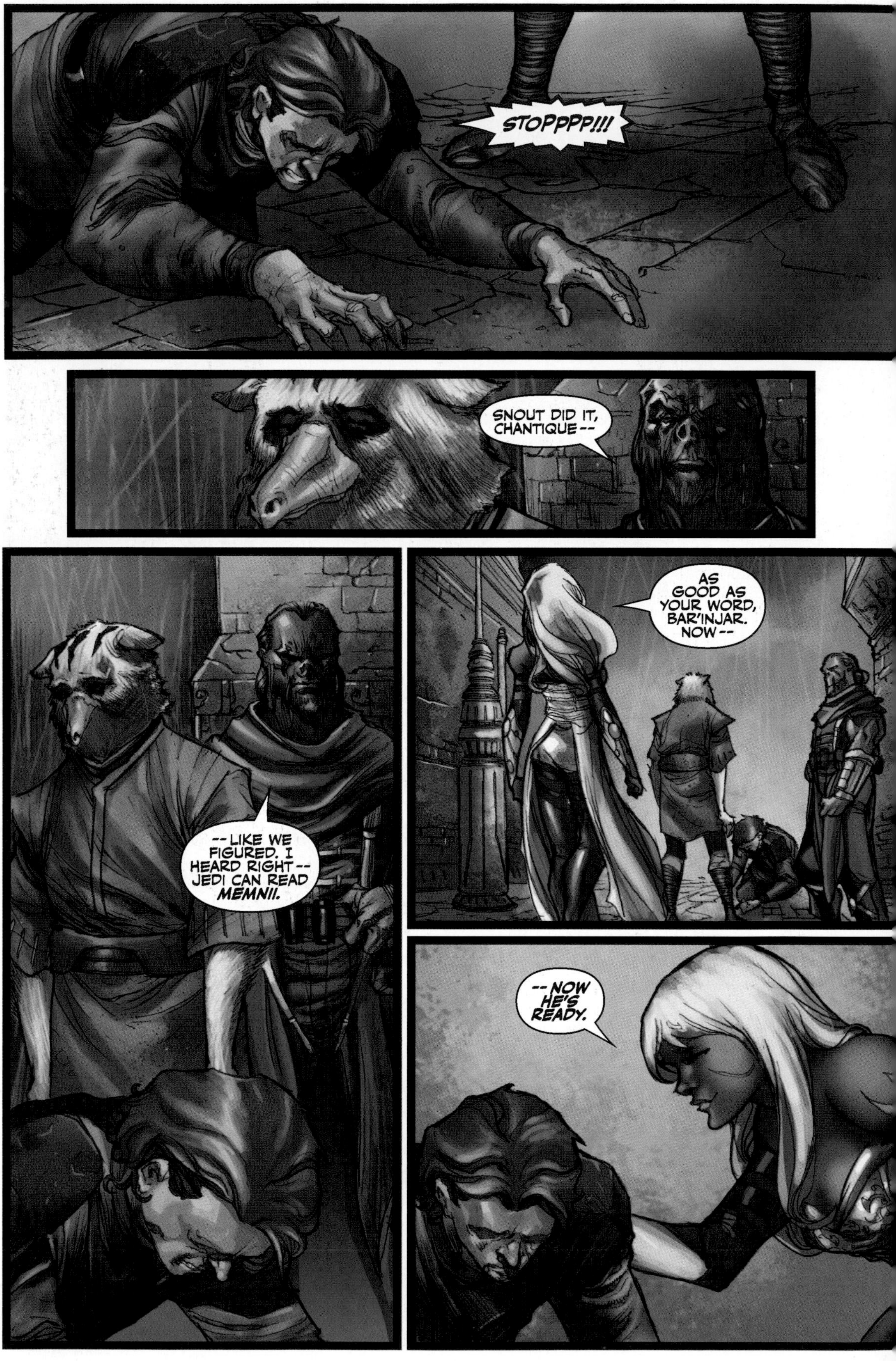
STOPPPP!!!
SNOUT DID IT, CHANTIQUE--
--LIKE WE FIGURED. I HEARD RIGHT--JEDI CAN READ MEMNII.
AS GOOD AS YOUR WORD, BAR'INJAR. NOW--
--NOW HE'S READY.

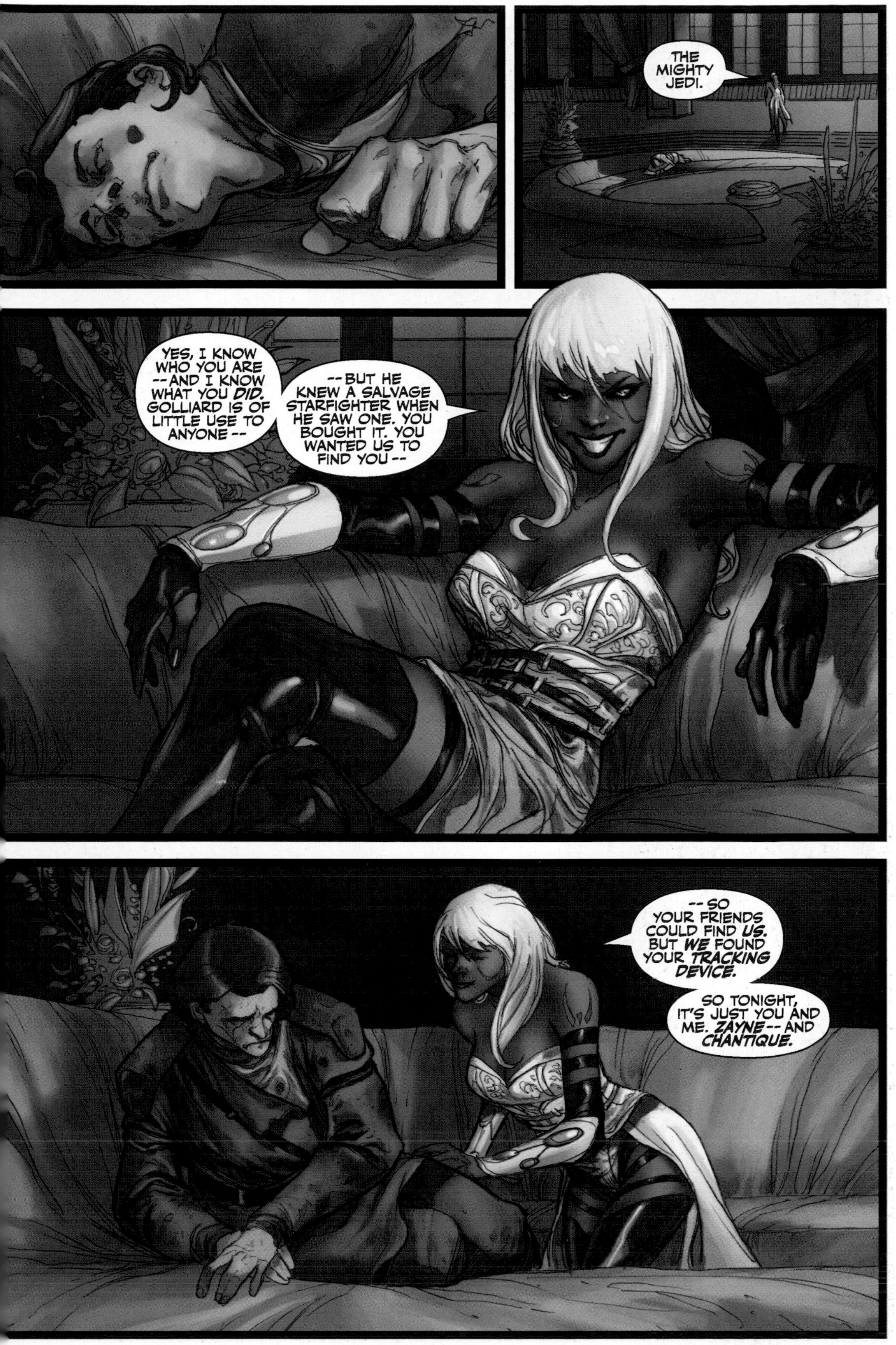
THE MIGHTY JEDI.
YES, I KNOW WHO YOU ARE --AND I KNOW WHAT YOU *DID.* GOLLIARD IS OF LITTLE USE TO ANYONE --
--BUT HE KNEW A SALVAGE STARFIGHTER WHEN HE SAW ONE. YOU BOUGHT IT. YOU WANTED US TO FIND YOU --
--SO YOUR FRIENDS COULD FIND *US.* BUT *WE* FOUND YOUR *TRACKING DEVICE.*
SO TONIGHT, IT'S JUST YOU AND ME. *ZAYNE*-- AND *CHANTIQUE.*

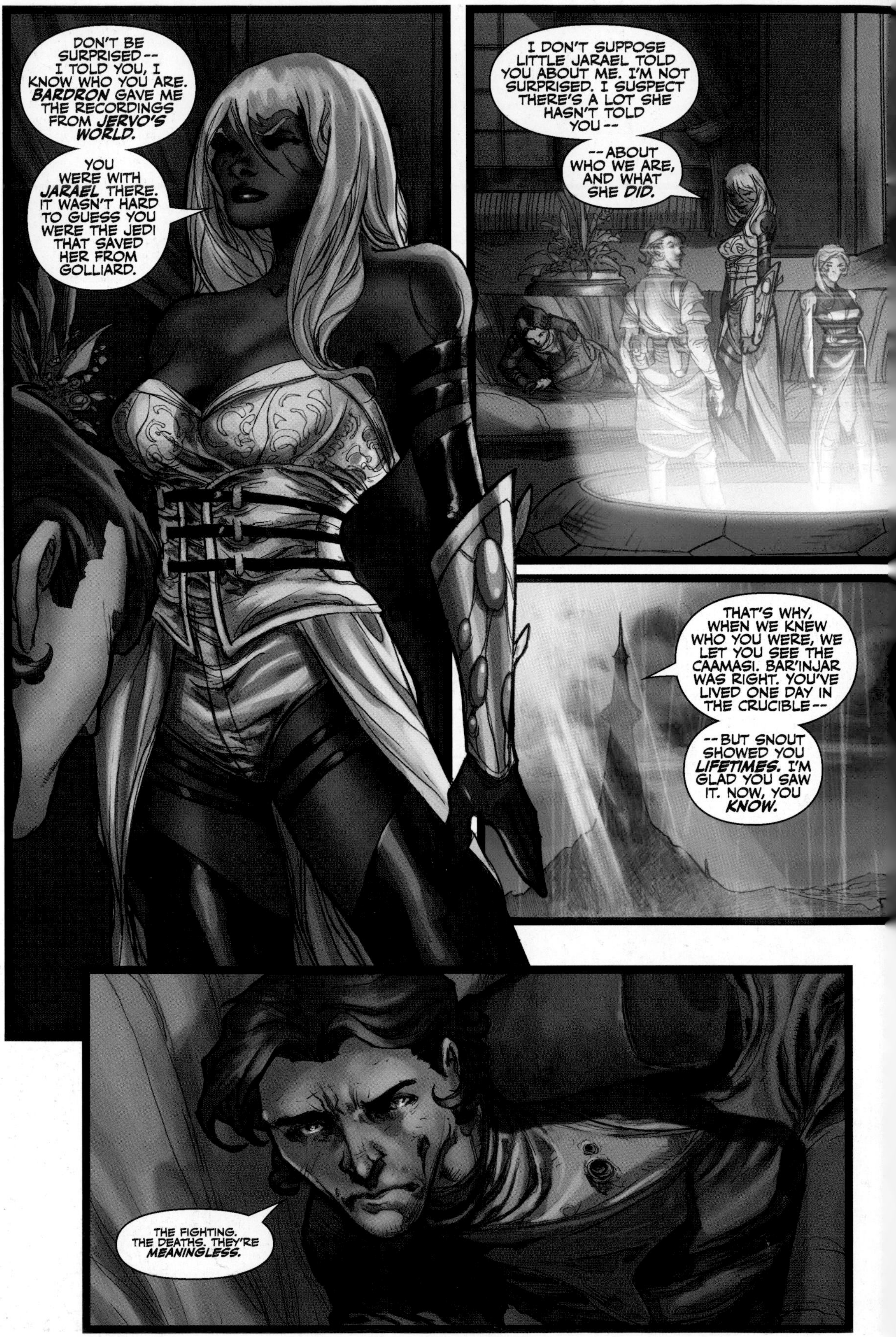
DON'T BE SURPRISED-- I TOLD YOU, I KNOW WHO YOU ARE. BARDRON GAVE ME THE RECORDINGS FROM JERVO'S WORLD.
YOU WERE WITH JARAEL THERE. IT WASN'T HARD TO GUESS YOU WERE THE JEDI THAT SAVED HER FROM GOLLIARD.
I DON'T SUPPOSE LITTLE JARAEL TOLD YOU ABOUT ME. I'M NOT SURPRISED. I SUSPECT THERE'S A LOT SHE HASN'T TOLD YOU --
--ABOUT WHO WE ARE, AND WHAT SHE DID.
THAT'S WHY, WHEN WE KNEW WHO YOU WERE, WE LET YOU SEE THE CAAMASI. BAR'INJAR WAS RIGHT. YOU'VE LIVED ONE DAY IN THE CRUCIBLE--
--BUT SNOUT SHOWED YOU LIFETIMES. I'M GLAD YOU SAW IT. NOW, YOU KNOW.
THE FIGHTING. THE DEATHS. THEY'RE MEANINGLESS.

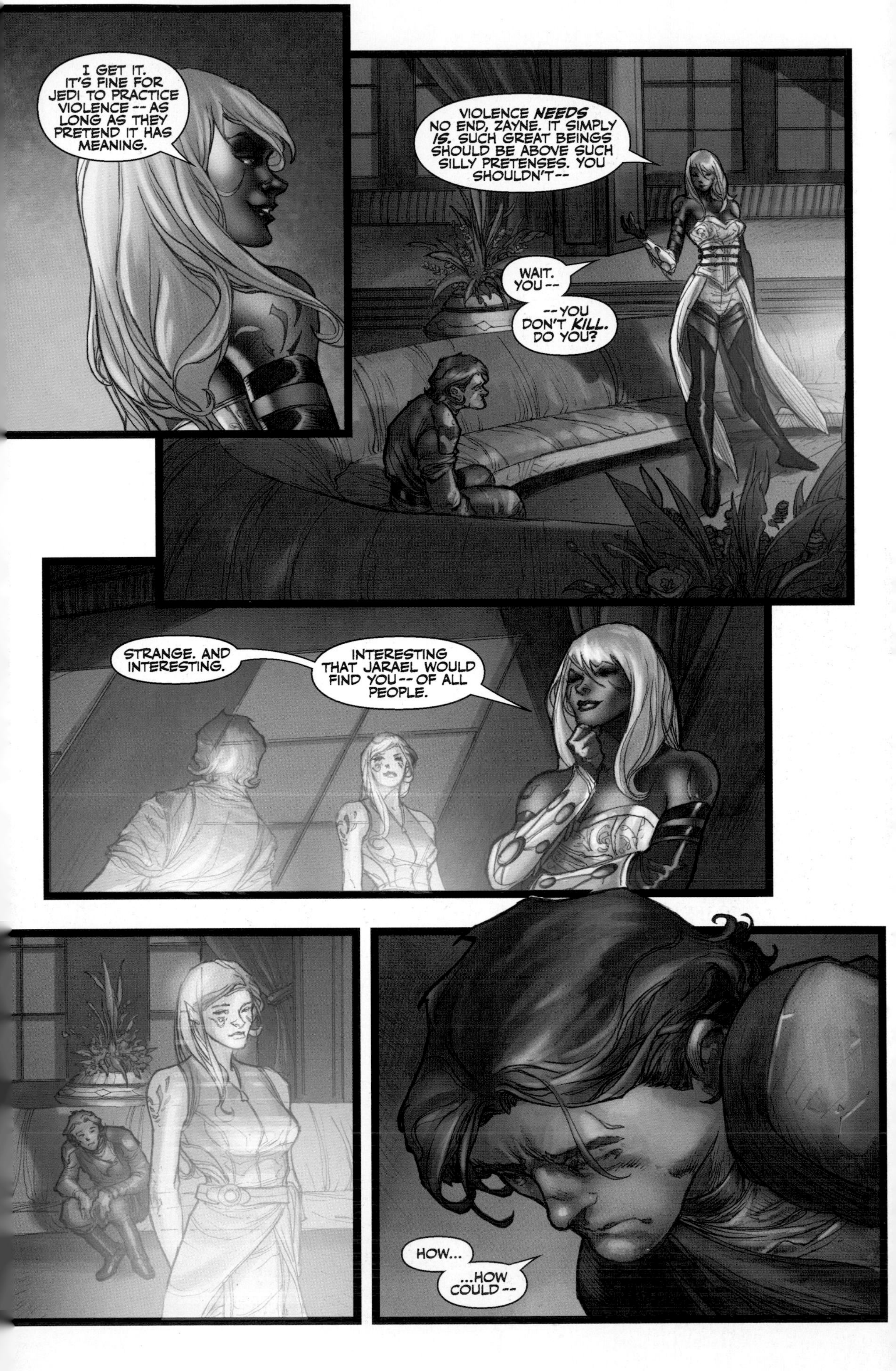

I GET IT. IT'S FINE FOR JEDI TO PRACTICE VIOLENCE -- AS LONG AS THEY PRETEND IT HAS MEANING.
VIOLENCE NEEDS NO END, ZAYNE. IT SIMPLY IS. SUCH GREAT BEINGS SHOULD BE ABOVE SUCH SILLY PRETENSES. YOU SHOULDN'T --
WAIT. YOU --
-- YOU DON'T KILL. DO YOU?
STRANGE. AND INTERESTING.
INTERESTING THAT JARAEL WOULD FIND YOU -- OF ALL PEOPLE.
HOW...
...HOW COULD --

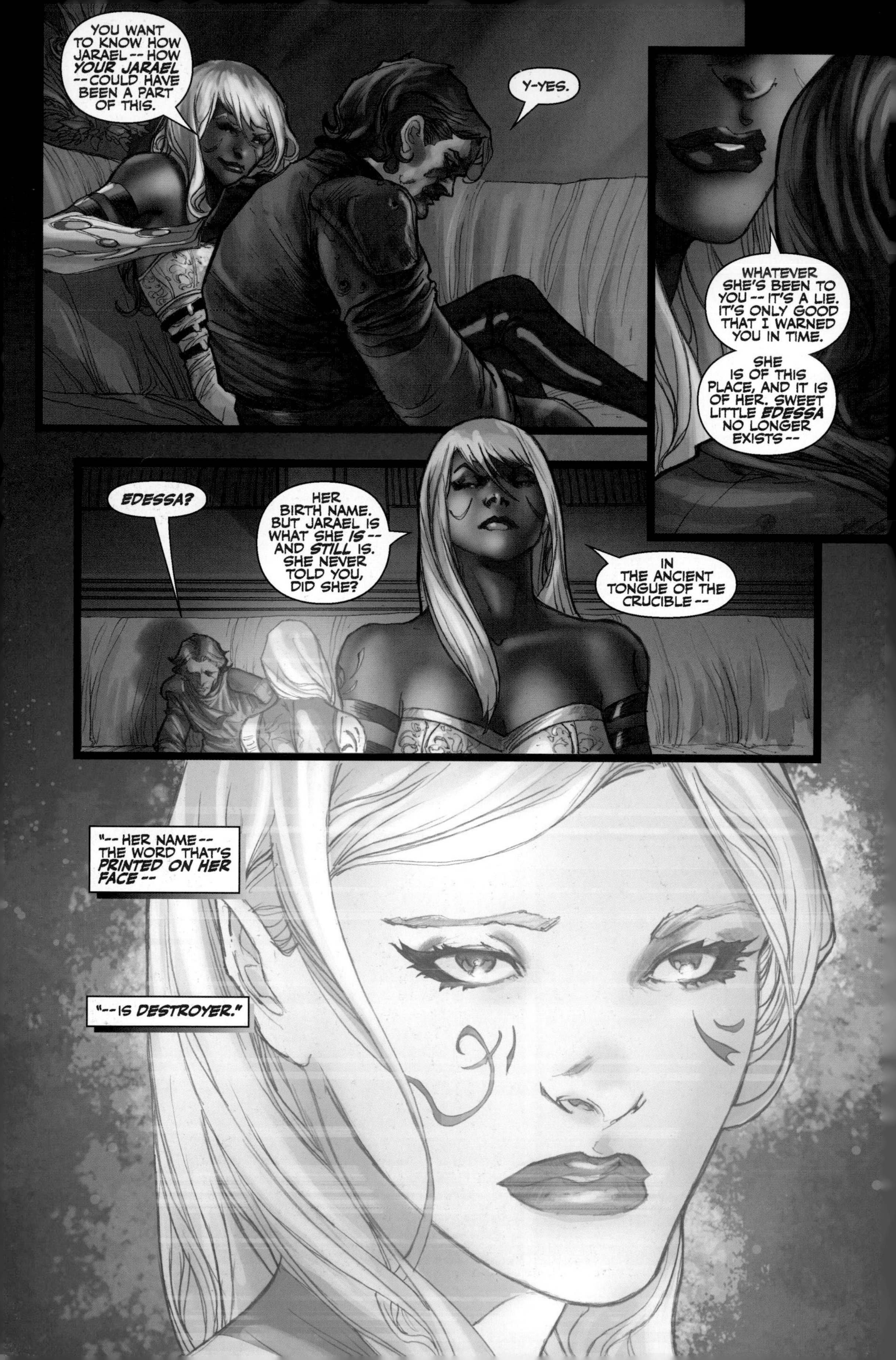
YOU WANT TO KNOW HOW JARAEL -- HOW *YOUR JARAEL* -- COULD HAVE BEEN A PART OF THIS.
Y-YES.
WHATEVER SHE'S BEEN TO YOU -- IT'S A LIE. IT'S ONLY GOOD THAT I WARNED YOU IN TIME.
SHE IS OF THIS PLACE, AND IT IS OF HER. SWEET LITTLE *EDESSA* NO LONGER EXISTS --
EDESSA?
HER BIRTH NAME. BUT JARAEL IS WHAT SHE *IS* -- AND *STILL* IS. SHE NEVER TOLD YOU, DID SHE?
IN THE ANCIENT TONGUE OF THE CRUCIBLE --
"-- HER NAME -- THE WORD THAT'S *PRINTED ON HER FACE* --
"-- IS *DESTROYER.*"

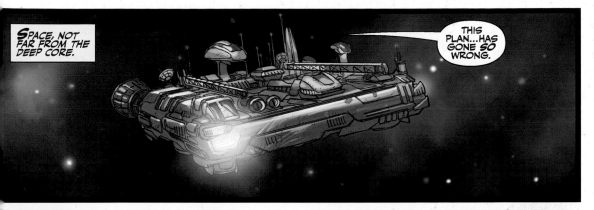

SPACE, NOT FAR FROM THE DEEP CORE.

THIS PLAN...HAS GONE *SO* WRONG.

THE TRACKING DEVICE WE HID ON ZAYNE'S FIGHTER WAS WORKING FINE WHEN WE LEFT HIM! HOW COULD IT GIVE OUT SO FAST?

THE *CRUCIBLE* LOVES TO PICK OFF STRAY SHIPS FROM CONVOYS. HIS SHIP *SHOULD* HAVE LED US TO THEIR LATEST HIDEOUT--

--BUT NOW, THEY COULD HAVE TAKEN HIM ANYWHERE!

I TRIED TO WARN YOU BOTH, *JARAEL.* DON'T BAIT TRAPS WITH ANYONE YOU HOPE TO *SEE* AGAIN!

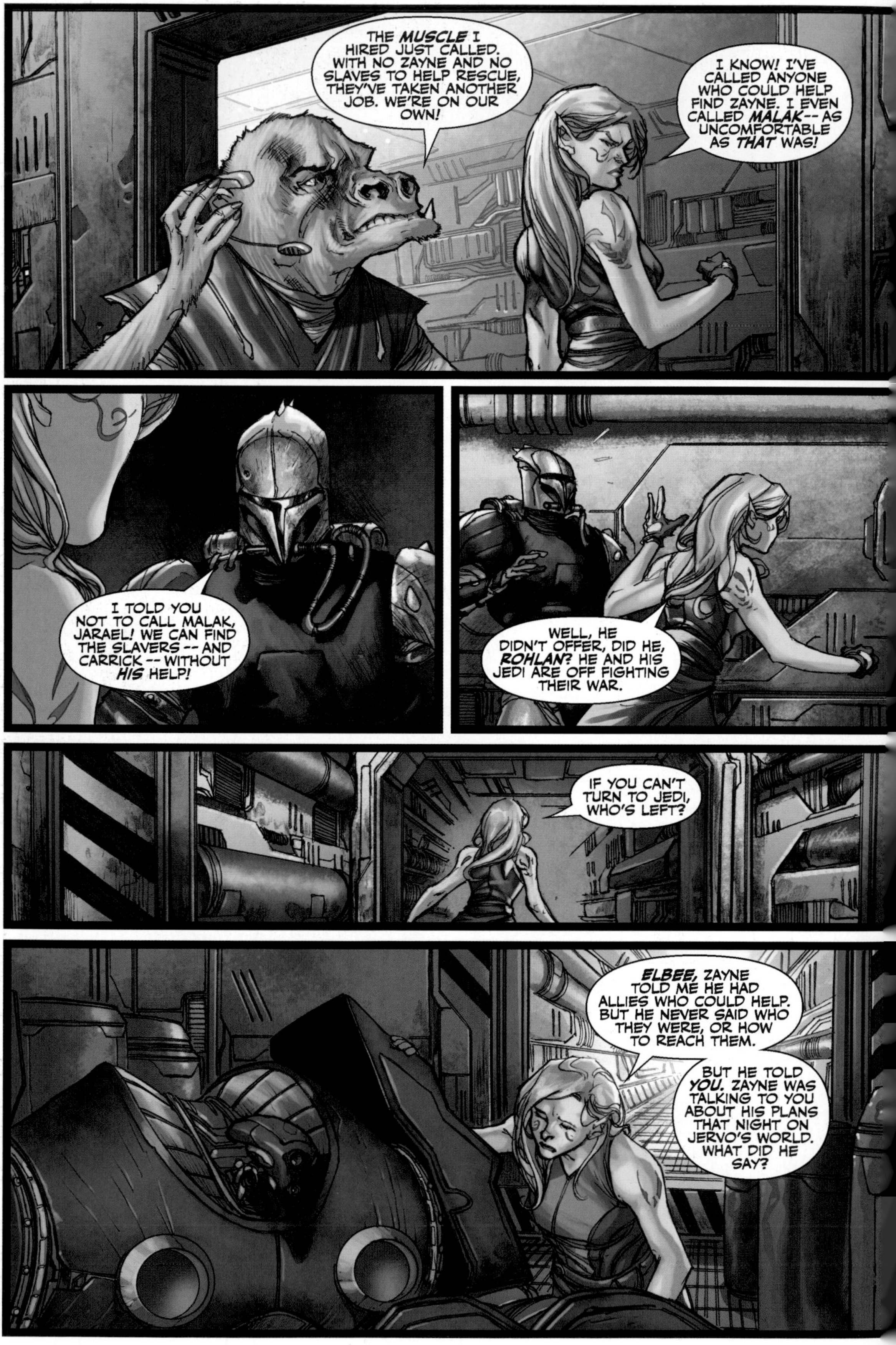
THE MUSCLE I HIRED JUST CALLED. WITH NO ZAYNE AND NO SLAVES TO HELP RESCUE, THEY'VE TAKEN ANOTHER JOB. WE'RE ON OUR OWN!
I KNOW! I'VE CALLED ANYONE WHO COULD HELP FIND ZAYNE. I EVEN CALLED MALAK-- AS UNCOMFORTABLE AS THAT WAS!
I TOLD YOU NOT TO CALL MALAK, JARAEL! WE CAN FIND THE SLAVERS -- AND CARRICK -- WITHOUT HIS HELP!
WELL, HE DIDN'T OFFER, DID HE, ROHLAN? HE AND HIS JEDI ARE OFF FIGHTING THEIR WAR.
IF YOU CAN'T TURN TO JEDI, WHO'S LEFT?
ELBEE, ZAYNE TOLD ME HE HAD ALLIES WHO COULD HELP. BUT HE NEVER SAID WHO THEY WERE, OR HOW TO REACH THEM.
BUT HE TOLD YOU. ZAYNE WAS TALKING TO YOU ABOUT HIS PLANS THAT NIGHT ON JERVO'S WORLD. WHAT DID HE SAY?

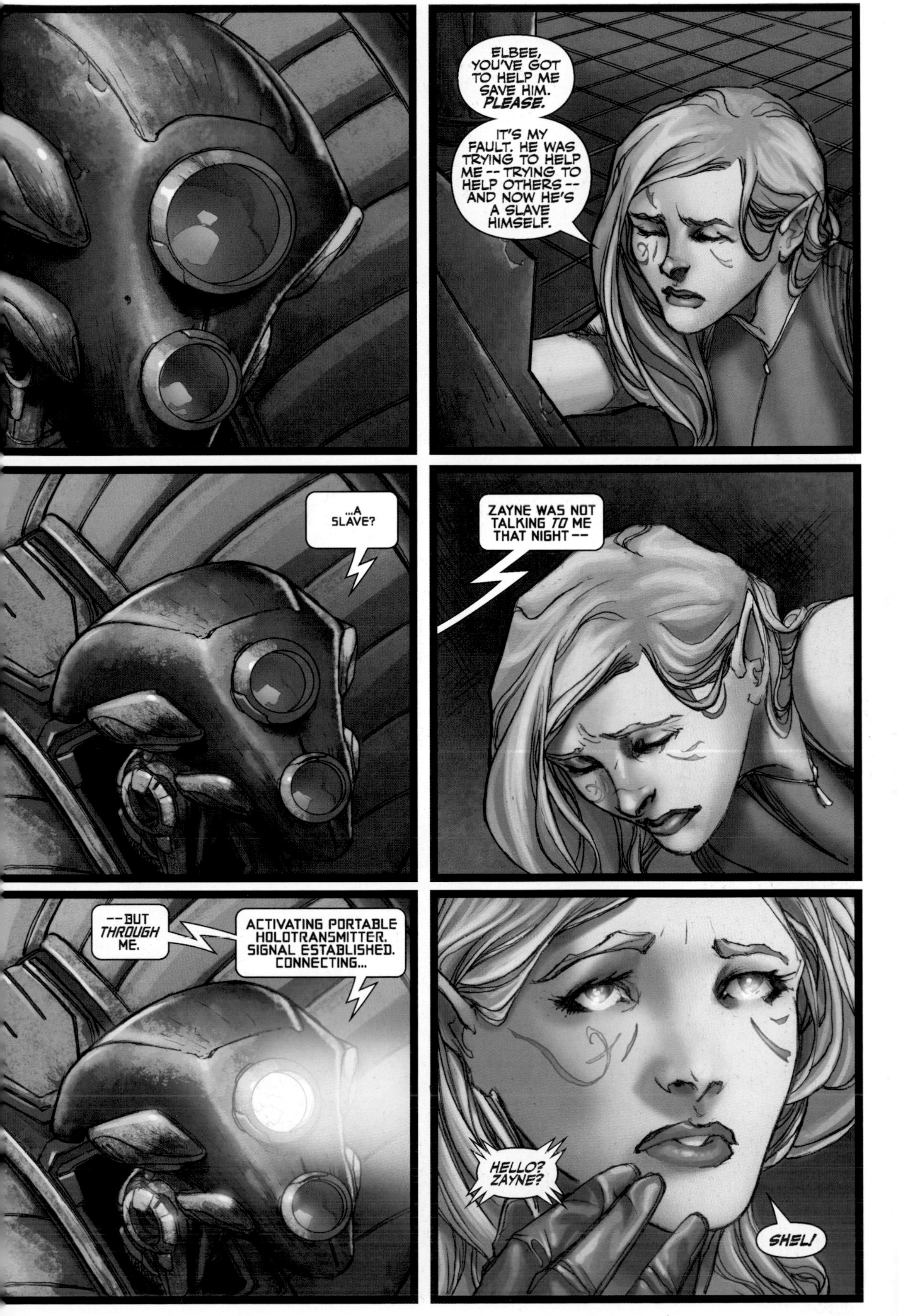
ELBEE, YOU'VE GOT TO HELP ME SAVE HIM. *PLEASE.*
IT'S MY FAULT. HE WAS TRYING TO HELP ME -- TRYING TO HELP OTHERS -- AND NOW HE'S A SLAVE HIMSELF.
...A SLAVE?
ZAYNE WAS NOT TALKING *TO* ME THAT NIGHT --
-- BUT *THROUGH* ME.
ACTIVATING PORTABLE HOLOTRANSMITTER. SIGNAL ESTABLISHED. CONNECTING...
HELLO? ZAYNE?
SHEL!

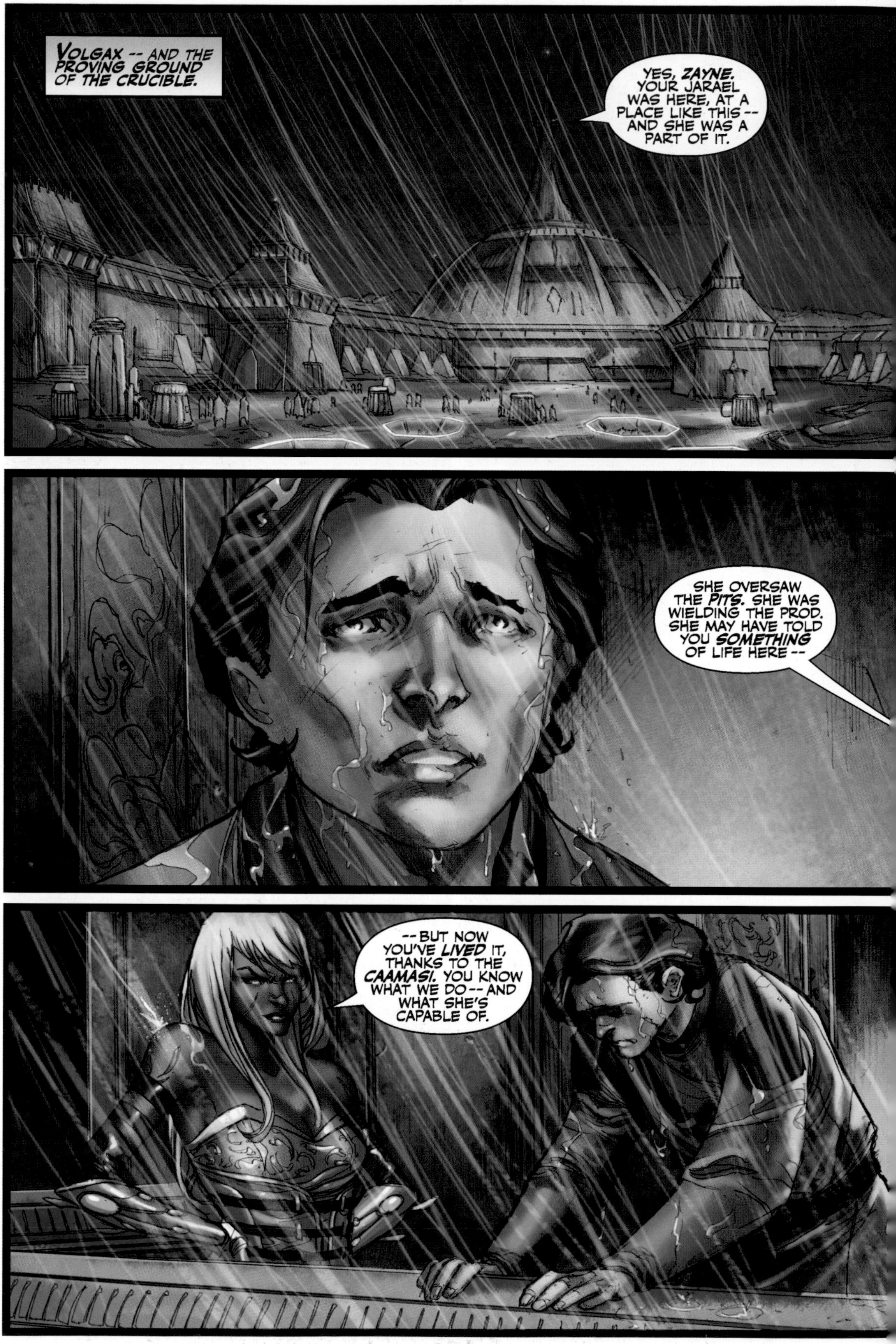
VOLGAX -- AND THE PROVING GROUND OF THE CRUCIBLE.
YES, ZAYNE. YOUR JARAEL WAS HERE, AT A PLACE LIKE THIS -- AND SHE WAS A PART OF IT.
SHE OVERSAW THE PITS. SHE WAS WIELDING THE PROD. SHE MAY HAVE TOLD YOU SOMETHING OF LIFE HERE --
-- BUT NOW YOU'VE LIVED IT, THANKS TO THE CAAMASI. YOU KNOW WHAT WE DO -- AND WHAT SHE'S CAPABLE OF.

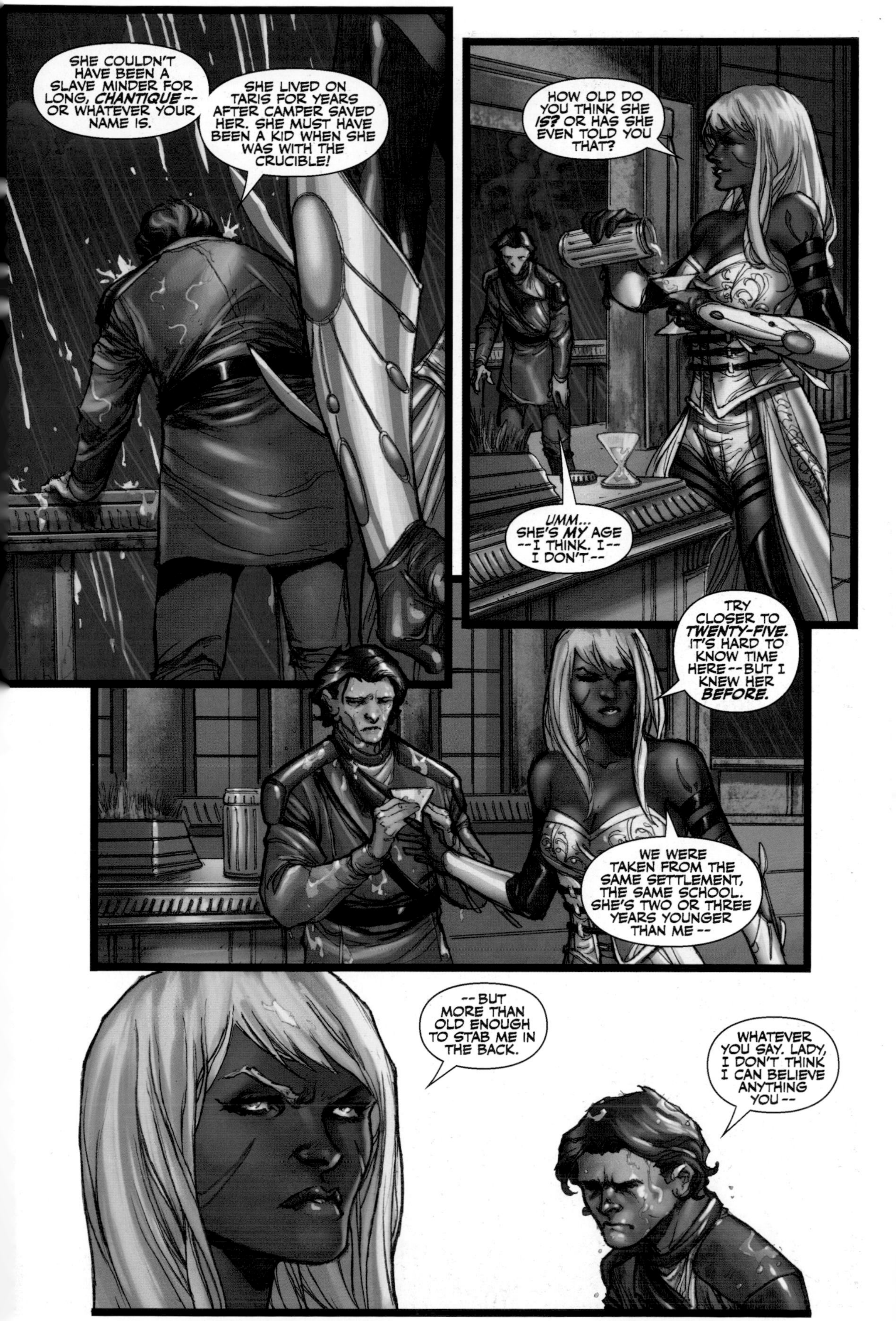
SHE COULDN'T HAVE BEEN A SLAVE MINDER FOR LONG, *CHANTIQUE* -- OR WHATEVER YOUR NAME IS.
SHE LIVED ON TARIS FOR YEARS AFTER CAMPER SAVED HER. SHE MUST HAVE BEEN A KID WHEN SHE WAS WITH THE CRUCIBLE!
HOW OLD DO YOU THINK SHE *IS?* OR HAS SHE EVEN TOLD YOU THAT?
UMM... SHE'S *MY* AGE --I THINK. I-- I DON'T--
TRY CLOSER TO ***TWENTY-FIVE.*** IT'S HARD TO KNOW TIME HERE--BUT I KNEW HER ***BEFORE.***
WE WERE TAKEN FROM THE SAME SETTLEMENT, THE SAME SCHOOL. SHE'S TWO OR THREE YEARS YOUNGER THAN ME --
--BUT MORE THAN OLD ENOUGH TO STAB ME IN THE BACK.
WHATEVER YOU SAY. LADY, I DON'T THINK I CAN BELIEVE ANYTHING YOU --

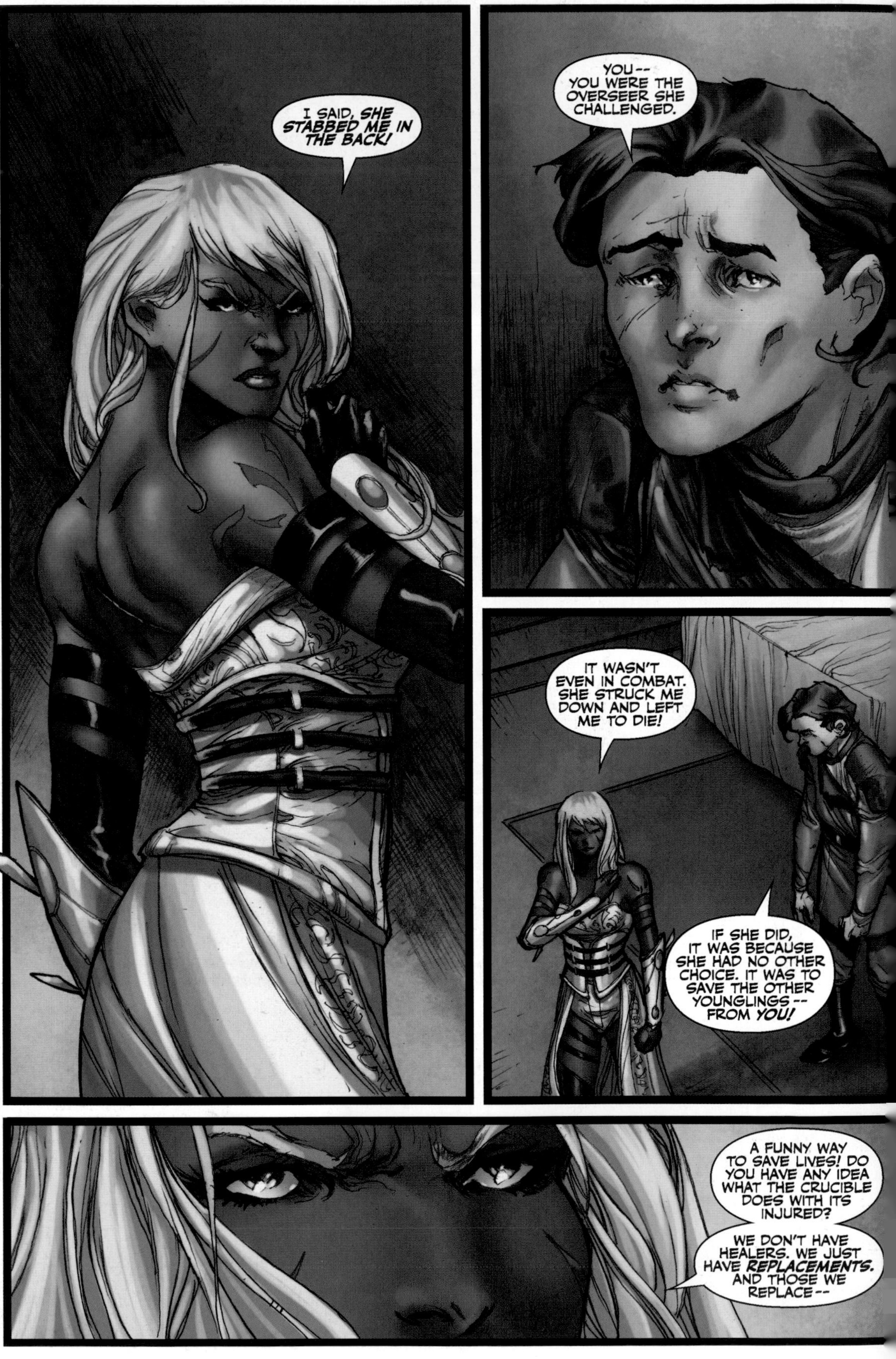
I SAID, SHE STABBED ME IN THE BACK!
YOU-- YOU WERE THE OVERSEER SHE CHALLENGED.
IT WASN'T EVEN IN COMBAT. SHE STRUCK ME DOWN AND LEFT ME TO DIE!
IF SHE DID, IT WAS BECAUSE SHE HAD NO OTHER CHOICE. IT WAS TO SAVE THE OTHER YOUNGLINGS-- FROM YOU!
A FUNNY WAY TO SAVE LIVES! DO YOU HAVE ANY IDEA WHAT THE CRUCIBLE DOES WITH ITS INJURED?
WE DON'T HAVE HEALERS. WE JUST HAVE REPLACEMENTS. AND THOSE WE REPLACE--

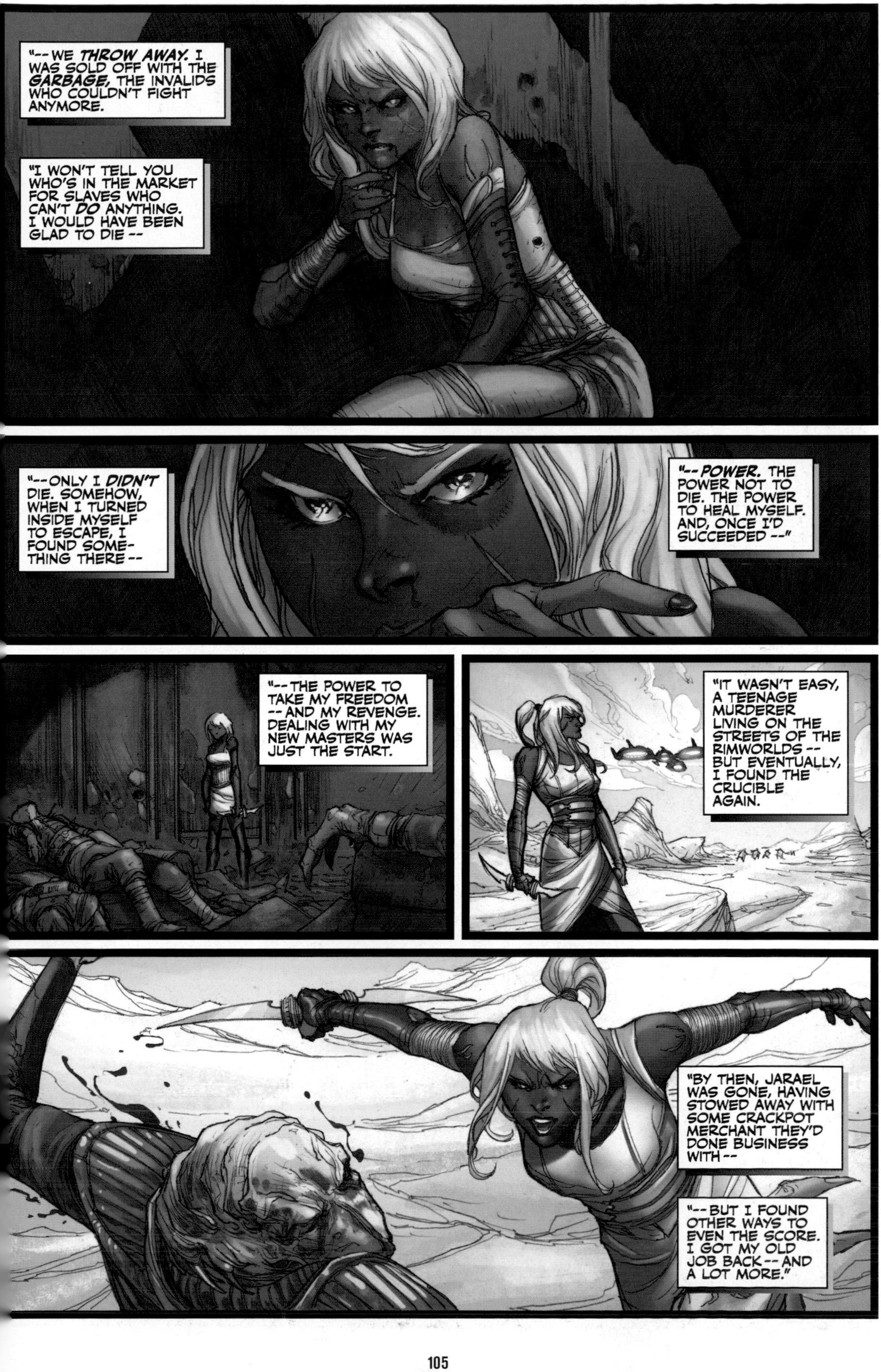
"--WE THROW AWAY. I WAS SOLD OFF WITH THE GARBAGE, THE INVALIDS WHO COULDN'T FIGHT ANYMORE.
"I WON'T TELL YOU WHO'S IN THE MARKET FOR SLAVES WHO CAN'T DO ANYTHING. I WOULD HAVE BEEN GLAD TO DIE --
"--ONLY I DIDN'T DIE. SOMEHOW, WHEN I TURNED INSIDE MYSELF TO ESCAPE, I FOUND SOMETHING THERE --
"--POWER. THE POWER NOT TO DIE. THE POWER TO HEAL MYSELF. AND, ONCE I'D SUCCEEDED --"
"--THE POWER TO TAKE MY FREEDOM --AND MY REVENGE. DEALING WITH MY NEW MASTERS WAS JUST THE START.
"IT WASN'T EASY, A TEENAGE MURDERER LIVING ON THE STREETS OF THE RIMWORLDS --BUT EVENTUALLY, I FOUND THE CRUCIBLE AGAIN.
"BY THEN, JARAEL WAS GONE, HAVING STOWED AWAY WITH SOME CRACKPOT MERCHANT THEY'D DONE BUSINESS WITH --
"--BUT I FOUND OTHER WAYS TO EVEN THE SCORE. I GOT MY OLD JOB BACK--AND A LOT MORE."

YOU CAME *BACK?* I KNOW YOU COULDN'T GO HOME TO JARAEL'S SCHOOL -- GOLLIARD ABDUCTED OR KILLED EVERYONE THERE.

BUT WHY WOULD YOU COME BACK *HERE?*

BECAUSE IT'S DIFFERENT THIS TIME. I'M *MAGISTER IMPRESSOR.* I OVERSEE THE CAPTURE OF *NEW RECRUITS* --

-- THE PLACEMENT OF OUR SUCCESSFUL TRAINEES, AND THE DISPOSAL OF OUR FAILURES. NO ONE WILL HAVE THAT POWER OVER ME, EVER AGAIN.

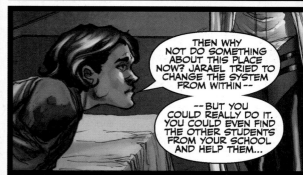

THEN WHY NOT DO SOMETHING ABOUT THIS PLACE NOW? JARAEL TRIED TO CHANGE THE SYSTEM FROM WITHIN --

-- BUT YOU COULD REALLY DO IT. YOU COULD EVEN FIND THE OTHER STUDENTS FROM YOUR SCHOOL AND HELP THEM...

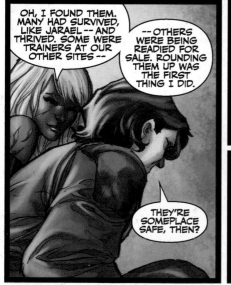

OH, I FOUND THEM. MANY HAD SURVIVED, LIKE JARAEL -- AND THRIVED. SOME WERE TRAINERS AT OUR OTHER SITES --

-- OTHERS WERE BEING READIED FOR SALE. ROUNDING THEM UP WAS THE FIRST THING I DID.

THEY'RE SOMEPLACE SAFE, THEN?

I WOULDN'T SAY THAT. MORE LIKE --SOMEPLACE *IRONIC.*

MANY OF THEM WERE FRIENDS OF JARAEL'S. KNOWING HOW THEY'RE LIVING NOW IS ONE OF THE PERKS OF THE JOB.

JARAEL'S NOT SOMEONE YOU WANT TO ASSOCIATE WITH, ZAYNE. LOOK AT THE NAME HER SLAVES GAVE HER IN CRUCIBLE CANT-- *DESTROYER.*

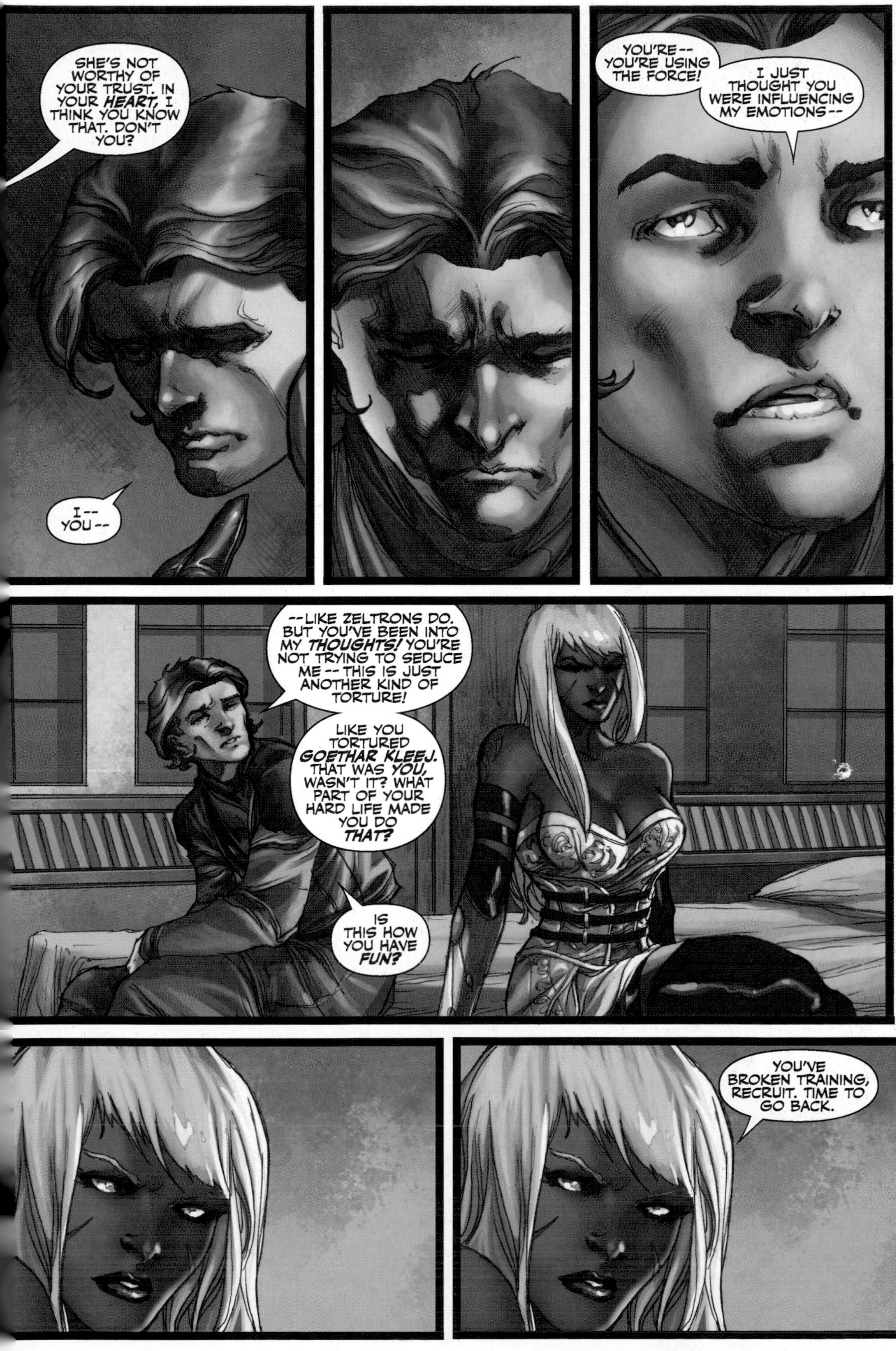
SHE'S NOT WORTHY OF YOUR TRUST. IN YOUR *HEART,* I THINK YOU KNOW THAT. DON'T YOU?
I-- YOU--
YOU'RE-- YOU'RE USING THE FORCE!
I JUST THOUGHT YOU WERE INFLUENCING MY EMOTIONS--
--LIKE ZELTRONS DO. BUT YOU'VE BEEN INTO MY *THOUGHTS!* YOU'RE NOT TRYING TO SEDUCE ME--THIS IS JUST ANOTHER KIND OF TORTURE!
LIKE YOU TORTURED *GOETHAR KLEEJ.* THAT WAS *YOU,* WASN'T IT? WHAT PART OF YOUR HARD LIFE MADE YOU DO *THAT?*
IS THIS HOW YOU HAVE *FUN?*
YOU'VE BROKEN TRAINING, RECRUIT. TIME TO GO BACK.

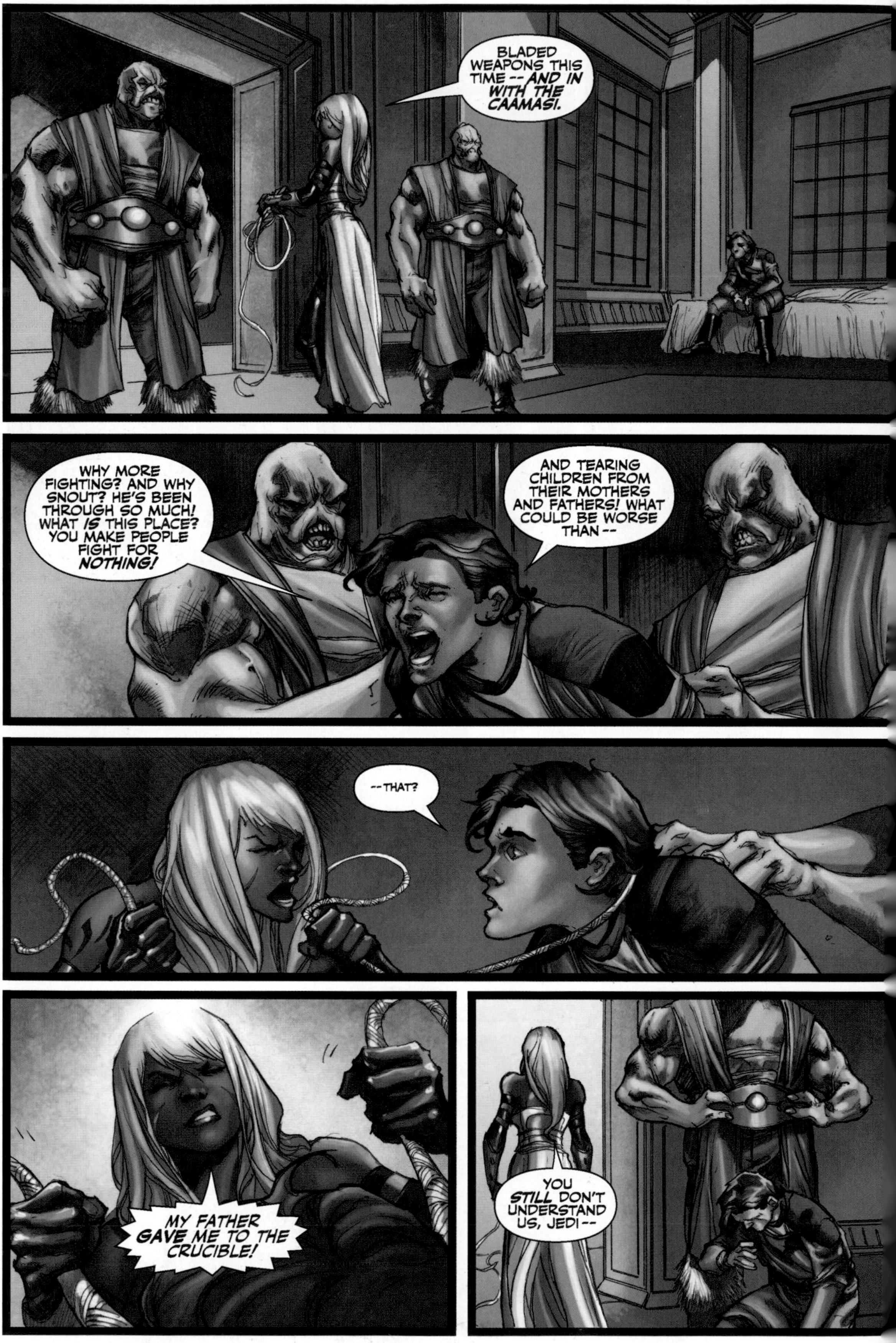
BLADED WEAPONS THIS TIME -- AND IN WITH THE CAAMASI.
WHY MORE FIGHTING? AND WHY SNOUT? HE'S BEEN THROUGH SO MUCH! WHAT IS THIS PLACE? YOU MAKE PEOPLE FIGHT FOR NOTHING!
AND TEARING CHILDREN FROM THEIR MOTHERS AND FATHERS! WHAT COULD BE WORSE THAN --
-- THAT?
MY FATHER GAVE ME TO THE CRUCIBLE!
YOU STILL DON'T UNDERSTAND US, JEDI --

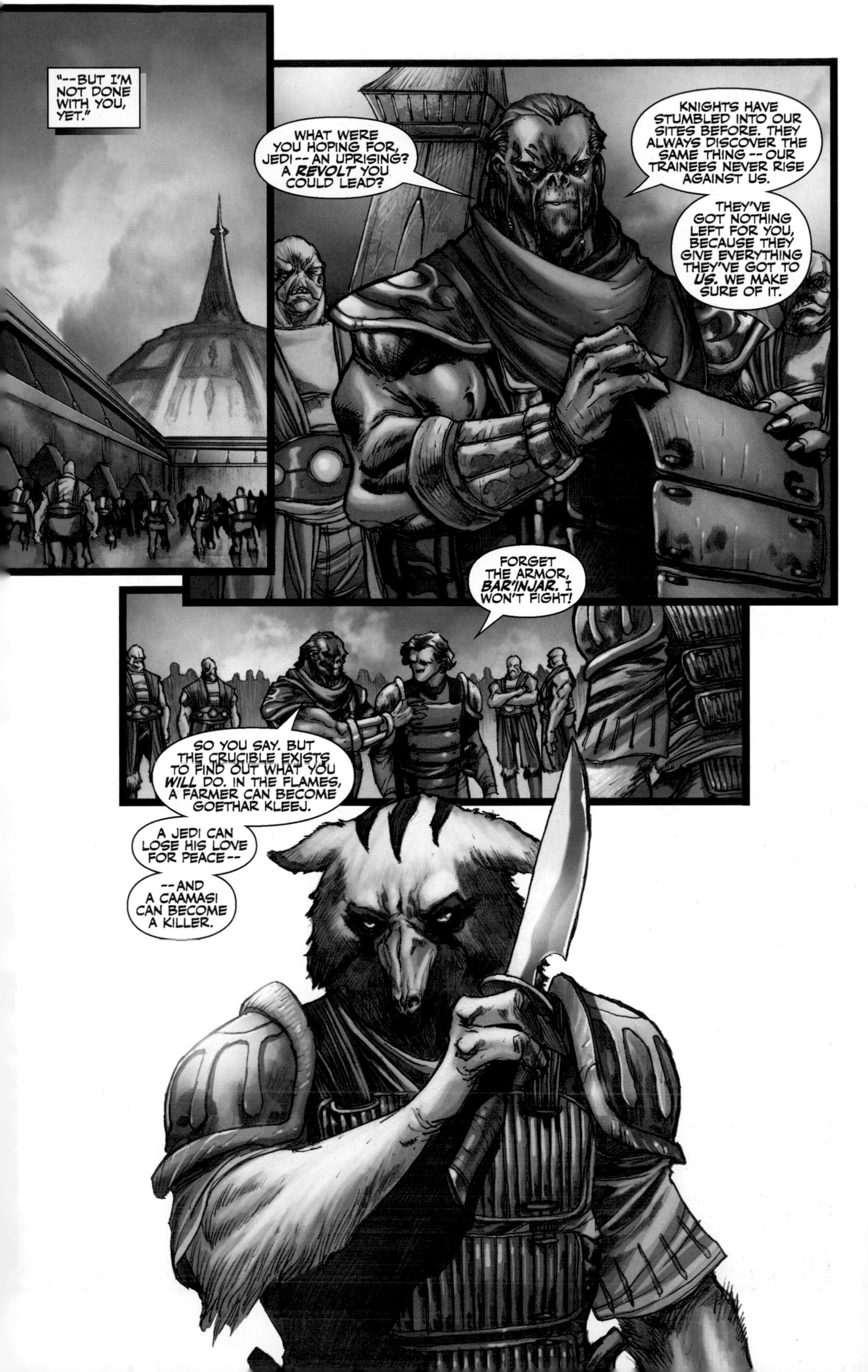
"--BUT I'M NOT DONE WITH YOU, YET."
WHAT WERE YOU HOPING FOR, JEDI -- AN UPRISING? A REVOLT YOU COULD LEAD?
KNIGHTS HAVE STUMBLED INTO OUR SITES BEFORE. THEY ALWAYS DISCOVER THE SAME THING -- OUR TRAINEES NEVER RISE AGAINST US.
THEY'VE GOT NOTHING LEFT FOR YOU, BECAUSE THEY GIVE EVERYTHING THEY'VE GOT TO US. WE MAKE SURE OF IT.
FORGET THE ARMOR, BAR'INJAR. I WON'T FIGHT!
SO YOU SAY. BUT THE CRUCIBLE EXISTS TO FIND OUT WHAT YOU WILL DO. IN THE FLAMES, A FARMER CAN BECOME GOETHAR KLEEJ.
A JEDI CAN LOSE HIS LOVE FOR PEACE --
-- AND A CAAMASI CAN BECOME A KILLER.

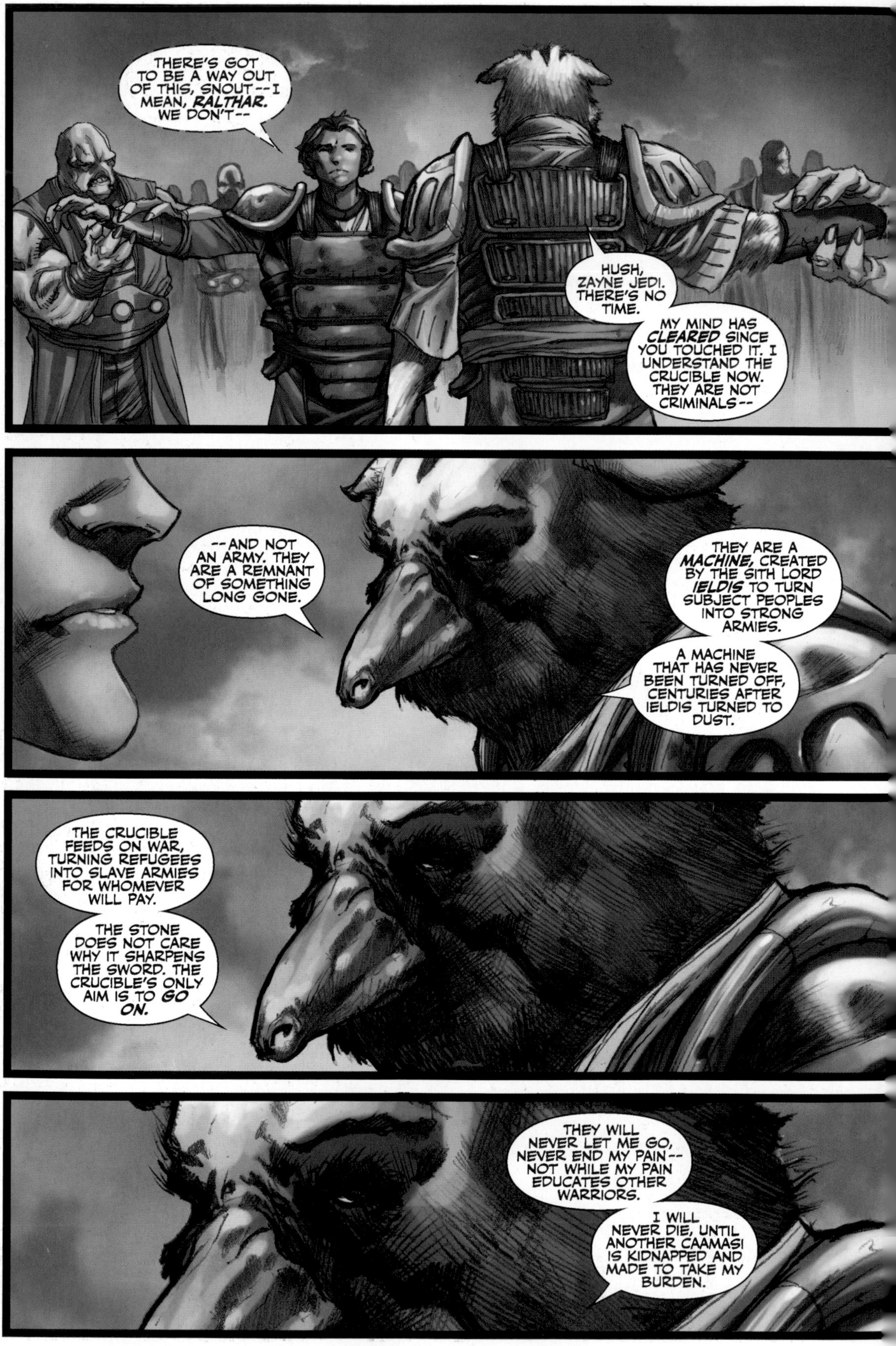
THERE'S GOT TO BE A WAY OUT OF THIS, SNOUT--I MEAN, RALTHAR. WE DON'T--
HUSH, ZAYNE JEDI. THERE'S NO TIME.
MY MIND HAS CLEARED SINCE YOU TOUCHED IT. I UNDERSTAND THE CRUCIBLE NOW. THEY ARE NOT CRIMINALS--
--AND NOT AN ARMY. THEY ARE A REMNANT OF SOMETHING LONG GONE.
THEY ARE A MACHINE, CREATED BY THE SITH LORD IELDIS TO TURN SUBJECT PEOPLES INTO STRONG ARMIES.
A MACHINE THAT HAS NEVER BEEN TURNED OFF, CENTURIES AFTER IELDIS TURNED TO DUST.
THE CRUCIBLE FEEDS ON WAR, TURNING REFUGEES INTO SLAVE ARMIES FOR WHOMEVER WILL PAY.
THE STONE DOES NOT CARE WHY IT SHARPENS THE SWORD. THE CRUCIBLE'S ONLY AIM IS TO GO ON.
THEY WILL NEVER LET ME GO, NEVER END MY PAIN--NOT WHILE MY PAIN EDUCATES OTHER WARRIORS.
I WILL NEVER DIE, UNTIL ANOTHER CAAMASI IS KIDNAPPED AND MADE TO TAKE MY BURDEN.

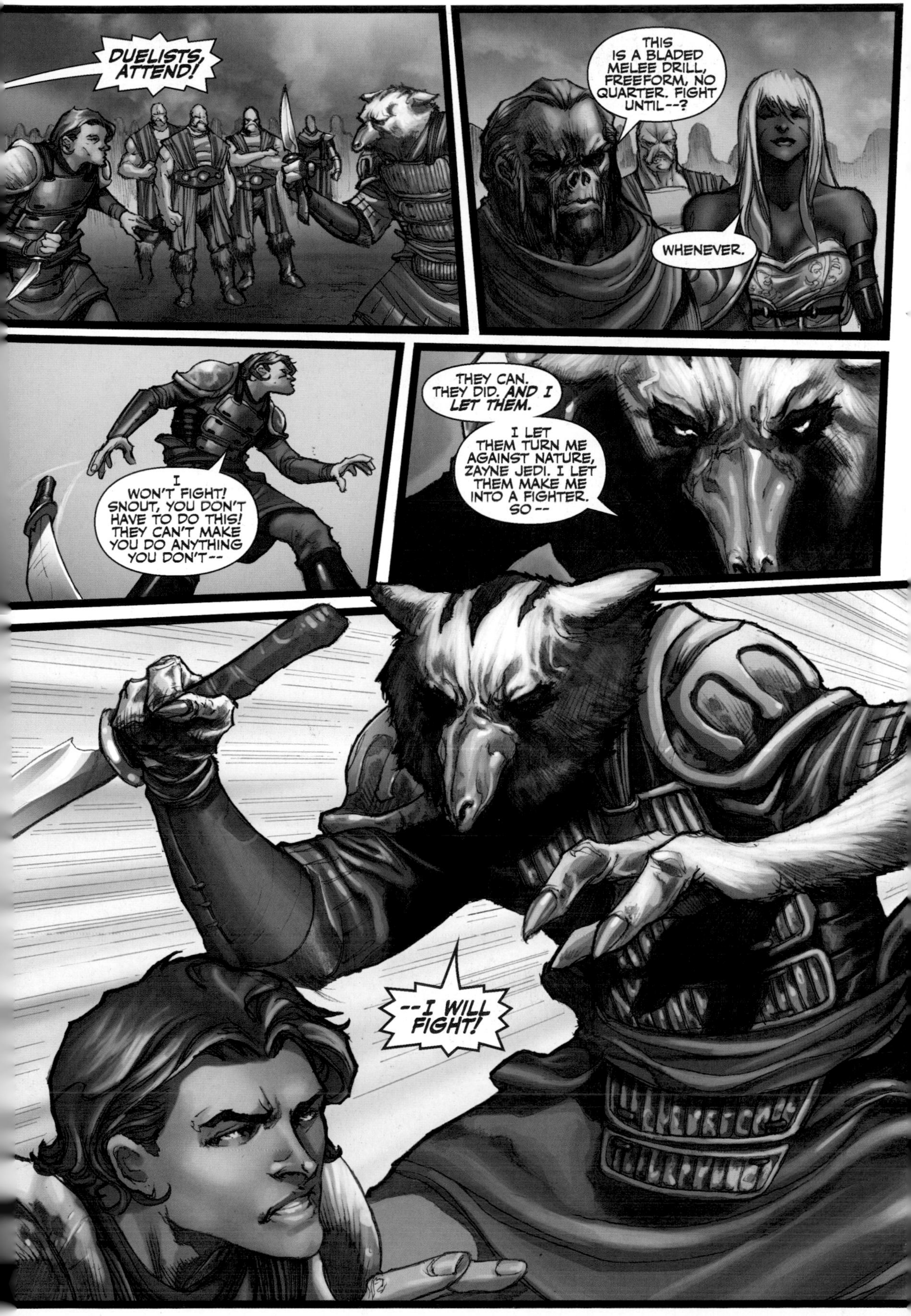
DUELISTS, ATTEND!
THIS IS A BLADED MELEE DRILL, FREEFORM, NO QUARTER. FIGHT UNTIL--?
WHENEVER.
I WON'T FIGHT! SNOUT, YOU DON'T HAVE TO DO THIS! THEY CAN'T MAKE YOU DO ANYTHING YOU DON'T--
THEY CAN. THEY DID. AND I LET THEM.
I LET THEM TURN ME AGAINST NATURE, ZAYNE JEDI. I LET THEM MAKE ME INTO A FIGHTER. SO --
--I WILL FIGHT!

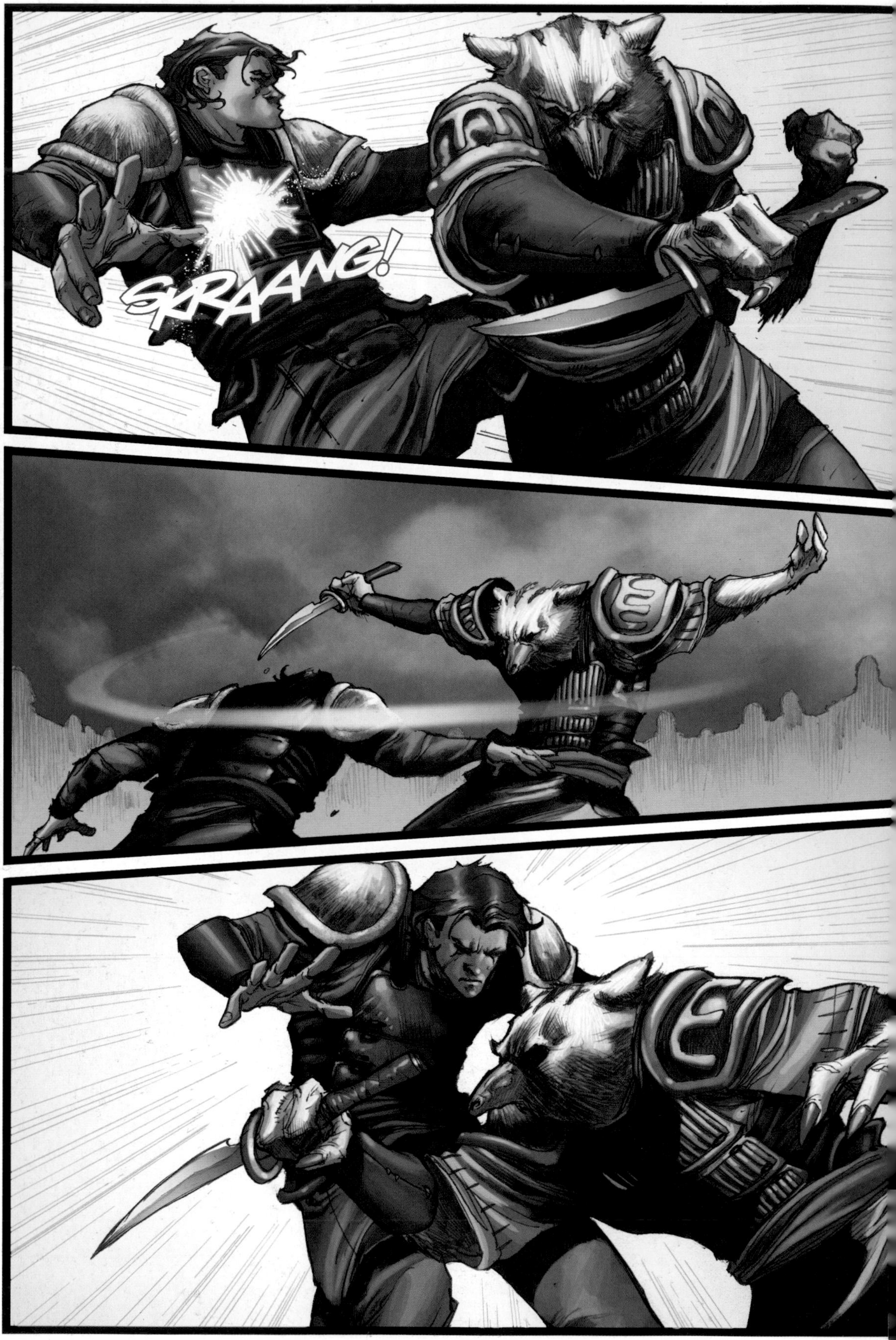
SKRAANG!

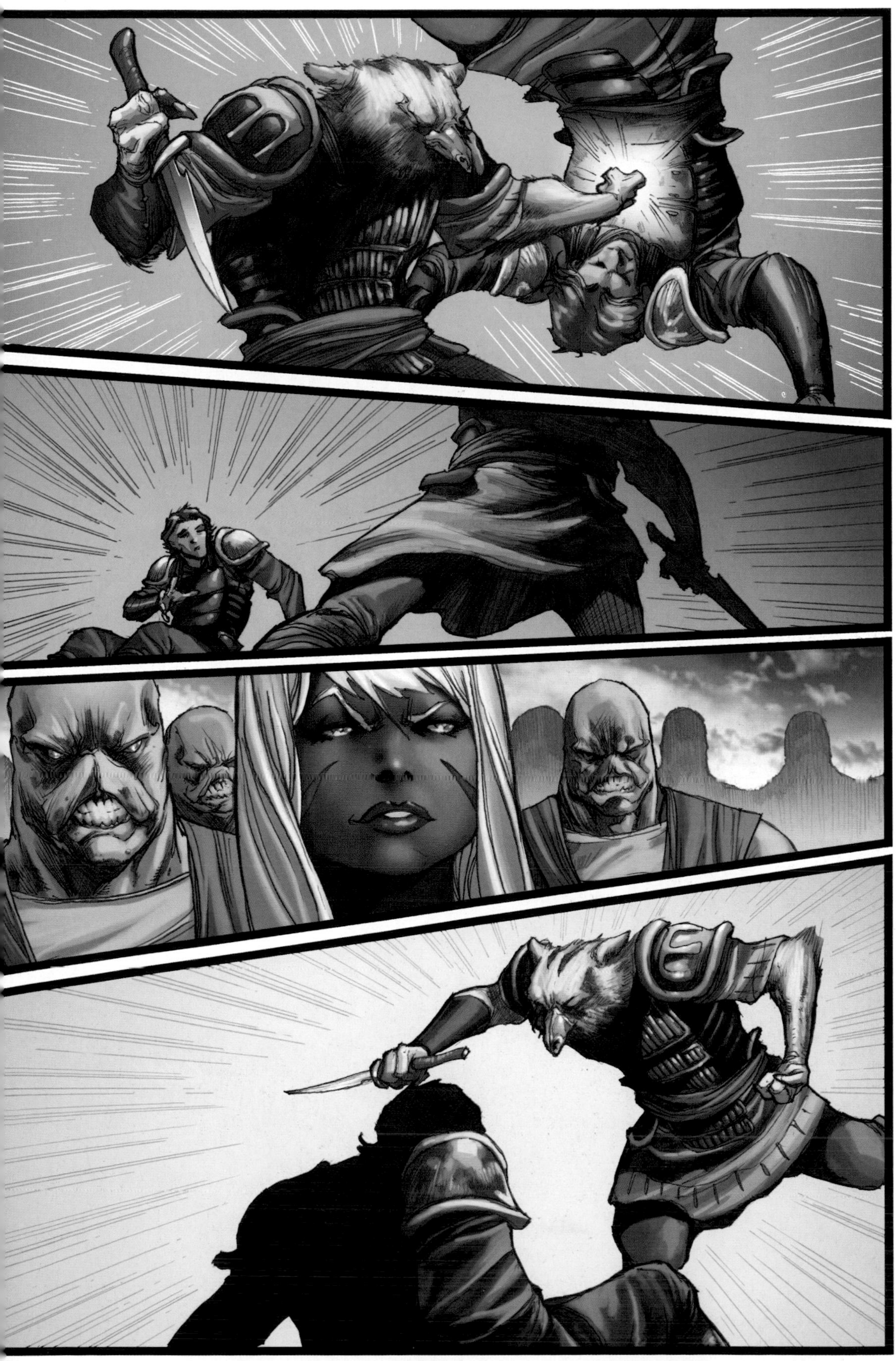

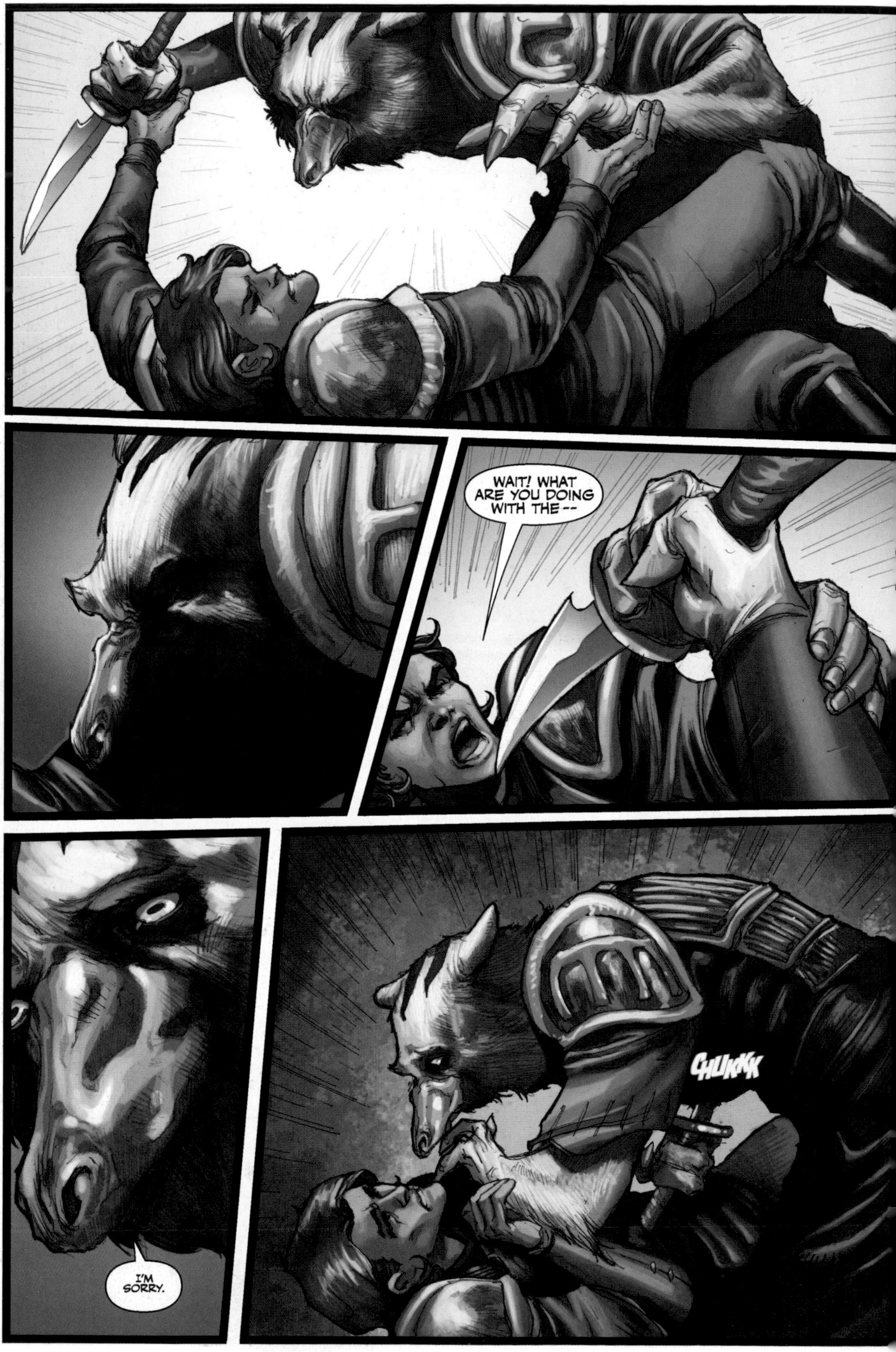
WAIT! WHAT ARE YOU DOING WITH THE--
I'M SORRY.
CHUKKK

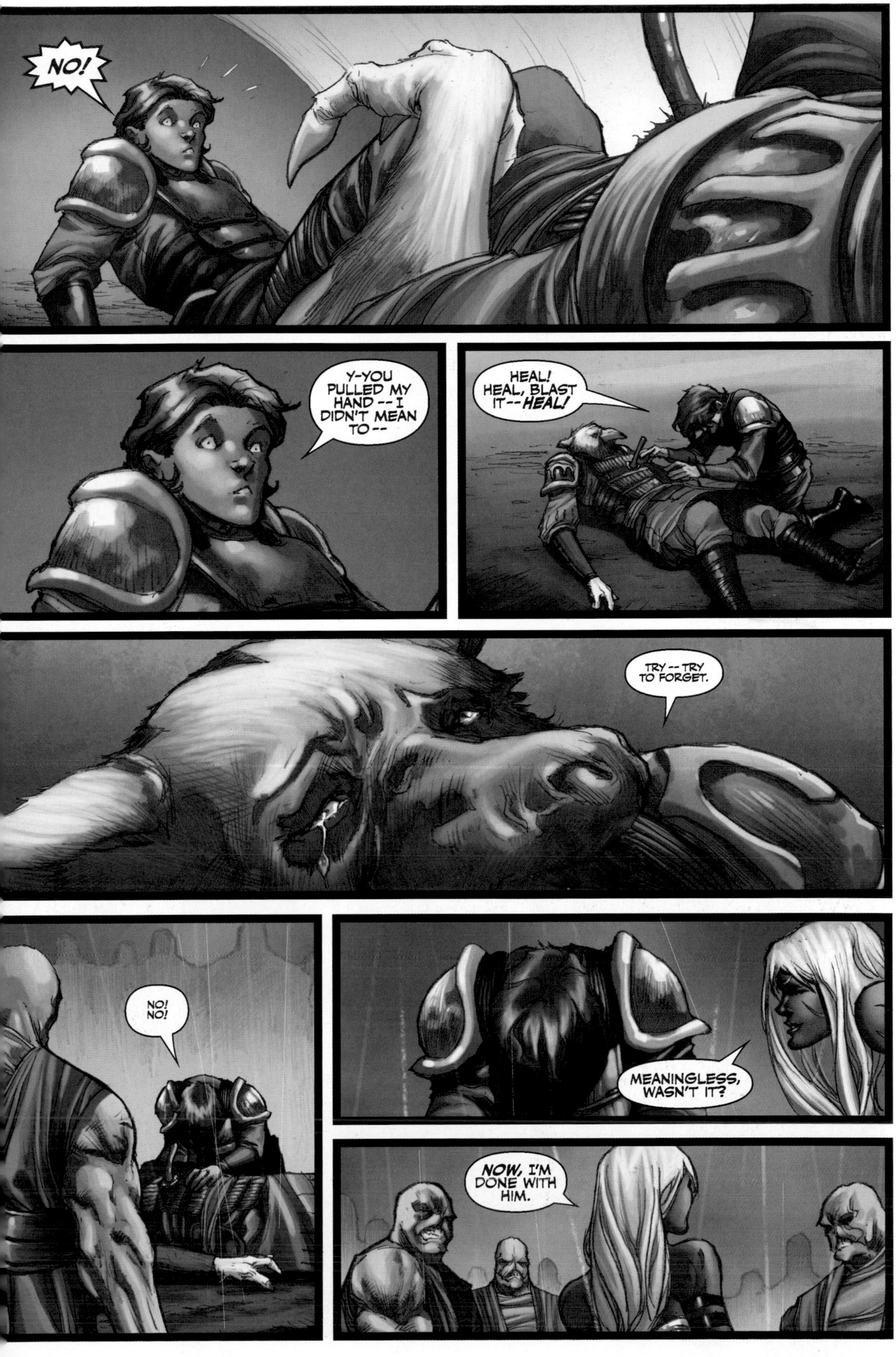
NO!
Y-YOU PULLED MY HAND -- I DIDN'T MEAN TO --
HEAL! HEAL, BLAST IT--*HEAL!*
TRY -- TRY TO FORGET.
NO! NO!
MEANINGLESS, WASN'T IT?
NOW, I'M DONE WITH HIM.

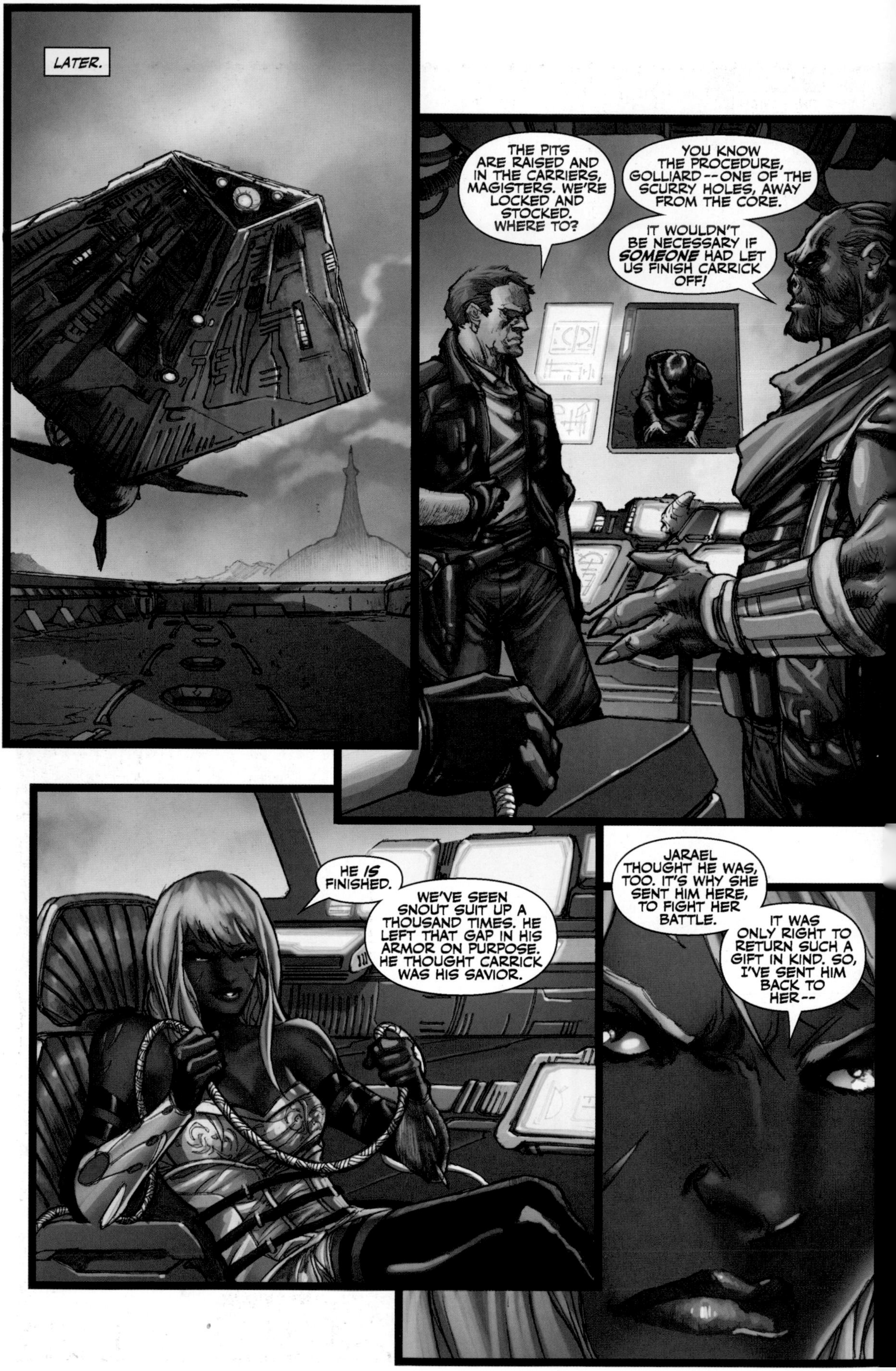
LATER.
THE PITS ARE RAISED AND IN THE CARRIERS, MAGISTERS. WE'RE LOCKED AND STOCKED. WHERE TO?
YOU KNOW THE PROCEDURE, GOLLIARD--ONE OF THE SCURRY HOLES, AWAY FROM THE CORE.
IT WOULDN'T BE NECESSARY IF *SOMEONE* HAD LET US FINISH CARRICK OFF!
HE *IS* FINISHED.
WE'VE SEEN SNOUT SUIT UP A THOUSAND TIMES. HE LEFT THAT GAP IN HIS ARMOR ON PURPOSE. HE THOUGHT CARRICK WAS HIS SAVIOR.
JARAEL THOUGHT HE WAS, TOO. IT'S WHY SHE SENT HIM HERE, TO FIGHT HER BATTLE.
IT WAS ONLY RIGHT TO RETURN SUCH A GIFT IN KIND. SO, I'VE SENT HIM BACK TO HER--

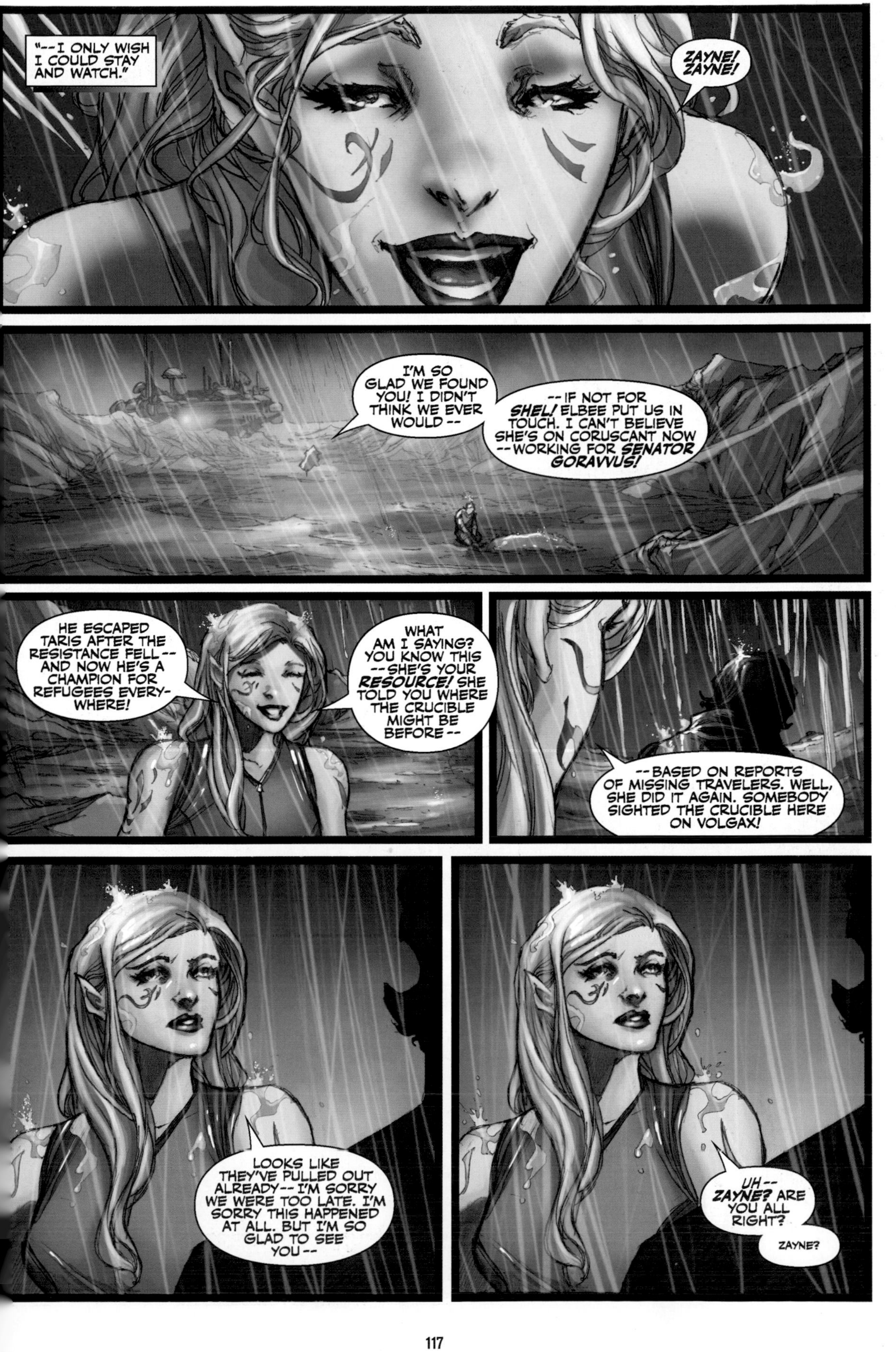
"--I ONLY WISH I COULD STAY AND WATCH."
ZAYNE! ZAYNE!
I'M SO GLAD WE FOUND YOU! I DIDN'T THINK WE EVER WOULD --
--IF NOT FOR SHEL! ELBEE PUT US IN TOUCH. I CAN'T BELIEVE SHE'S ON CORUSCANT NOW --WORKING FOR SENATOR GORAVVUS!
HE ESCAPED TARIS AFTER THE RESISTANCE FELL-- AND NOW HE'S A CHAMPION FOR REFUGEES EVERY-WHERE!
WHAT AM I SAYING? YOU KNOW THIS --SHE'S YOUR RESOURCE! SHE TOLD YOU WHERE THE CRUCIBLE MIGHT BE BEFORE--
--BASED ON REPORTS OF MISSING TRAVELERS. WELL, SHE DID IT AGAIN. SOMEBODY SIGHTED THE CRUCIBLE HERE ON VOLGAX!
LOOKS LIKE THEY'VE PULLED OUT ALREADY-- I'M SORRY WE WERE TOO LATE. I'M SORRY THIS HAPPENED AT ALL. BUT I'M SO GLAD TO SEE YOU--
UH-- ZAYNE? ARE YOU ALL RIGHT?
ZAYNE?

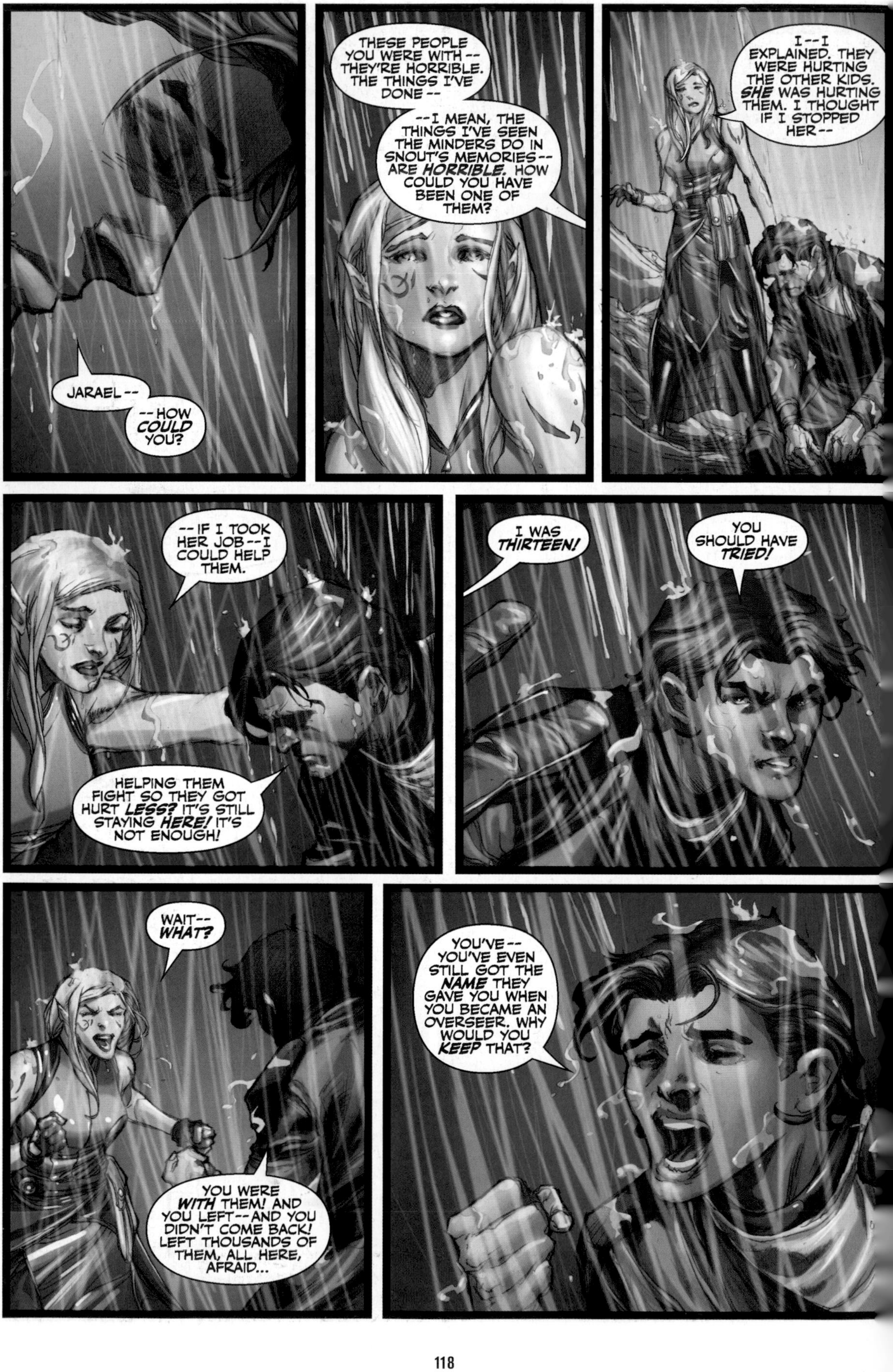
JARAEL--
--HOW COULD YOU?
THESE PEOPLE YOU WERE WITH--THEY'RE HORRIBLE. THE THINGS I'VE DONE--
--I MEAN, THE THINGS I'VE SEEN THE MINDERS DO IN SNOUT'S MEMORIES--ARE HORRIBLE. HOW COULD YOU HAVE BEEN ONE OF THEM?
I--I EXPLAINED. THEY WERE HURTING THE OTHER KIDS. SHE WAS HURTING THEM. I THOUGHT IF I STOPPED HER--
--IF I TOOK HER JOB--I COULD HELP THEM.
HELPING THEM FIGHT SO THEY GOT HURT LESS? IT'S STILL STAYING HERE! IT'S NOT ENOUGH!
I WAS THIRTEEN!
YOU SHOULD HAVE TRIED!
WAIT--WHAT?
YOU WERE WITH THEM! AND YOU LEFT--AND YOU DIDN'T COME BACK! LEFT THOUSANDS OF THEM, ALL HERE, AFRAID...
YOU'VE--YOU'VE EVEN STILL GOT THE NAME THEY GAVE YOU WHEN YOU BECAME AN OVERSEER. WHY WOULD YOU KEEP THAT?

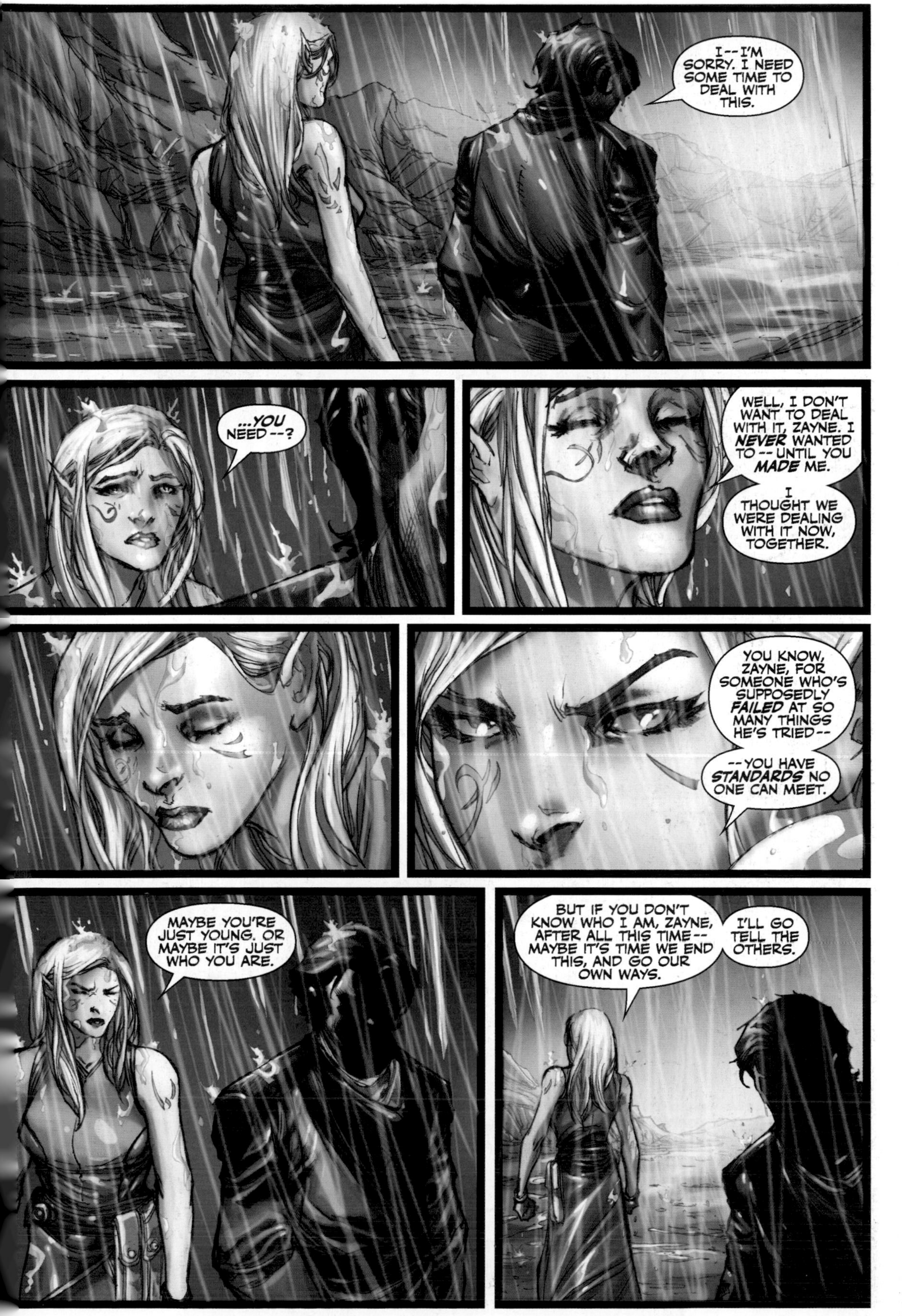
I--I'M SORRY. I NEED SOME TIME TO DEAL WITH THIS.
...YOU NEED--?
WELL, I DON'T WANT TO DEAL WITH IT, ZAYNE. I NEVER WANTED TO--UNTIL YOU MADE ME.
I THOUGHT WE WERE DEALING WITH IT NOW, TOGETHER.
YOU KNOW, ZAYNE, FOR SOMEONE WHO'S SUPPOSEDLY FAILED AT SO MANY THINGS HE'S TRIED--
--YOU HAVE STANDARDS NO ONE CAN MEET.
MAYBE YOU'RE JUST YOUNG. OR MAYBE IT'S JUST WHO YOU ARE.
BUT IF YOU DON'T KNOW WHO I AM, ZAYNE, AFTER ALL THIS TIME-- MAYBE IT'S TIME WE END THIS, AND GO OUR OWN WAYS.
I'LL GO TELL THE OTHERS.

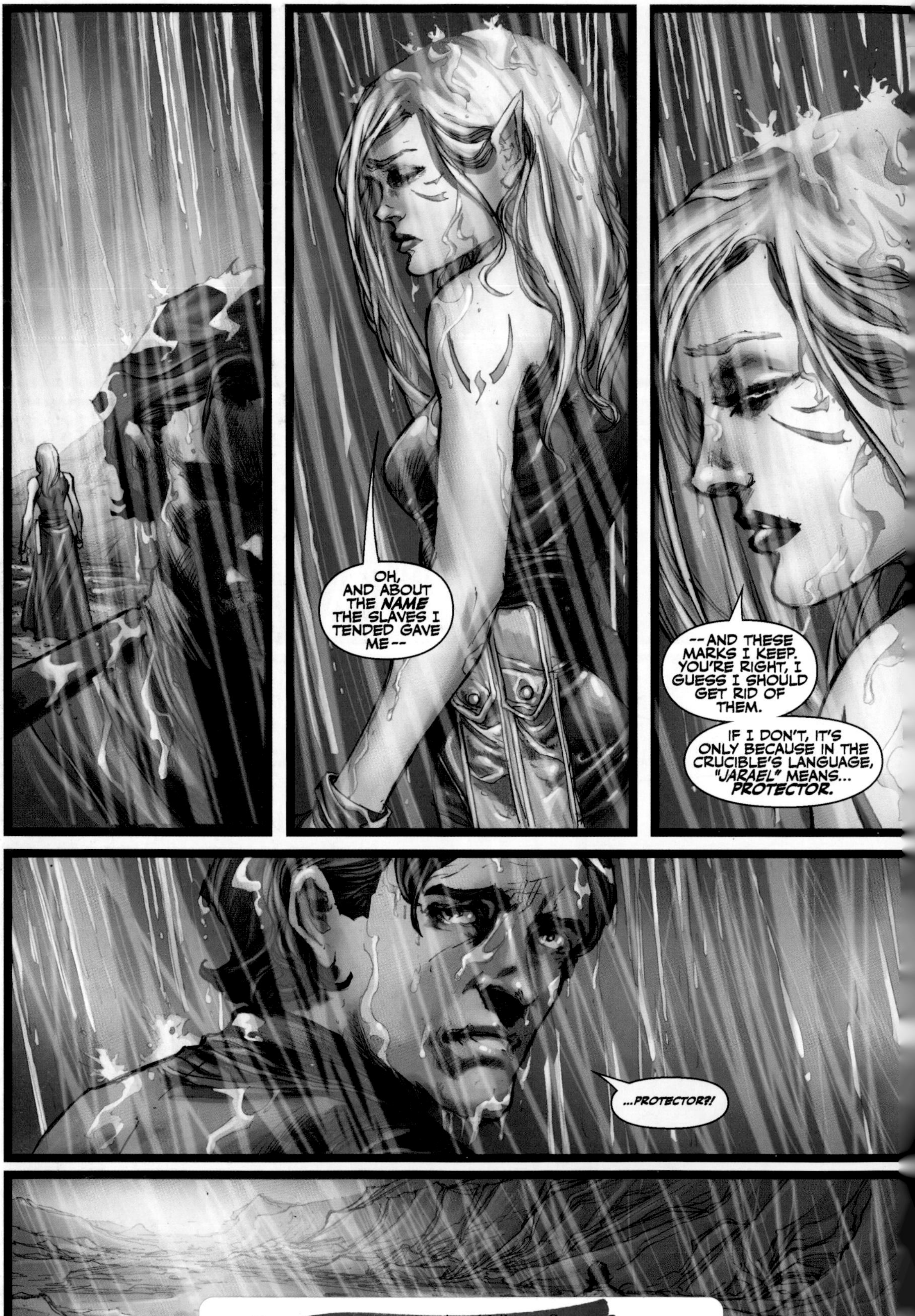
OH, AND ABOUT THE *NAME* THE SLAVES I TENDED GAVE ME--
--AND THESE MARKS I KEEP. YOU'RE RIGHT, I GUESS I SHOULD GET RID OF THEM.
IF I DON'T, IT'S ONLY BECAUSE IN THE CRUCIBLE'S LANGUAGE, "*JARAEL*" MEANS... *PROTECTOR.*
...PROTECTOR?!